The *Familia Urbana* during the Early Empire

A Study of *Columbaria* Inscriptions

Kinuko Hasegawa

BAR International Series 1440
2005

Published in 2016 by
BAR Publishing, Oxford

BAR International Series 1440

The Familia Urbana *during the Early Empire*

ISBN 978 1 84171 876 7

© K Hasegawa and the Publisher 2005

The author's moral rights under the 1988 UK Copyright,
Designs and Patents Act are hereby expressly asserted.

All rights reserved. No part of this work may be copied, reproduced, stored,
sold, distributed, scanned, saved in any form of digital format or transmitted
in any form digitally, without the written permission of the Publisher.

BAR Publishing is the trading name of British Archaeological Reports (Oxford) Ltd.
British Archaeological Reports was first incorporated in 1974 to publish the BAR
Series, International and British. In 1992 Hadrian Books Ltd became part of the BAR
group. This volume was originally published by Archaeopress in conjunction with
British Archaeological Reports (Oxford) Ltd / Hadrian Books Ltd, the Series principal
publisher, in 2005. This present volume is published by BAR Publishing, 2016.

Printed in England

BAR titles are available from:

BAR Publishing
122 Banbury Rd, Oxford, OX2 7BP, UK
EMAIL   info@barpublishing.com
PHONE +44 (0)1865 310431
FAX   +44 (0)1865 316916
www.barpublishing.com

Table of Contents

Abbreviations		page ii
List of tables		iii
List of figures		iv

Chapter 1	Introduction	page 1
Chapter 2	The *columbaria* and the aristocratic families	4
Chapter 3	The occupations of slaves and freedmen	30
Chapter 4	Legal status and ownership structure in elite Roman households	52
Chapter 5	The women, children, and servile families	62
Chapter 6	Slave names	73
Chapter 7	The burial clubs for slaves and freedmen	81
Conclusion		89
Appendix	Inscriptions from the *columbarium* of the Statilii	92
Concordance		108
Bibliography		112

Abbreviations

Unless otherwise stated, translations of Justinian's *Digest* are those of A. Watson, in *The Digest of Justinian*, 4 vols., Latin text edited by T. Mommsen with the aid of Paul Krueger (Philadelphia, 1985). Likewise, translations of Gaius' *Institutiones* are those of W.M. Gordon and O.F. Robinson, in *The Institutes of Gaius* (London, 1988).

Unless otherwise stated, translations of other ancient texts are those of the Loeb Classical Library, with some modifications.

Inscriptions from the Statilian *columbarium* are cited on a numeration based on that of Caldelli and Ricci, 1999; for convenience, the inscriptions are reproduced with this numeration in Appendix, followed by a concordance to *CIL* VI. See further Chap.2.

AE	*Année Epigraphique*
AJAH	*American Journal of Ancient History*
ZPE	*Zeitschrift für Papyrologie und Epigraphik*
CIL	*Corpus Inscriptionum Latinarum* (Berlin, 1863-)
CP	*Classical Philology*
CQ	*Classical Quarterly*
FIRA	*Fontes Iuris Romani Anteiustiniani*, 3 vols., eds., S. Riccobono, J. Baviera, C. Ferrini, J. Furlani and V. Arangio-Ruiz (Florence, 1940-43)
G&R	*Greece and Rome*
GARS	*Greek and Roman Slavery*, ed. T. Wiedemann (London, 1981)
IG	*Inscriptiones Graecae* (Berlin, 1873-)
ILLRP	*Inscriptiones Latinae Liberae Rei Publicae*, ed. A. Degrassi (Florence, 1957-)
ILS	*Inscriptiones Latinae Selectae*, ed. H. Dessau (Berlin, 1892-1916)
JRS	*Journal of Roman Studies*
LTUR	*Lexicon Topographicum Urbis Romae*, ed. E. M. Steinby (Rome, 1993-2000)
MAR	*Mapping Augustan Rome*, directed by L. Haselberger (Portsmouth, 2002)
PCPS	*Proceedings of the Cambridge Philological Society*
PIR	*Prosopographia Imperii Romani*
PIR^2	*Prosopographia Imperii Romani*. 2nd edn.
PFOS	T. Raepsaet-Charlier, *Prosopographie des femmes de l'ordre sénatorial* (Ier-IIe siècles). M.- (Lovain, 1987)
RE	*Real-Encyclopädie der classischen Altertumswissenschaft*, ed. A. Fr. von Pauly, rev. G. Wissowa *et al.* (Stuttgart, 1884-1980)
TAPA	*Transactions and Proceedings of the American Philological Association*
TLG	*Thesaurus Linguae Graecae*
TLL	*Thesaurus Linguae Latinae*
WLGR	*Women's Life in Greece and Rome*, ed. M. R. Lefkowitz, M. B. Fant, 2nd edn. (Trowbridge, 1992)

Figures

2.1	The map of Rome: locations of the *columbaria*	6
2.2	The ground plan of the sepulchral complex in the area of Porta Maggiore	8
2.3	The chronological shift of the sepulchral complex	9
2.4	The plan of the *Monumentum Statiliorum*	11
2.5	The *gens Statilia*	13
2.6	The *columbarium* of the Arruntii viewed from outside	18
2.7	The *columbarium* of the Arruntii inside	18
2.8	The *gens Volusia*	21
2.9	The *columbarium* of Livia's staff on the via Appia (1)	23
2.10	The *columbarium* of Livia's staff on the via Appia (2)	23
2.11	The *columbarium* II of the Vigna Codini	24
2.12	The *columbarium* III of the Vigna Codini	24
2.13	Livia's family	25
3.1	Provision of clothes: the Statilii	41
3.2	Provision of clothes: the Volusii	43
3.3	Provision of clothes: Livia	43
4.1	Euticus family	57
4.2	Hesychus family	57
4.3	Phileros ownership	57
4.4	Familial-ownership unit of Auctus the *dispensator*	59
4.5	Attalus	60
4.6	Livia Musa	60
4.7	Antonia Lyde	60
5.1.1	Recorded age of death: the Statilii	66
5.1.2	Recorded age of death: the Volusii, Iunii, Abuccii, Arruntii, Annii, Caecilii, Livia	66
5.1.3	Recorded age of death: all	66
5.2	The commemorative pattern of Euticus family	69
5.3	The commemorative pattern of Hesychus' family	69

Tables

Table		
2.1	The *columbaria* of known individuals or families in *CIL* VI	5
2.2	Named *domini* and *dominae* (the Statilii)	15
2.3	Named *domini* and *dominae* (the Volusii)	17
2.4	Named *domini* and *dominae* (Livia)	21
3.1	The proportion of job-title holders in the *columbaria*	32
3.2	List of job titles: bodyguards and servants of transport	34
3.3	List of job titles: personal servants	35
3.4	List of job titles: child care	36
3.5	List of job titles: on finance	37
3.6	List of job titles: secretaries	38
3.7	List of job titles: medical service	39
3.8	List of job titles: on clothes and accessories	41
3.9	List of job titles: on foods	45
3.10	List of job titles: builders	47
3.11	List of job titles: property managers / keepers	48
4.1	Legal status of individuals in the *columbaria*	53
4.2	Proportions of those under aristocratic masters and under sub-owners in the *columbaria*	56
5.1	Patterns of commemoration (Statilii, Volusii, and Livia)	64
5.2	The types of relationship in the *columbaria*	64
5.3	Proportion of male and female in the *columbaria*	65
5.4	Brothers and Sisters in the *columbaria*	67
5.5	The number of epitaphs recording the death of male and female with family relationship specified	78
5.6	The number of *verna* in the *columbaria*	71
6.1	Proportion of Greek, Latin, and others names	74
6.2.1	The most common servile names (male)	74
6.2.2	The most common servile names (female)	74
6.2.3	Total readable names in seven *columbaria*	75
6.3	'Barbarian' names in the *columbaria*	76
6.4	Individuals with clear indication of *nation*	77
6.5	Naming practice from father to son	79
7.1	Signs of operations of the *collegia* in each *columbarium*	82
7.2	Comparison of the prices relating to slaves and freedmen	84

Chapter 1

Introduction

For slaves, the household is a sort of state and citizenship.
servis res publica quaedam et quasi civitas domus est. (Plin. *Ep.* 8, 16)

They (our ancestors) held that the household was a miniature state.
domum pusillam rem publicam esse iudicaverunt. (Sen. *Ep.* 47, 14)

(C. Cassius Longinus' speech at the senate) "But now that our households comprise nations – with customs the reverse of our own, with foreign cults or with none, you will never coerce such a medley of humanity except by terror."
postquam vero nationes in familiis habemus, quibus diversi ritus, externa sacra aut nulla sunt, conluviem istam non nisi metu coercueris. (Tac. *Ann.* 14, 44)

It was claimed by Pliny and Seneca that a household (*domus*) be the *res publica* for slaves. As its members might have become more diverse in terms of places of origin (*nationes*) as we are told by Tacitus' Cassius Longinus, a large aristocratic household must ideally operate under discipline, led by the *dominus* as *pater*. The idea of the household as a self-contained, tightly-knit community was widely held.[1] The *domus* gave slaves responsibilities and basic welfare (food, clothes, and shelter), and was sustained by their service and labour.[2] Socially, slaves' associations with their fellows, if any, and especially the process of their finding their consorts, were mainly conducted within the bar of the household. The household was also the place of justice, in the sense that the *paterfamilias* could exercise judicial power over the crimes or misdeeds of slaves (as he did theoretically over the sons or daughters in his *potestas*). Instead of being brought into the public, they might be interrogated and given sentence at a domestic court (*tribunal domesticum*), which was presided over by the *paterfamilias* and usually assisted by friends or members of the *gens* (or *familia*) as advisors.[3] Even though such a domestic 'court' was not necessarily a regular procedure, its formality and degree of deliberation distinguish it from the arbitrary punishments that masters sporadically imposed upon them.

The aim of this book is to investigate the lives of servile dependants, and their role in the large households of the elite Romans. In parallel to the public and political lives of the aristocracy under constant public gaze, there had been other lives led that were totally different but closely connected to them as if the other side of the coin - the usually unseen world of servile dependants. An uneasy proximity created by the cohabitation of the two opposite status groups (aristocratic masters and slaves) brought conflicts and contradiction. Several important studies have been already undertaken on aspects of this theme of 'slavery and household'. Recent studies include K. Bradley (1987; 1994) and R. Saller (1987a; 1994; 1996; 1998) on the relationships of slaves and masters in a household. Earlier, J. Vogt (1974, 103-121) looked at

---

[1] A similar thought is also found in Florus, a historian during the reigns of Trajan and Hadrian; when he gives an account of the early administrations of Servius Tullius (1, 6, 3), which enrolled the whole *populus Romanus* on the census-roll by dividing them into *classes*, and distributed them to *decuriae* and *collegia,* he comments that as a result, the great State (*maxima civitas*) came to be governed exactly 'like a small household' (*ac sic maxima civitas minimae domus diligentia contineretur*). The discipline and order in the household were to affect those of the state.
[2] *Dig.* 7, 1, 15, 2 (Ulpian): *sufficienter autem alere et uestire debet secundum ordinem et dignitatem mancipiorum.*
[3] The *tribunal domesticum* (family council) for slaves; Cic. *Clu.* 176-185, a matron held inquiries into the circumstances of her husband's death before the *consilium* of the family's friends and associates, and interrogated slaves with torture; Plut. *Cat. Mai.*, 21, 4, Cato tried slaves who committed crimes in the presence of other dependants and might even give the death sentence; minor crimes such as theft committed by slaves, freedmen, or hired workers were judged by their master/patron/employer: *Dig.* 48, 19, 11, 1 (Marcian); Petr. 70, Trimalchio presides as a judge over the quarrel between slaves; Petr. 53, his slave Mithridates was crucified for cursing the *genius* of Trimalchio; The inscription from Puteoli (*lex Libitinae Puteolana, AE* 1971, 88) attests to a public funeral contractor which also undertook punishment and execution of slaves for a master; Wallon, 1988, 126; Wiseman, 1985b, 14-16; cf. the *tribunal domesticum* for sons: Dion. Hal. *Ant. Rom.* 2, 26; but in practice, the extreme power of a *paterfamilias* was reasonably restricted. Gardner and Wiedemann, 1991, 12-13; Sen. *Clem.* 1, 15.

individual cases from historical sources and emphasised actual humane relationships between masters and slaves, though this was opposed by M. Finley (1980, 93-122) who insisted on the ultimate cruelty of slavery in its fundamental ideology and structure. From the literary perspective, W. Fitzgerald (2000) explored highly subtle and sophisticated perceptions of the slave-master relationship.[4] Moreover, an article of Flory (1978) uniquely illustrated kinship and community among servile members of the *domus*, aspects of their lives which were quite separate and remote from the intervention of masters.

In attempting a new inquiry into such historically anonymous individuals and their *res publica*, the *domus*, then, what kinds of sources are available for us? This book confines itself to analysis of a particular group of inscriptions, that is the epitaphs from the *columbaria*, collected in *CIL* vol. VI, section 6 '*Monumenta columbariorum integra reperta*' (pp.877-1110, n.3926-8397). The uniqueness of this type of inscription might be highlighted by the nature of the subsequent two sections of the same volume, the *CIL* vol. VI section 7 '*tituli officialium et artificum*' (pp.1113-1346, n.8398-10228), and the section 8 '*tituli sepulcrales reliqui*' (pp.1349-2872, n.10229-29680). These are collections of epitaphs, many of whose find-spots are unknown, and comprise a wide range of epitaphs set up individually, from very wealthy freedmen to commoners of modest means. Unlike these inscriptions, in contrast, the *columbaria* inscriptions allow us to suppose their common archaeological background. The '*columbarium*', a dovecote-like burial structure, was designed to accommodate a number of epitaphs and urns of ashes and became particularly popular during the Julio-Claudian period. Such a communal burial structure appears to have been shared by people with a common background, in many cases the slaves and freedmen staff of a noble family. In other words, the set of epitaphs from a given *columbarium* is arguably representative of the *familia urbana* of a certain noble family. Once the group of individuals is thus given an identity, it opens the way to systematic examination of their lives and status from multiple angles. These inscriptions, relatively unexplored until recent decades, offer researchers unique insights into otherwise anonymous people.

Certainly, there have been many productive studies that used non-*columbaria* type inscriptions. For instance, S. Joshel (1992) selected her main sample from the above-mentioned 'officiales' section for her study of the occupations of the people in Rome. Others such as Hermann-Otto on *vernae* (home-born slaves) (1997), F. Merola on *vicarii* (under-slaves) (1990), H. Solin for the catalogue of servile names (1996), and B. Rawson on various aspects of lower-class families (1966; 1986a;

1986b), took samples widely, at the same time including *columbaria* inscriptions within their scope. P. Huttunen (1974) undertook statistical analysis of his randomly selected samples (one in five of *CIL* vol. VI section 6-8) and thematically analysed them. R. Saller and B. Shaw produced a series of articles (1984 etc.) that brought important sociological insights from larger scale samples of epigraphic data. Lastly, P. R. C. Weaver (1972) examined the inscriptions of imperial slaves and freedmen, chronologically and regionally wide-ranging, and shed light upon the increasingly institutionalised body of the Familia Caesaris, mainly focusing on their epigraphic styles.

Though not infrequently referred to in these excellent studies, however, the *columbaria* inscriptions have not been taken as seriously as they deserve, and their treatment has been often only marginal. Fortunately, there has been important progress in recent decades on the basic understanding of the structure and inscriptions of the *columbaria*. A series of archaeological and epigraphic studies of the major *columbaria* have come out as revised editions, primarily based on the reports of archaeologists of previous centuries. I am greatly indebted to Caldelli and Ricci for their edition of the inscriptions from the *columbarium* of the Statilii (1999) based on the earlier accounts of E. Brizio (1876), M. Buonocore (1984) on that of the Volusii, and the reprint (1991) of F. Bianchini's report on the *columbarium* of Livia (1727) with introduction and synopsis by J. Kolendo. These publications certainly enhanced a great deal our access to and understanding of these epigraphic materials. Acknowledging the importance of their contributions, however, it can be said that these authors' interest was primarily in the material evidence, rather than its sociological implications. In other words, further contribution can be made by turning more attention to the protagonists of the inscriptions themselves, that is to say, slaves and freedmen. In this respect, the aim and subject-matters of this discussion are essentially prompted from elsewhere, that is a series of earlier articles by S. Treggiari (1973; 1975a; 1975b; 1976). While systematically focusing on the *columbaria* inscriptions (mainly those of Livia and the Volusii), her questions were asked from the perspective of social themes: the range of jobs and the family lives of the domestic staff of the aristocratic households.

Building on the works of these predecessors, this book focuses on the *columbaria* evidence and the above-stated social groups, namely the servile dependants of the Roman aristocracy. The '*familia urbana*' that I took up in the title of this thesis is meant to cover a broader range of people than that in a scrupulous legal definition.[5] As will

---

[4] Other scholars, P. Veyne (1961), F. Millar (1981), K. Hopkins (1993), and K. Bradley (2000), have attempted to research the reality of social background and structure in fictions containing themes of slavery, such as Petronius' *Satyricon* or Apuleius' *Metamorphosis* etc.

[5] Apparently by legal definition, a slave was to enter either *familia urbana* or *familia rustica* according to his *genus* or *opus* (namely, the kind of work he did), rather than by *locus*, the place where one lived or worked: *Dig.* 32, 99 (Paul), *non loco sed opere*; id. 50, 16, 166 (Pomponius), '*urbana familia*' et '*rustica*' non loco, sed genere

be shown in subsequent chapters, the *columbaria* actually include not only strictly 'domestic slaves/servants', but also freedmen and even their free-born descendants, and those who apparently lived and worked outside the *domus*. As a matter of course, the thesis aims not to discuss the subjects with primary concern for their legal statuses, either slave or freed or free-born, but to explore the 'social group', defined as the subordinates, labour force, and the protégées, of some of the most prominent families in Rome. One category this book positively excludes by naming its subject-matter as the '*familia urbana*', is the '*familia rustica*': it is supposed that the majority of those named in the epitaphs in the *columbaria* were urban dwellers as they were located in the outskirts of the city.[6] In other words, the picture that will be drawn here from the *columbaria* inscriptions is largely descriptive of those who worked and lived in the city or in the suburb of the city, but we are largely ignorant of the agricultural workers belonging to the same owners.[7]

Analysis based on comparison between several *columbaria* will be central throughout the thesis, though special emphasis will be placed on that of the Statilii in view of its size and availability of information. The chapters are structured thematically.

First, in order to conduct the investigation into the *columbaria* inscriptions, it will be essential for us to understand the funerary structures from which our sources originate. Chapter 2 'The *columbaria* and the aristocratic families' is an examination of the funerary structures, their location, their epitaphs, and the family history of *columbaria*-owning families. The archaeological and topographic information of the *columbaria* is discussed with what we know about the background history of patron families, namely the master's/mistresses' rise and fall, acquisition and loss of their property, and their effect on their servile dependants.

From the following chapter on, the focus will gradually shift onto the protagonists of our sources, slaves and freedmen. The third chapter is 'The occupations of slaves and freedmen', where the occupational activities of slaves/freedmen will be reconstructed from the job-titles in epitaphs. The job-titles found there are so extensive that the large households of the period appear to have been filling their own need within their own branches, virtually attaining a certain degree of the traditionally ideal self-sufficiency.

The following two chapters are concerned with personal connections between slaves/freedmen in a *columbarium*. Chapter 4 'Legal status and ownership structure in elite Roman households' examines the ties of ownership and hierarchy of the *columbaria* population at a personal level. In the same chapter, I will also attempt to find a category that frames and defines the individuals in the *columbarium* as a group, that is to say, the composition of legal status or the application of terms such as *familia* or *domus*. Chapter 5 'The women, children, and servile families' is about the familial ties of the *columbaria* populations. In particular, my concern is to find the conditions of servile women, how they appear in epitaphs of the *columbaria*.

As the other side of that reality that yields abundant evidence of families, some of the *columbaria* individuals were certainly foreigners, cut off from all pre-existing kinship ties. Chapter 6 'Slave names' is an attempt to trace servile dependants originating from outside Rome, as some personal names might present a clue to the bearers' places of origins.

Chapter 7 'The burial clubs for slaves and freedmen' examines the funeral clubs supposedly organised for the management of each *columbarium*, chiefly by those associated to a certain *domus*. The purpose of such a corporate organisation was primarily to ensure burial for all the members and manage the *columbarium*, but it is also significant in terms of group unity among the servile dependants.

---

distinguitur (but the text of this passage is problematic); cf. *Dig.* 7, 8, 10, 4 (Ulpian).

[6] The extant epitaphs in general are largely those of urban dwellers: Saller and Shaw, 1984, 127; for a rare exception, see *ILS* 7367 (=*CIL* IX 3028, from Teate Marrucinorum) *Hippocrati Plauti vilic(o), familia rust(ica) quibus imperavit modeste.*

[7] In this sense, we do not find in the *columbaria* epitaphs such job-title holders as *vilicus* (supervisor of the farm) or *magister pecoris* (supervisor of cattle / shepherds) known from agricultural writers. Admittedly, of course, some job-titles found in the *columbaria* epitaphs are at the same time the ones attested by an agricultural writer and a legal expert as belonging to a rural household, such as *topiarius, ostiarius, cellarius, fartor, actor, aquarius*, etc. We cannot tell how much mobility existed between distant households. But there seems to be a strong emotional barrier between an urban slave and a rural slave. A *vilicus*' nostalgia for urban life, who as an urban slave used to yearn for rural life, Hor. *Ep.* 1, 14, 14f., *tu mediastinus tacita prece rura petebas, nunc urbem et ludos et balnea vilicus optas*; the discord and repulsion between the *armiger* as a town slave and the *vilicus* as a country slave in Plautus' *Casina* is discussed by Fitzgerald, 2000, 82.

Chapter 2

The *columbaria* and the aristocratic families

The word *columbarium*, deriving from '*columba*' ('pigeon'), is descriptive of a structure whose internal wall was furnished with rows of niches with the appearance of a pigeon-house (dovecote).[1] In this peculiar sepulchral structure, a type that became particularly popular during the Julio-Claudian period, each niche was occupied by one or two urns of ashes. The *columbarium*, therefore, was a refined and economical use of sepulchral space for the city dwellers in terms of its capacity.[2]

Such a communal burial facility was constructed either under the initiative of a single (wealthy) individual patron, or of a co-operative body such as a funeral club. In the latter case, the niches within the structure were sometimes sold piecemeal or allocated by lot to individual purchasers or members of a *collegium*. As a result, people who had no connection whatsoever with one another might end up sharing the same *columbarium*.[3] For the present purpose, our concern is with the former, the *columbaria* occupied mostly by members of the same households. We know of at least sixteen *monumenta* of this type, whose inscriptions are collected in the *CIL* vol. VI (though some of them might not be strictly '*columbarium*', since the structures or the reports of the structures are now lost and it is difficult to assess). Among them, the *columbarium* of the Statilii will be given particularly close attention in this thesis. This burial structure was located on the Esquiline region, and preserved the epitaphs of the slaves and freedmen (and also their free-born descendants, the second generation of the freed) of the senatorial family Statilii. The number of its extant inscriptions exceeds that of any other known *columbaria* of private *domus*. This set of inscriptions is collected under the heading *Monumentum Statiliorum* in *CIL* VI 6213-6640, and other relevant inscriptions omitted in the section have been recently gathered and compiled together by Italian scholars Caldelli and Ricci. Two other *columbaria* in use during the same period will serve as good comparative materials; the *Monumentum Liviae* (3926-4326) and *Monumentum Volusiorum* (7281-7394), both situated on the west side of the *via Appia*. In close relation to the former, we also know of the *columbaria* of Marcellae and Nero Claudius Drusus, categorised as imperial households. Beside these major sources, other minor *columbaria* will also be set within the scope of analysis, whose epitaphs are known to us only in small number: these were the *columbaria* of the dependants of certain senatorial families (L. Arruntius, Iunius Silanus, C. Annius Pollio, L. Caninius Gallus), and others of unknown social standing (Abuccii, Caecilii) (vd. Table 2.1 with brief descriptions of the structures).

The central theme of the current chapter is the *columbaria* and aristocratic families whose dependants were buried in them. In order to investigate the *familia urbana* and their epitaphs, it is essential for us to grasp the information regarding the surroundings of their sepulchral structures, locations, public careers of their elite masters, and not least the course of family destiny that must have had an enormous effect on slaves and freedmen, facilitating the establishment and closure of the *columbaria*. I will first discuss the *columbaria* in the Esquiline region, mainly that of the Statilii, and secondly those on the *via Appia* (the Volusii, Livia, and others), and finally the epitaphs as material evidence, particularly those of the Statilii and the Volusii.

I. The *columbaria* on the Esquiline: the Statilii and the Arruntii

Location and topography: the Esquiline necropolis

For reasons of sanitation and religious prohibition, it was ordered in the Twelve Tables that the disposal of the body or ashes had to take place outside the city. This principle had been observed since the Republican period, allowing exceptions only for emperors or others who were specially honoured.[4] For the majority of city dwellers, their dead bodies had to be carried to the

---

[1] vd. Fig. 2.10-13; *TLL* vol. iii, 1991-1912, 1733-1734: The '*aviarium columbarum*' (the place where pigeons were kept) is referred to by agricultural writers such as Varro or Columella, whereas the '*columbarium*' as '*caverna in pariete aedis, in quo ollae cinerum reponuntur*', i.e. as funeral structure, is exclusive to epitaphic evidence.

[2] The emergence of the *columbarium* or collective tomb and its social impact is discussed by Hopkins, 1983, 211-217; Morris, 1992, 42-69.

[3] Ownership of some of the *columbaria* remains ambiguous, one of which is the *columbarium* on the Via Latina just outside Porta Latina. The epitaph on the 'entrance' (*CIL* VI 5552) attests to its owner Cn. Pomponius Hylas (related to C. Pomponius Hylas, *PIR*² P 542, the *procurator* of Augustus?) and his wife Pomponia Cn. l(iberta) Vitalis. But twenty-nine epitaphs from 'inside' the structure record *nomina* apparently unrelated to the Pomponii, including that of a freedman of Antoninus Pius; cf. The *columbarium* of Ti. Claudius Vitalis *architectus* (*CIL* VI 9151), with no other epitaph found from inside the structure. Perhaps these *columbaria* were abandoned or sold to another party in the course of time; Nash, 1968, ii, 324-26; Richardson, 1992, 354, 358; Toynbee, 1971, 115; Nielsen, 1995.

[4] *FIRA*, I, p.66 (*Lex XII Tabularum*, X.1), *hominem mortuum in urbe ne sepelito neve urito*; cf. id. I, no.21, §73 (*lex coloniae Genetivae*, a.710); Crook, 1967, 135.

CHAPTER 2: THE *COLUMBARIA* AND THE ARISTOCRATIC FAMILIES

Table 2.1: The *columbaria* of known individuals or families in *CIL* VI

columbaria	note on the site and aristocratic patrons	*CIL* no., page number	Number of *tituli*
Statilii	On the Esquiline Hill	6213-6640 pp.994-1013	429
Volusii	On the *via Appia*	7281-7394 pp.1043-1050	158
Livia	On the *via Appia*	3926-4326 pp.877-899	401
L. Arruntius	On the Esquiline Hill	5931-5960 pp.978-981	30
Iunius Silanus	On the *via Appia* (in vinea Randaninia) M. Iunius Silanus (*cos.* A.D.46) (*PIR*[1] I 833) and his son L. Silanus	7600-7643 pp.1066-1067	44
Nero Claudius Drusus	Between the *via Appia* and *via Latina* near the Aurelian wall The masters include wife Antonia, mother Livia, brother Tiberius etc.	4327-4413 pp.899-907	87
Marcella	Between the *Via Latina* and *via Appia*, one of the *columbaria* of 'Vigna Codini' The masters include Marcella (Augustus' niece, second wife of Agrippa), and her daughter Marcella the younger	4414-4880 pp.908-926	467
Iunius Silanus	On the *via Appia* (in vinea Randaninia) M. Iunius Silanus (*cos.* A.D.46) (*PIR*[1] I 833) and his son L. Silanus	7600-7643 pp.1066-1067	44
Carvilii	On the *via Appia* (in vinea Randaninia) The patrons are not clear.	7590-7599 pp.1065-1066	10
C. Annius Pollio	On the *via Appia* (in the vinea Amendolae) C. Annius Pollio (*PIR*[1] A 679) or (*PIR*[1] A 677)	7395-7429 pp.1051-1052	35
Caecilii	On *via Appia* (in vinea Amendolae)	7430-7442 pp.1052-1054	13
Passienii	On the west side of the *via Appia* (in Vigna Moroni). During 1-2 century AD	7257-7280, 33248-49 pp.1040-1042	26
Bruttii	Between *via Appia* and *via Ardeatina* The masters include C. Bruttius Praesens (*cos.* II AD 180) and his son L. Bruttius Quintius Crispinus (*cos.* 187)	7582-7589 pp.1064-1065	8
L. Caninius Gallus	On the *via Salaria* L. Caninius Gallus (*cos.* 37BC) or (*cos.* 2BC) (*PIR*[2] C 390)	7987-7996 pp.1088	10
L. Abuccii	no report on the site is known	8117-8172 pp. 1096-1099	56
Q. Sallustii	no report on the site is known	8173-8210 pp.1100-1102	38

The *Familia Urbana* During the Early Empire

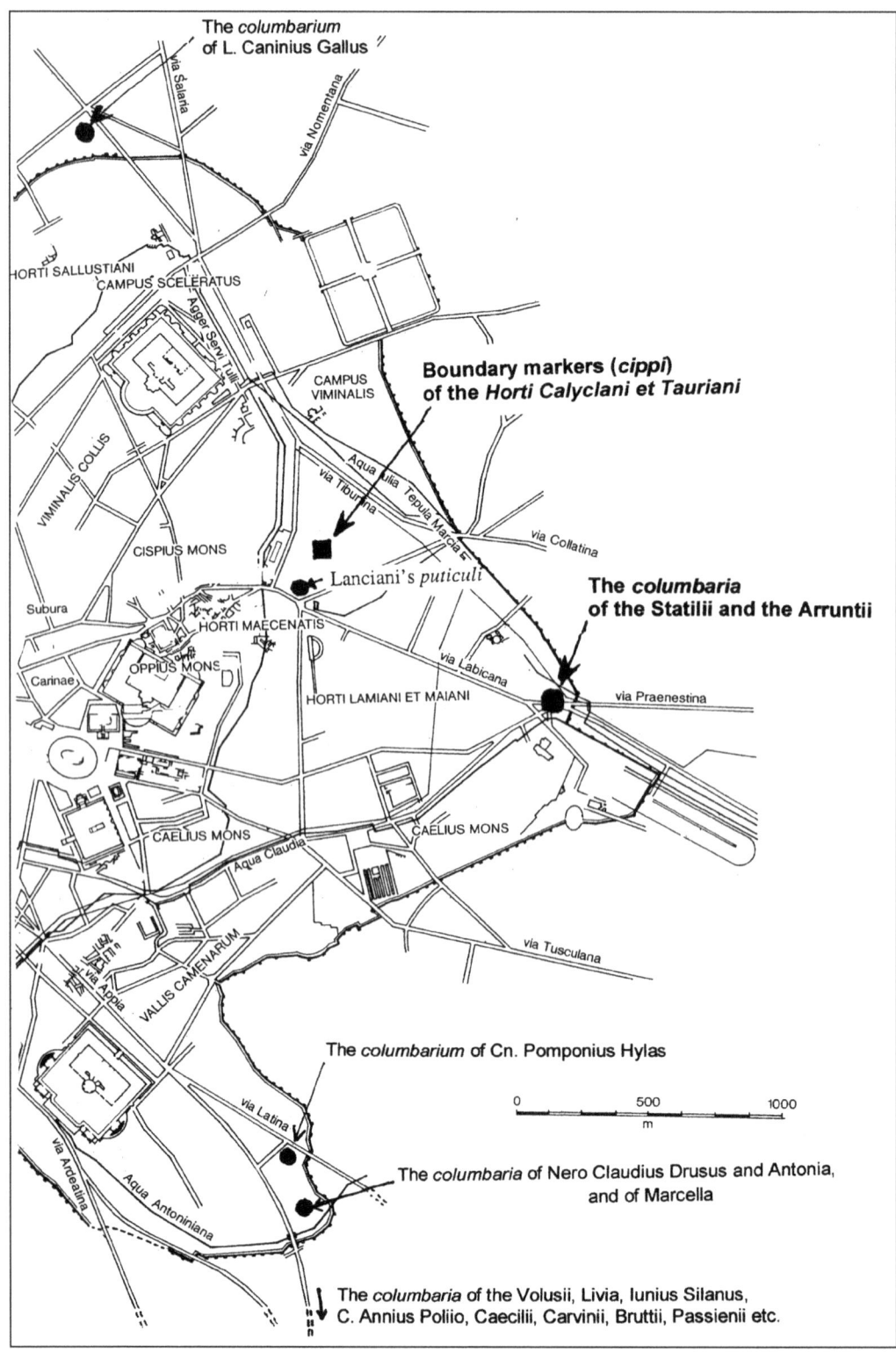

Fig. 2.1 The map of Rome: locations of the *columbaria*
(the Esquiline in the centre; the Servian Wall running vertical across the hill;
part of the via Latina and via Appia)

Extracted and modified from Coarelli (1974), *Guida archeologica di Roma*, Verona.

outside of the Servian walls. Part of the Esquiline Hill, the area close to the Servian walls just outside the *Porta Esquilina*, had been known as the graveyard of the paupers. In excavations carried out between 1874 and 1885, R. Lanciani discovered more than seventy pits full of bones of humans and animals. These pits were presumably what Varro called *puticuli*, where the bodies of the poor, slaves or the free, were dumped without cremation.[5] Such unrestricted disposal of the corpses, an inevitable consequence of poverty and death, apparently brought serious destitution to the Esquiline. The *cippi* (pillars) inscribed with the edict of the praetor L. Sentius (in the early first century BC), which prohibited the burning or dumping of corpses and throwing excrement (*stercus*), have been found from the area along the Servian walls.[6] Attempts to improve the conditions went on, and at the time of Augustus, some visible change was introduced when beautiful gardens of the aristocrats came to occupy the area. The gardens of the wealthy equestrian Maecenas were the most notable ones (*horti Maecenatis*).[7] According to Horace, himself the *amicus* of Maecenas, the gardens contributed to improve the sanitation and landscape of the gloomy Esquiline necropolis.[8] The actual improvement might have been mere side-product of the luxury of a wealthy man, and certainly, the dark side of the landscape did not disappear overnight; the Esquiline continued to retain a parallel land use.[9] Nonetheless, at the same time, the fact that the Esquiline common graveyard (*commune sepulchrum*) underwent a certain degree of transformation during the early Empire, with the refurbishment of magnificent aristocratic gardens, needs to be noted.

In this context, the Statilii, one of our *columbaria*-owning families, played a role similar to that of Maecenas. The area further down to the south-east corner of the Esquiline, just inside the *porta Praenestina*, had been long occupied by numerous sepulchral structures. Among them was the *columbarium* for the family's slaves and freedmen (Fig. 2.1-4). But this was not the only property in the Esquiline that belonged to the Statilii. At a close distance from this district, in the same Regio V outside the Servian walls, the Statilii owned pleasure gardens or suburban residences (*horti*).

Two kinds of evidence locate their ownership of the *horti* on the spot. First, two *cippi* (pillars), designating the boundary 'between the *horti Calyclani* and the *horti Tauriani*', were discovered *in situ* (and two close together) between the modern *via Cappellini* and *via Mamiani* (the area between the ancient *via Labicana* and *via Tiburtina*), that is about 800m. north-west of the family's *columbarium*.[10] The other evidence, which further corroborates the association of the Statilii with this area, is a fragment of a *fistula aquaria* (water-pipe): the stamp on the *fistula* reads "T. Statili Tauri" (*CIL* XV 7542), and is said to have been found in the same Esquiline region. As generally understood, in order to receive water from public aqueducts for private use, the water pipes were procured by the owner of the house to which the water was being piped and were designated with the stamp of their name. In this regard, it is reasonable to consider the *fistula* with the name 'T. Statilius Taurus' as part of a water-supplying facility for his residence, namely the *horti Tauriani* that would have stood nearby according to the boundary *cippi*.[11] In all, it is plausible that the gardens of T. Statilius Taurus occupied the area of Regio V, alongside the *columbarium* of their staff in close proximity (Fig. 2.1).[12]

Since the *horti* were eponymously called '*Tauriani*', the Statilii either constructed them or gave them a first substantial refurbishment. The area was now the frontier of a changing landscape. There stood the *horti Maecenatis* on the south-west, and the *Macellum Liviae* (Market Hall of Livia, built by Augustus and dedicated by Tiberius in 7 BC) on the west. Together with them, I think that the *horti Tauriani* made some contribution to pushing back the destitute area of *puticuli* (pit-holes) of dead animals and the poor.

Another point in regard to the Statilii's *horti* is its coordination with the location of the *columbarium*. In less than a kilometre to the south-east, the Statilian *horti* met the sepulchral structures of the family's slaves and freedmen. The Statilian slaves and freedmen whose relatives or colleagues (and eventually themselves) were buried in the *columbarium* must have enjoyed the convenience of a close proximity to their master's estates where probably many of them actually lived and worked as members of the staff. The suburban residences of the powerful individuals in this period, rather than the forum of Republican times, came to play a more and more central political role. Moreover, if we observe that several prominent figures inadvertently met their end in their *horti* and were buried there as a private resting-place (vd. Chap. 3), it is possible that the *horti Tauriani* were also the place where the Statilian *domini* had their tombs. Thus in terms of their location, the family's possession of the *horti* and the *columbaria* appears to be, to say the

---

[5] Varro, *Ling.* 5, 25.
[6] *ILS* 8208=*CIL* I² 838f; cf. Degrassi, *ILLRP*, 485; Lanciani, 1889, 66-67; Hopkins, 1983, 207-211; Toynbee, 1971, 48-50; Bodel, 1994, 38-54: an inscription on a travertine block, which recorded the *senatusconsultum* aimed to protect the area of the *pagus Montanus* from similar kinds of wrongdoings, was also found from the area.
[7] Dio, 55, 7, with Rich, 1990, 225; Suet. *Vita Hor.*; Richardson, 1992, 200-201.
[8] Hor. *Sat.* I, 8, 6-16.
[9] It is referred to as a place of execution of criminals in the time of Claudius: Suet. *Claud.* 25, 3, *civitatem R. usurpantes in campo Esquilino securi percussit*.

[10] *CIL* VI 29771=*ILS* 5998, *cippi hi finiunt hortos Calyclan(os) et Taurianos*.
[11] On the *fistula aquaria*, Loane, 1938, 110-111; cf. Eck, 1997b, 172ff.; on the *horti Tauriani*: E. Papi, *LTUR*, iii, 85.
[12] Apart from the *horti Tauriani*, the Statilii in fact had more than one garden in Rome. We know at least that the *horti Pompeiani* (on the Campus Martius) and certain *horti Scatoniani* were in their possession according to the epitaphs of slaves (A090; A280). We are not sure which one was the target of Agrippina's jealousy that drove T. Statilius Taurus (*cos*. AD 44) into suicide.

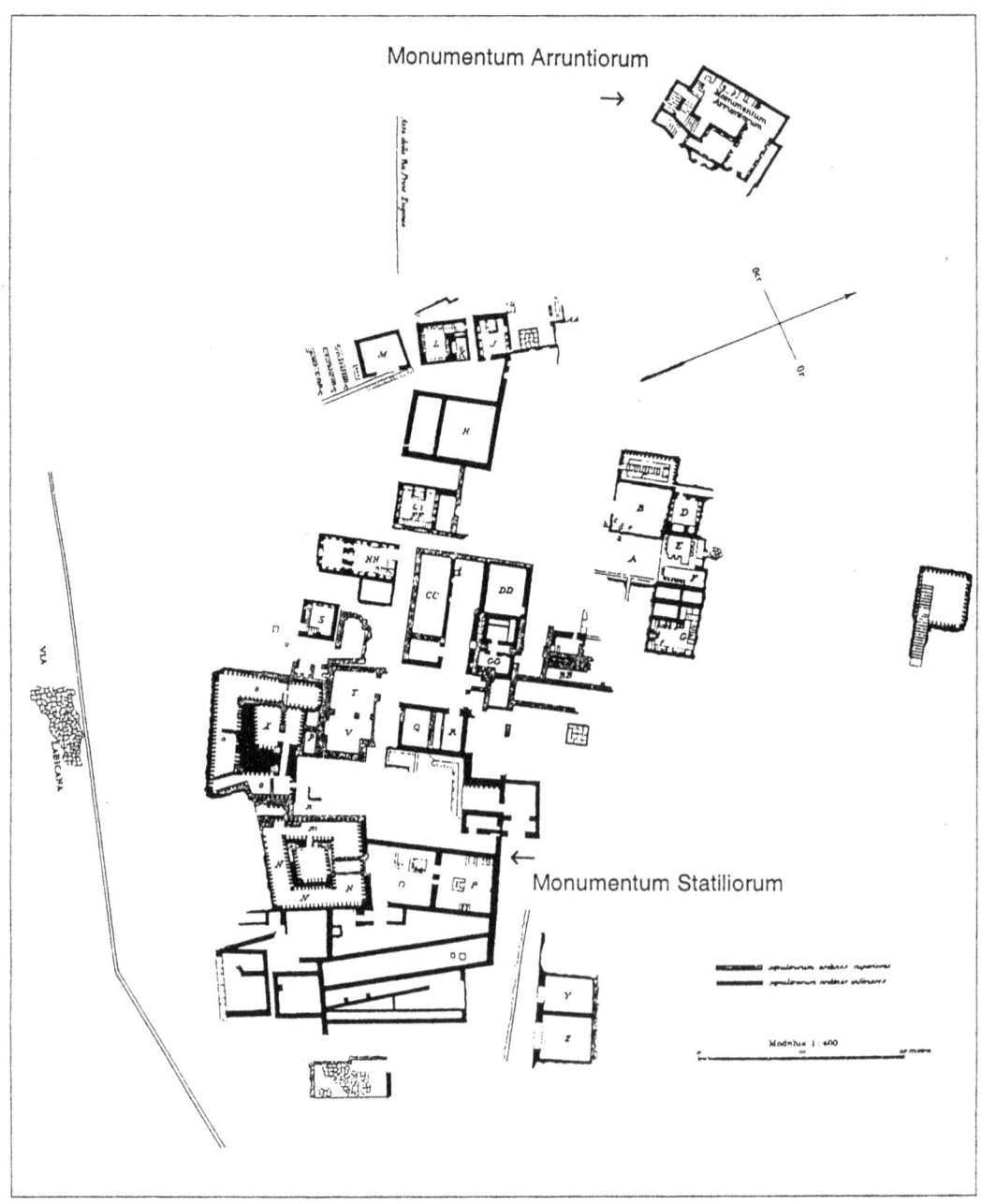

Fig. 2.2 The ground plan of the sepulchral complex in the area of Porta Maggiore
Extracted from *CIL* VI, p. 982

least, nicely co-ordinated for connecting the masters and their dependants. One could say the arrangement of the family estates on the Esquiline, which contained the living, working, and burial places of masters and household staff in proximity, was good planning. A further possible speculation is that the Statilii were virtually the owners of the whole area, stretching from the west boundary to the *horti Calyclani* down to the *columbarium* of their servants.[13]

The *columbarium*: surrounding sepulchral buildings

Let us now look closely at the site and structures of the Statilian *columbarium*. It was part of larger sepulchral complex in the area about 100 metres inside from the *porta Praenestina* (also known as *porta Maggiore* since the tenth century), facing on the south the ancient *via Labicana* (presently the *via Praenestina*).[14] A systematic archaeological survey of the site was first undertaken in

---

[13] Cf. 'Forum Tauri' and 'Caput Tauri' on the Esquiline, mentioned only in medieval documents: Richardson, 1992, 175.

[14] On the *Porta Praenestina*, Nash, 1968, ii, 225-228; it is not clear whether the so-called Basilica of the Porta Maggiore outside the Porta, discovered in 1917, dated to the same period of the *columbarium*, and whose neo-Pythagorean connection has been suggested, has anything to do with the Statilii.

CHAPTER 2: THE *COLUMBARIA* AND THE ARISTOCRATIC FAMILIES

Fig. 2.3 The chronological shift of the sepulchral complex in the Esquiline
Extracted with some modification from Caldelli and Ricci, 1999, n.10-13

1875, and uncovered a number of closely adjacent *columbaria* and other sepulchral buildings (Fig. 2.2-4). Unfortunately, after a series of excavations, the whole necropolis complex was either destroyed or buried under Piazza di Porta Maggiore without being preserved, due to the construction and enlargement of the adjacent roads at the end of the nineteenth century.[15] The result of the excavation of the *Monumentum Statiliorum* was subsequently published by the late nineteenth century archaeologist E. Brizio; this work remains our primary source of information, with its accounts of the structures, topography of the site, and analysis of the inscriptions. A century later, with growing interest in the subjects of less privileged social groups, the Italian scholars Caldelli and Ricci (1999) published the study of the *columbarium* of the Statilii, which gathered together and reassessed the fragmented nineteenth century archaeological reports.[16]

The report of Rodolfo Lanciani, the director of the excavation, cited by Caldelli and Ricci, gives a general view of the site: "...the stratification of the sepulchral buildings consisted of three phases; one during the Republic, one at the beginning of the Empire, and one in the third century...One must note that while the *columbaria* overlap with the republican *sepulcra*, and the buildings of the late imperial period with the *columbaria*,

---

[15] Caldelli and Ricci, 1999, 18f.

[16] For other succinct accounts of the *monumentum Statiliorum*, see D. Mancioli, s.v. "Sepulcrum: Statilii", in *LTUR*, iv, 299; A. G. Thein, s.v. "Sepulcrum: Statilii", in *MAR*, 229; Nash, 1968, ii, 359-369; Richardson, 1992, 360; Mommsen's report based on Brizio in *CIL* VI, pp.994-995.

each respects the ashes and the memory of the deceased as much as possible..."[17] It appears that the whole sepulchral complex did not exist simultaneously (Fig. 2.3). Mainly from the evidence of the epitaphs recovered from certain structures, architectural techniques, or directions of the buildings, Caldelli and Ricci (originally E. Brizio) established the chronological relationship between each structure. Here I will cite their argument (N.B., the translation is my own and my supplementary comments are shown in square brackets):[18]

> 'The first *sepulcra* to be constructed (50-20 BC) seems to be (BB), datable around 50 BC., on the basis of *CIL* VI 33087-33088 (which record Q. Pompeius Sosius, freedman of Q. Pompeius Bitinicus, *quaestor* or *legatus* in Bithynia in 75 or 74 BC.); the *sepulcra* (J), (K), (L), (M), each structure standing separately, may be dated on the basis of *CIL* VI 6184 (which records a freedwoman of Agrippa) and on the techniques of construction (*opus reticulatum* of the end of the Republican period or the beginning of the Principate); the *monumentum* (X) may be dated, at the latest, to the first years of the reign of Augustus, on the basis of *CIL* VI 6687 (which records Eros and Felix, the *pistores* [bakers] of Autronius Paetus, who triumphed in 26 BC [sic, in fact, 28BC])...; the *sepulcra* (Q-R) may be dated to the beginning of the Augustan period, on the basis of *CIL* VI 6671 (which records a freedman of L. Volcacius Tullus, consul with Augustus in 26 BC).

> 'During the main Augustan period (20 BC – 14 AD), the *sepulcra* (A), (B), (C), (D), (E), (F), (G), were successively constructed side by side: of these, only the *monumentum* (A) is datable on basis of *CIL* VI 6030 (which records the slave or freedman of A. Caecina Severus, suffect consul in 2 BC), while the *sepulcrum* (DD) may be dated on the basis of *CIL* VI 33102 (which records Cn. Sentius, suffect consul in 4 AD).

> 'Towards the end of the Augustan period or the beginning of Tiberius' reign, the *sepulcra* (S), (T), (V), were constructed, datable on the basis of techniques of construction and of *CIL* VI 6677 (which records a freedman of Sex. Pompeius, identified with the consul in 14 AD); and the first structure (N) of the sepulchral building of the Statilii was established, backing onto *monumentum* (X).

> 'From the end of the Neronian age, after the marriage of Statilia Messalina with the emperor, were constructed the structures (O-P), which will have adjoined and functionally replaced the *monumentum* of the Statilii properly so called, and the *sepulcrum* (FF), datable in particular on the basis of *CIL* VI 33131 (which records a *Ti. Iulius Aug. lib. Xanthus*, *tractator* of the deified Claudius and of Nero).

> 'We do not have firm chronological indications regarding the *sepulcra* (H), (Y-Z), (AA), (CC), (GG), (HH), the epigraphic materials from which, where extant and legible, attest respectively to frequentation from the end of republican period to the end of Claudius' reign (CC and HH), from the period of Claudius to the end of the second century AD (GG), and to in the middle of the second century AD (AA).

Thus, according to the argument of Caldelli and Ricci (and originally of Brizio), the area where the *columbarium* of the Statilii was located had been long in use for sepulchral purposes by those associated with other different families. Even after the Statilian *columbarium*, the place continued to be used for the funerals and burials of relatively prosperous individuals (who could afford to pay for the building or the space in it), up to the end of the second century. Among these numerous sepulchral structures, the three structures (N, O, P) are established as the *Monumentum Statiliorum* (Fig. 2.4), on the basis of the fact that the majority of epitaphs recovered from the three structures clearly designated their connection to the Statilii. The structure (N) is dated to the early Empire (late Augustan or early Tiberian) in relation to the surrounding sepulchral buildings.[19] In this regard, the *columbarium* of the Statilii most likely saw its foundation during the time of the brothers Taurus (*cos.* AD 11) and Sisenna (*cos.* AD 16), i.e., one or two generations later than the new man T. Statilius Taurus (*cos.* 26 BC), a prominent Augustan general.

The *columbarium*: the three structures ascribed to the Statilii (N, O, P)

The main structure (N), the earliest of the three, consisted of two floor levels, with several rooms on the upper level and on the lower level a gallery, a rectangular of about 80 m², surrounding a central room. According to Brizio, there was no direct communication between the two levels, each of which had its own separate access.[20]

The structure (N) had in total more than 700 loculi (niches for ashes). The upper level rooms and the central room on the lower level were furnished with five rows of loculi, while the gallery on the lower level had only three rows of loculi. From the structure (N) as a whole, 381 inscriptions are known, though we do not have reports describing their exact locations within the structure, and we do not even hear of any recovery of urns of ashes.

---

[17] Caldelli and Ricci, 1999, 16-17.
[18] Caldelli and Ricci, 1999, 17.
[19] Caldelli and Ricci, 1999, 15-20, 55-56.
[20] Brizio, 1875, 49-50; Caldelli and Ricci, 1999, 18-19.

CHAPTER 2: THE *COLUMBARIA* AND THE ARISTOCRATIC FAMILIES

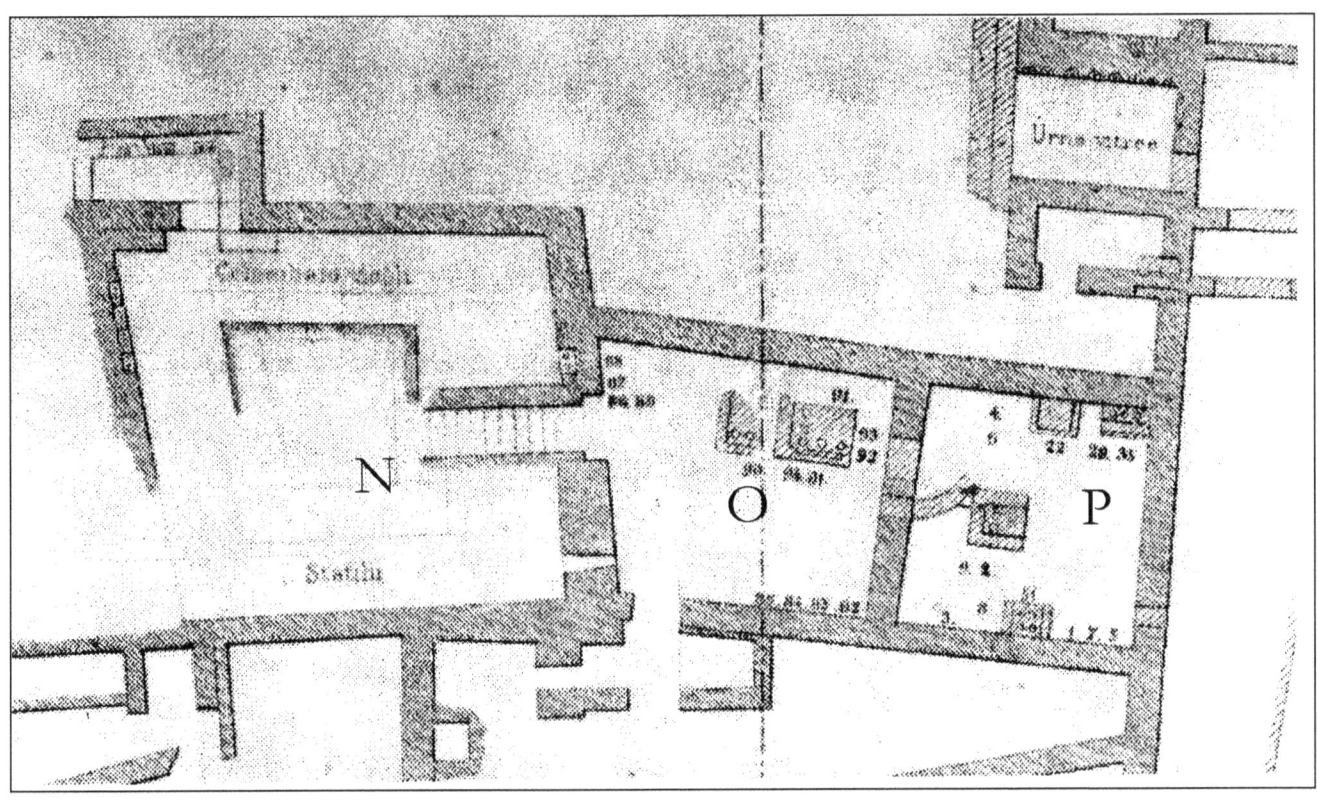

Fig. 2.4 The plan of the *Monumentum Statiliorum*: from the left, N, O, P
Extracted and modified from Caldelli and Ricci, 1999, Fig. 14 (plan by Lanciani, 1877)

The newer and smaller sepulchral structures (O and P) were excavated in 1877 under Lanciani's direction. As to the structure (O) (5.20× 5.55m. square), we can see from the plan in Lanciani's report that it contained at least two small cells or altars. From the structure (O), twenty-six inscriptions were recovered, and fortunately, the exact finding places of some epitaphs were recorded by Lanciani.[21] Structure (P), next to structure (O), appears to have four similar cells or possibly altars inside, in spite of the discrepancy with Lanciani's report, which claims that there was only one such object. A total of 20 inscriptions were recovered from (P), and we are also informed of some of their find spots (Fig. 2.4).[22]

The point of consideration here is that a total of only 381 epitaphs are known from structure (N), which had the capacity of 700 loculi. It seems that the structure (N) ceased to function as a sepulchral chamber at a stage when a large number of the loculi still remained unoccupied. If the structure (N) was prematurely closed, was there perhaps some kind of unexpected intervention to halt the use of the *columbarium*? We have seemingly matching historical incidents that occurred in later generations of the Statilii, namely the clashes of two brothers Statilius Taurus (*cos.* AD 44) and Corvinus (*cos.* AD 45) against the imperial power: that is Corvinus' attempted revolt against Claudius in AD 46, and the accusation made against Taurus (allegedly schemed by Agrippina) and his subsequent suicide in 53 AD. It has been speculated that if the loculi were never filled up, the structure (N) was most probably confiscated from the Statilii, at the time of Taurus' suicide in 53; after that date, the *columbarium* could no longer admit new burials but remained open only for commemorative rituals for those already buried in it; after thirteen years' interval, however, the marriage of Statilia Messalina (daughter of Corvinus or Taurus) to Nero reinvigorated the once fallen *familia*, and they succeeded in constructing the new buildings (O) and (P) - as we saw above, the adjacent structures (O) and (P) were built slightly later than the structure (N) - next to the sepulchral structure (N) which had been closed down.[23] The memorials of the deceased were now to be accommodated in these new structures.

---

[21] To cite Caldelli and Ricci, 1999, 20, "*CIL* VI 6595, 6596, 6602, 6602, 6609, were discovered at the north-west angle; *CIL* VI 6610 lay at the north of a small funeral structure described above; *CIL* VI 6605, 6612 had been instead toward the east of it; *CIL* VI 6603, 6611, 6619 had been at the south of it, the last one resting against it; *CIL* VI 6617, 6618, had been posted at the southern wall: *CIL* VI 6620, 6621, instead had been in the south-oriented angle, laid on to the southern wall." Other epitaphs, according to R. Lanciani, were scattered in the various levels of the grounds.

[22] Again, to cite Caldelli and Ricci, 1999, 20, who referred to the report of R. Lanciani, "*CIL* VI 6635, 6640, 6624, 6639, 6629 had been found near the northern wall; *CIL* VI 6634 was in proximity to the small structure in the centre; *CIL* VI 6628, 6625, 6632, 6633, 6638, 6637 lay near the southern wall."

[23] Caldelli and Ricci, 1999, 99, 55-59, attribute those epitaphs found outside the *columbarium* as belonging to the slaves and freedmen who died during the interval and also before the opening of the *columbarium*; D. Mancioli, s.v. "Sepulcrum: Statilii", in *LTUR*, iv, 299; Mommsen, *CIL* VI, pp.994-995.

If there is any doubt in the view addressed by Caldelli and Ricci and others, it concerns the use of the *columbarium*. Despite Taurus' suicide to save the family fortune, it is unlikely that the Statilii kept possession of their *horti*; for the subsequent emergence of the *horti Pallantiani* and *horti Epaphroditiani* on the Esquiline hill, the names of which were presumably taken from the freedmen of Claudius and Nero respectively, overrode part of the *horti Tauriani*.[24] Unlike the fate of such grand family properties, however, I think that the *columbarium* was quite possibly left untouched, since, above all, in Roman law, sepulchral structures formed a *locus religiosus*, protected from changes in ownership. Certainly, we know of some sepulchral structures which came to be occupied by those other than the family initially buried. But they were likely to be the result of legitimate purchase or the natural conclusion of a household rather than the abrupt confiscation of dubious motives. In the first place, there is no recognisable trace of buried alien individuals who might have subsequently taken over: names of outsiders are found in a very limited number, and several inscriptions that suggest individuals associated to the *familia* of emperor Claudius are only attributed to the adjacent sepulchral structures in the complex (not to the main chamber of the Statilian *columbarium*).[25] In the circumstances, it is reasonable to infer that the *columbarium* was practically open for burial and rituals as long as the staff and their family were alive. But before we consider more on this issue, it is necessary for us to look more closely into the rise of this *columbarium* owner and the situations surrounding the family's fall from the public scene.

The *gens Statilia*

T. Statilius Taurus (*cos. suff.* 37 BC; *cos. ord.* 26 BC), probably born in 70s BC, arose from unknown ancestry, and turned out to be an extremely successful *homo novus*. The contemporary historian Velleius Paterculus described him as the most trusted friend of Augustus, 'only second to Agrippa.'[26] Though he might not have been alive at the time of the construction of the *columbarium*, the new man Taurus was to exercise a far-reaching effect upon descendants and their slaves and freedmen, as the first of the family who established prestige and influence in politics.[27]

Taurus established himself through a distinguished military career, fighting a series of wars for Octavian.[28] His prominence as a triumphant general brought him the honour of undertaking a public building project: he dedicated Rome's first stone amphitheatre in 29 BC at his own expense according to Cassius Dio, and perhaps using the spoils from his campaigns - Africa and Illyricum. For this benefaction, Taurus was granted the right to nominate one of the praetors each year.[29] He was then entrusted with the informal supervision of Rome and Italy in 16 BC during Augustus' absence, a post yet in a premature phase before the formal office of city prefect (*praefectus urbi*) was created as a permanency from AD 13 onward.[30] This appointment probably continued until 13 BC, and then Taurus disappears from the record, perhaps dying soon afterward. For Taurus' meritorious service, the Statilii were probably one of the plebeian families that were raised to patrician rank by Augustus in 29 BC.[31]

After Taurus the *novus homo*, the next family members known to have reached the consulship are T. Statilius Taurus (*cos.* AD 11) and his brother Sisenna Statilius Taurus (*cos.* AD 16) (Fig. 2.5). The problem, however, is that there appears to be a gap of one generation between the two Tauri. The figure who might fill this lost generation is Taurus (*PIR*[1] S 616), known from the tenure of the junior post of *monetalis*. Unfortunately, his location in the family tree is highly obscure; some scholars identify him as the son of Taurus the *novus homo* and father of Taurus (*cos.* AD 11) and Sisenna (*cos.* AD 16), while others locate him as the brother of Taurus and Sisenna.[32] The latter proposition might be favoured over the former if we credit the usual dating of his coinage as *monetalis* to around 8 BC.[33] Taurus must have been in his early twenties as *monetalis*, born no earlier than 30 BC. In that sense, he cannot have had a son who was consul in AD 11 or AD 16, but would rather belong to the same generation as Taurus and Sisenna. If so, the *monetalis* might be a brother who died young before he could reach the consulship or, alternatively, it is possible that the *monetalis* Taurus was not a separate individual at all, but identical to Taurus (*cos.* AD 11).[34]

---

[24] Caldelli and Ricci, 1999, 15; cf. Frontin. *Aq.* 19; 20; 68; 69.
[25] Two epitaphs of the emperor's freedmen or with the nomen Claudius or Iulius are found from the main structure (N) (A332), (A244), three from (O) (A392) (A402) (A407), and one *dispensator* of an emperor from the new structure (P) (A426).
[26] Vell. 2, 127.
[27] Taurus as a *homo novus*, Wiseman, 1971, 263; as an *amicus* of Augustus, Crook, 1955, no.310; Syme, 1939, 237, from an inscription dedicated to Taurus by the Volceii in Lucania (*ILS* 893a), a speculation is made about the old ancestry of the Statilii from Lucania; other inscriptions of Taurus in connection to his wife Cornelia are discussed by Kajava, 1989, 147 *et al.* See also *PIR*[1] S 615.

---

[28] Taurus' military achievement: the war against Sex. Pompeius (Appian, *B.C.* V 97-99, 103, 105, 108); against Antony (Dio, 50, 13, 3; Vell. 2, 85; Plut. *Ant.* 65); in Africa (Dio, 49, 14, 6); against Hispanic tribes, the Cantabri, the Vaccaei, and the Astures (Dio, 51, 20, 5).
[29] Taurus' construction of the amphitheatre, Dio, 51, 23, 1; Suet. *Aug.* 29, 5; Tac. *Ann.* 3, 72.
[30] Dio, 53, 23, 1; 54, 19, 6; Rich, 1990, 157, 196-7; Kienast, 1982, 272-273; cf. Tac. *Ann.* 6, 11; Taurus' responsibility over Rome and Italy was probably tentative and was not accompanied by the formal title *praefectus urbi*.
[31] *RG* 8.1; Dio 52, 42, 5; Syme, 1939, 382; Vogel-Weidemann, 1982, 155-156.
[32] The former hypothesis is held by Dessau (*PIR*[1] S 616), Mommsen (*CIL* VI p.994), and Benario, 1970, while the latter by Syme, 1986, 376-7 etc., Kajava, 1989, Caldelli and Ricci, 1999.
[33] Sutherland, 1984, 75, nos. 423-5; according to Syme, 1986, 376-7, n. 54, no numismatist dates Taurus the monetalis earlier than 10 BC.
[34] Kajava, 1989, 141-142; on the view that the *monetalis* is identical to Taurus (*cos.* AD 11), Wiseman, 1971, 150 and 263, no.413.

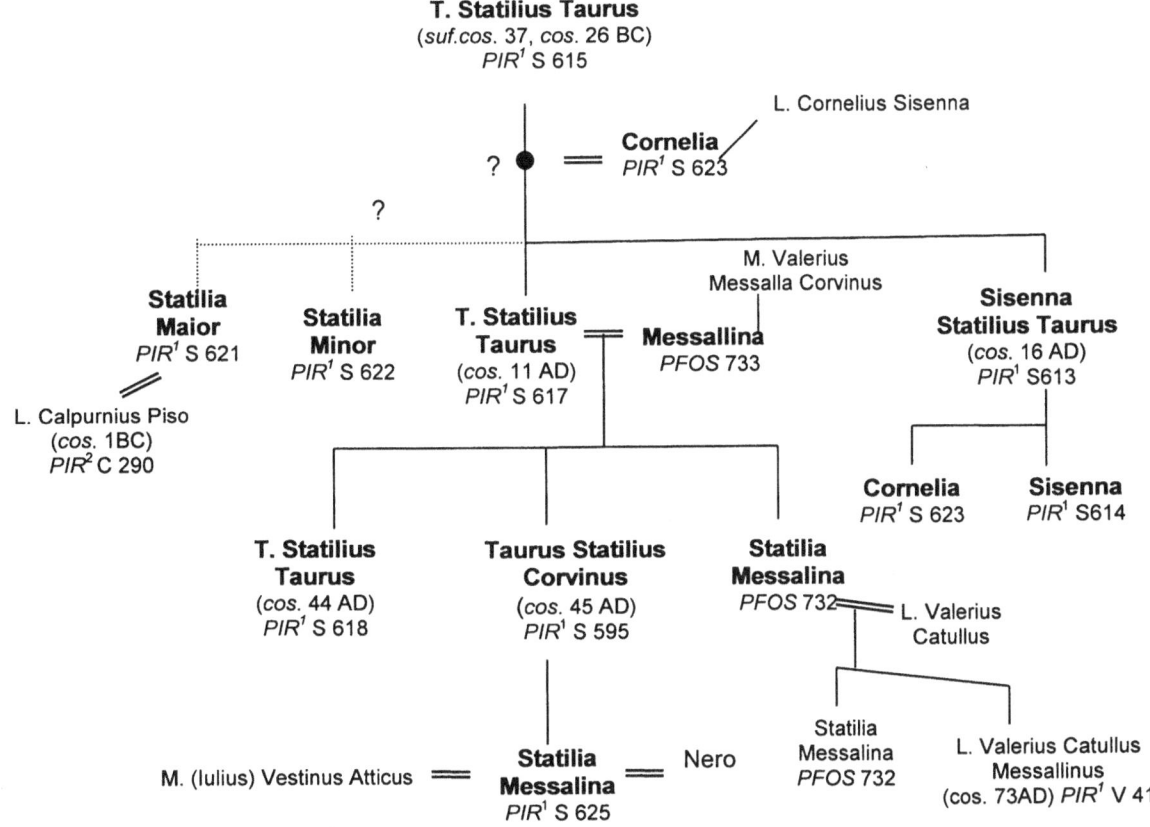

Fig. 2.5: The *gens Statilia*
(adapted from *PIR*¹ S, p.264 and Caldelli and Ricci, 1999, 44)

According to archaeological and epigraphic evidence, the construction of the *columbarium* is probably attributed to the generation of Taurus (*cos.* AD 11) and Sisenna (*cos.* AD 14), about whose career we do not have much to say. It was then during the following generation when the family met an unfortunate end. First, Corvinus (*cos.* AD 45), the younger son of Taurus (*cos.* AD 11), immediately after his consulship, turned into a rebel who attempted to overthrow the emperor Claudius in AD 46. Suetonius gives a brief account of the conspiracy led by Corvinus and Asinius Gallus, joined by 'his (Claudius') own slaves and freedmen.'[35] The outcome of this failed revolt is only explicitly stated for Asinius Gallus, whose punishment was unusually moderate and merciful. Claudius pardoned him for the charge of high treason because, according to Dio, it was rather an erratic action, and Gallus collected neither an army nor money beforehand (Dio, 60, 27-28); Asinius Gallus escaped execution and was instead merely exiled. If banishment was the case for Gallus, the co-leader Statilius Corvinus is also likely to have had his life spared. In fact, Corvinus was seen to be active between AD 50 and 54 as a member of the *fratres Arvales*, which suggests that he had been acquitted of the accusation.[36]

More fatal to the family than Corvinus' revolt against Claudius were the charges of extortion (*repetundae*) and practice of magic (*magicae superstitiones*) brought against the other brother Taurus (*cos.* AD 44). Tarquitius Priscus, the accuser (*delator*), had been the deputy (*legatus*) of Taurus in his proconsulship in Africa, and was personally supported by Agrippina. The real motivation behind the accusation, according to Tacitus, was that Agrippina wanted to seize the magnificent garden that Taurus owned. Taurus committed suicide in AD 53 without waiting for the verdict. Whether he was guilty or not, suicide was a common path taken by those accused of these kinds of charges during the period.[37]

After Taurus and Corvinus, we do not hear of any prominent heirs of the *gens Statilia*.[38] The last of the family to appear in the historical record was Statilia Messalina, the daughter of Corvinus or Taurus. She was renowned for her beauty, and became the third wife of the emperor Nero in AD 66. Before her marriage to Nero,

---

[35] Suet. *Claud.* 13, *assumptis compluribus libertis ipsius atque servis.*
[36] *AE* 1983, 95; Vogel-Weidemann, 1982, 156.
[37] On analysis of this case in a long line of bloodshed accusations thrown upon the noble families, Rutledge, 2001, 109-110, 272, suggests that the brother Corvinus' conspiracy rendered Taurus a potential enemy; Talbert, 1984, 183, 413, 508; Vogel-Weidemann, 1982, 154-160; Benario, 1970, 73-76; the senate as well as Tacitus was indignant at Agrippina's agent Tarquitius Priscus, and managed to expel him from the senate after Taurus' death: Tac. *Ann.* 12, 59; 14, 46.
[38] Cf. Statilius Cassius Taurinus, a *frater Arvalis* in AD 155 (*CIL* V 2086): *RE*, IIIa, 1929, 2190.

Messalina had been married to Vestinus Atticus, who was a bitter rival of the emperor and eventually forced to commit suicide. Messalina's marriage with Nero soon ended with his suicide in AD 68. She then nearly went on to remarry the subsequent emperor Otho. The marriage never took place, but Otho, on the verge of committing suicide, wrote a letter to Messalina, asking her to take care of his burial (Suet. *Otho*, 10, 2). Though he was eventually buried with a modest tomb in Brixellum, probably by his close associates (Plut. *Otho*, 18, 1-2; Tac. *Hist.* 2, 49), Messalina he trusted to the extent of asking her to ensure the disposition of his ashes and the construction and maintenance of his tomb.[39]

The question here is whether the confiscation of Taurus' property ever took place after his suicide, in accordance with Agrippina's wishes. Did they take all the property away from the family, as has often been assumed, not only the gardens coveted by Agrippina but also the houses and slaves and even their *columbarium*? Did this lead to a cessation in the use of the oldest main chamber (N) of the *columbarium*?

The general rule set during the reign of Tiberius drove the aristocrat who was accused of a capital offence to commit suicide before the court sentenced him to death. By doing so, he was not only saved from disgrace as a criminal whose burial was forbidden, but also a large part of his property could escape confiscation and be left to his heirs.[40] Dio reports as the situation following Sejanus' treason in AD 31 that the intention of defendants who took their own life was "partly that their children might inherit their property, since very few estates of those who voluntarily died before their trial were confiscated, Tiberius in this way inviting men to become their own murderers, so that he might avoid the reputation of having killed them…Most of the estates of those who failed to die in this manner were confiscated, only a little or even nothing at all being given to their accusers" (Dio, 58, 16). On the other hand, other sources attest to instances when part or all of the property was taken away by the accuser as reward, even though the accused committed suicide. It was once proposed by the Senate in AD 24 that the *delator* should forfeit his reward if a defender took his own life before the trial was finished, though on this occasion the proposal was rejected by Tiberius. The property of those who killed themselves was usually preserved from the hands of *delatores*, but it was "more by custom than by law."[41]

In such rather ambivalent situations, all we can speculate in Taurus' case is that his suicide might have reduced the possibility or degree of confiscation of the property, since that was what tended to happen. This at the same time means that it is also possible that the gardens including the *horti Tauriani* on the Esquiline and other grand parts of the property were taken away from the family.

Unlike these family estates, however, the treatment of the *columbarium* deserves further consideration. Setting aside the question of who actually owned the *columbarium*, it is usually assumed that the *horti* and the *columbarium* were both confiscated in 53 at the time of Taurus' suicide; and that this accounts for the cessation in the use of the structure (N), the largest and earliest of the sepulchral structures, with many of its 700 loculi still unfilled; new burials were no longer made in the structure (N), which remained open only to undertake commemorative rituals for those already buried in it. After an interval of thirteen years, the marriage of Statilia Messalina with Nero reinvigorated the once fallen *familia*, and they succeeded in constructing the new sepulchral buildings (O) and (P) next to the main sepulchral structure (N) that had been closed since Taurus' death.[42]

The discrepancy between the capacity of the niches and the number of *tituli* actually recovered, certainly suggests the premature closure of the *columbarium* (N); followed by a shift to the adjacent newer structures (O) and (P), as the epitaphs of later generations appear to concentrate there. In my view, however, this transition was not necessarily a result of the disruption caused by confiscation. Above all, and unlike other kinds of estate, the *sepulchrum* or *monumentum* was considered as rather special or inviolable. Roman law regarded places intended for burial as *loci religiosi*, which were "subject to divine law and therefore not susceptible of human ownership or alienation of any kind."[43] In this respect, an abrupt confiscation of the *columbarium*, already more than half of its total capacity filled with urns of ashes, seems highly questionable. The right of the family members left to perform commemorative ritual was well protected by law, and I suppose that nothing could have prevented the remaining slaves/freedmen from being buried there as they wished, even after the death of Taurus in AD 53.

---

[39] A series of relentless wife-swapping: Poppaea Sabina was married to Otho when Nero fell for her; Suet. *Nero*, 35, 1; Tac. *Ann.* 15, 68-69; about the reputation for beauty and marital life of Statilia Messalina, Syme, 1986, 240-241; Bauman, 1992, 209; but some statements that she married five times are probably incorrect, confused with Valeria Messallina, Claudius' wife (cf. Juv. 6, 434); Murison, 1992, 125-126; Kienast, 1990, 100.
[40] Tac. *Ann.* 6, 29, 2.
[41] Tac. *Ann.* 4, 30, 3; Chilton, 1955; Brunt, 1961, 203; Levick, 1976, 180-200; Rutledge, 2001, 42-3.

[42] Caldelli and Ricci, 1999, 55-59 and 99, suggested that the epitaphs found outside the *columbaria* might belong to those who died either during the interval (between Taurus' suicide and Messalina's marriage) or before the opening of the *columbaria*; Mommsen, *CIL* VI, p.994; D. Mancioli, s.v. "Sepulcrum: Statilii", in *LTUR*, iv, 299.
[43] Crook, 1967, 133-138; Gaius, *Inst*, 2, 2-9, *religiosum vero nostra uoluntate facimus mortuum inferentes in locum nostrum, si modo eius mortui funus ad nos pertineat…quod autem diuini iuris est, id nullius in bonis est*; *Dig.* 11, 7, 2, pr. (Ulpian), *locum in quo seruus sepultus est religiosum esse Aristo ait*; on theoretical contradiction between the *columbarium* as the ownership-free property and the individual niches inside as the object of sale, Crook suggests that "what was being bought and sold was not the tomb itself but the right to dispose of a place in it, the *ius sepulchri*."

Chapter 2: The *columbaria* and the aristocratic families

Table 2.2 Named *domini* and *dominae* (the Statilii)

Name	Number	Percentage	
Taurus	23	3.5%	
T. Statilius Taurus pater (*PIR*[1] S 617)	2	0.3%	
Taurus adulescens / filius (*PIR*[1] S 618)	3	0.5%	
T. Statilius [Taurus]	2	0.3%	
Sisenna (*PIR*[1] S 613)	6	0.9%	a. Total: 80
Sisenna augur / Sisenna filius (*PIR*[1] S 614)	3	0.5%	(12.40%)
Corvinus /Taurus Statilius (*PIR*[1] S 595)	12	1.8%	
Tauri soror	1	0.2%	
Cornelia (daughter of L. Cornelius Sisenna)	4	0.6%	
Cornelia (daughter or wife of Sisenna or Taurus?)	2	0.3%	
Statilia [Maior]	7	1.1%	
Statilia [Minor]	2	0.3%	
Messalina [Valeria?] (wife of Taurus, *cos*.11)	3	0.5%	
Messallina Tauri f. (daughter of Taurus, *cos*.11)	3	0.5%	
Messalina [Neronis]	7	1.1%	
b. Intermediate owners (owned by slaves/freedmen)	121	18.4%	
c. Unknown / others	456	69.4%	
Total (a, b, c)	657	100.0%	

The loss of a master was undoubtedly an enormous blow for slaves and freedmen.[44] After the incident, slaves who lost their master would have had to be sold off or passed on to others,[45] and naturally, as a result, the demand for burial in the *columbarium* reduced dramatically. But not to the extent of closure. For it must be noted that there were many freedmen or free-born buried in the *columbarium*, and not all of them actually belonged to Taurus, but many to the freedmen of the Statilii (vd. Table 2.2). These freedmen and other free dependants should not be affected and would suffer little disruption, since they were no longer legally the property of the Statilii. Moreover, if Taurus and Corvinus were allowed to make a will (a right usually preserved for the accused who commit suicide or who were exiled), they might have provided in their will for the manumission of as many slaves as possible within the limitation of the *lex Fufia Caninia*.

Why, then, were the two newer structures (O, P) built, or did they come into use while the structure (N) apparently still had substantial vacancies? I suggest the following scenario. Messalina's marriage with Nero in AD 66 brought a final major boost to the social status of the Statilii. At this point, only a reduced number of servants associated to the *gens Statilia* remained, consisting mainly of the servants of Statilia Messalina and of other remaining servants of the Statilii. For some reason, this last group of Statilian dependants shifted the main place of burial into the new sepulchral chambers (O and P), whether because smaller sepulchral structures were felt more suitable for a now smaller circle of members (certainly easier for the maintenance), or because, proud to be the servants of the emperor's wife, they wished to distinguish themselves from the fallen Statilii in the old grand chamber (N). I suspect that Messalina herself intended the establishment of the new *columbaria* because, like Livia, she anticipated the expansion of her servants by marriage with the emperor. Unfortunately, her grand marriage ended in less than two years with Nero's suicide in AD 68. The emperor Otho subsequently considered marrying her but the ceremony never took place in his brief reign.[46] Messalina witnessed and outlived the fall of the *gens Statilia* as a daughter, and also the end of the emperor of the Julio-Claudian dynasty as a wife. After Messalina, the use of the *columbarium* slowly came to a final end.

---

[44] Impact of change of master following the death of a current master: Apul. *Met.* 8, 15; Plut. *Ant.* 75; Appian, *B Civ.* 4, 24, when a certain Salassus, put on the proscription list of the second triumvirate, came back to his house from flight, was only recognised by his doorkeeper who had been sold together with the house; Cic. *Verr.* II, 1, 90-91, at the death of a master, a malicious guardian of a young master might seize control of the management of property, selling off or appropriating slaves for his own use.

[45] More unfortunately, slaves might have been sold to a public treasury-agent and interrogated for the master's *maiestas* charges with torture, as did happen to slaves of C. Iunius Silanus (*cos.* AD 10), who was charged with *repetundae* in AD 22: Tac. *Ann.* 3, 67; 2, 30; on slaves as witnesses, Schumacher, 1982, 134-136.

[46] Suet. *Otho*, 10, 2.

The masters and mistresses of the *gens Statilia* in the *columbaria* inscriptions

If the *tria nomina*, with a set of conventional *praenomen*, *nomen gentilicium*, and *cognomen* in order, was the exemplary form of Roman onomastics, the period of our *columbaria* inscriptions witnesses a diversion from its previous practice among some aristocratic families.[47] Here it is observed that the Statilii was one of those families that reinvented its standardised form of the *tria nomina* into something distinctive: while the standard *tria nomina* 'T. Statilius Taurus' were held by the eldest son of the Statilii, from Taurus (*suf. cos.* 37, *cos.* 26 BC) to Taurus (*cos.* AD 44), the names of their brothers replace the *praenomen* 'Titus' with the existing *cognomina*, thus as 'Sisenna Statilius Taurus' (*cos.* AD 16) and 'Taurus Statilius Corvinus' (*cos.* AD 45).

Slaves and freedmen in the *columbarium* mainly address their masters either as 'Taurus', 'Sisenna', or 'Corvinus'. While the former was the hereditary *cognomen* of the eldest son of the Statilii, the latter two in the collateral line were 'imports', originally the *cognomina* of their maternal grandfathers. 'Sisenna' was from the patrician family of the Cornelii Sisennae,[48] and 'Corvinus' was the hereditary second cognomen of his mother Messallina's family – her father was supposedly the respected orator M. Valerius Messalla Corvinus.[49] In the consular *fasti*, Taurus' (*cos.* AD 11) brother (*cos.* AD 16) was recorded as 'Sisenna Statilius (T.f.) Taurus' (cf. Tac. *Ann.* 2, 1, 'Sisenna Statilius'). One of his slave's epitaphs likewise recorded him as 'Sisenna Statilius' (A330).[50] As for Corvinus (*cos.* AD 45), Suetonius called him customarily 'Statilius Corvinus'.[51] But in the inscription from the Via Portuensis that recorded the *collegium* of *fratres Arvales*, Corvinus the *promagister* of the college appears as 'Taurus Statilius Corvinus'.[52] Despite some variation within the sources, both Sisenna and Corvinus set out to replace conventional *praenomina* with existing *cognomina*. H. Solin called them 'special *praenomima*' (*besondere Vornamen*), adopted by a handful of individuals of senatorial families during this period.[53] Taking up the names of long-standing aristocratic families into their own allowed the families of recent advancement to forge some authority to their *nouitas*.

Table 2.2 is the list of *domini* and *dominae* as designated in the epitaphs with the number of attestations. Often their identities remain obscure, due to the hereditary elements of nomenclature. Caldelli and Ricci attempted to address this problem with a set of rather problematic principles (1999, 44-49). First, as for 'Taurus', one may be reasonably ready to accept the designations 'Taurus pater' and 'Taurus filius/adulescens' as pointing to Taurus (*cos.* AD 11) and his son (*cos.* AD 44) respectively, but Caldelli and Ricci further proceed to attribute all those simply designated as 'Taurus' to the father (*cos.* AD 11), with the claim that those without the designation 'filius' are virtually the 'pater', the title merely omitted. Furthermore, the designation 'T. Statilius' (Taurus) is now attributed to the son (*cos.* AD 44), for the reason that it was differentiated from 'Taurus' (which they had already identified as the 'pater'). The main problem with this categorisation is that it disregards the shift of time during the use of the *columbarium*: what would have happened when Taurus *filius* became the *paterfamilias* after the death of the father? This is in fact no good reason to suppose that particular designations always refer to the same individual, let alone for identifying such an individual with a particular member of the family. Apart from '(T. Statilius) Taurus', other male members of the *gens* can be identified relatively straightforwardly. The designations of 'Sisenna' and 'Corvinus' would mean Sisenna (*cos.* AD 16) and Corvinus (*cos.* AD 45), and 'Taurus Statilius' might also point to Corvinus according to his distinctive *tria nomina* 'Taurus Statilius Corvinus'.

Uncertainties about identification occur for some of the *dominae*. For instance, there are probably two possible candidates for the name 'Cornelia', namely the elder Cornelia (daughter of L. Cornelius Sisenna)[54] and the younger Cornelia (either daughter or wife of Sisenna Taurus?). Two freedmen of Cornelii buried in the *columbarium*, 'L. Cornelius L. l. Alexander' (A316) and 'C. Cornelius Synneros' (A237), are likely to be associates of the former. Their presence in the *columbarium* might be explained as follows: originally slaves of the elder Cornelia's father L. Cornelius Sisenna or his son (her brother), they came into the new household with Cornelia as trusted servants and were eventually manumitted.[55] Others with agnomen 'Cornelianus', which indicates that the holders were

---

[47] Sandys, 1969, 207-221; Salway, 1994; Salomies, 2001.
[48] His mother Cornelia was probably the daughter of L. Cornelius Sisenna, proconsul of Sicily under Augustus. Cf. Dio, 54, 27, 4; they are descendants of the historian L. Cornelius Sisenna in the early first century; on the Etruscan origin of the family, Rawson, 1979, 364-366.
[49] *PIR*[1] V 90; On the Statilian descents of Messalla Corvinus, Syme, 1986, 240-241; Suet. *Claud.* 13; Messalla Corvinus, a friend of Brutus, reconciled with Augustus after the battle of Philippi: Plut. *Brutus*, 45; 53 et al.; cf. Tac. *Ann.* 4, 34; 6, 11.
[50] An epitaph from Parentium records a freedwoman of '*Sisenna Statilius Taurus pontifex*': *CIL* V 332; but see *CIL* V 409, *T. Statilius Sissene Tauri sibi et suis vivens fecit*.
[51] Suet. *Claud.* 13.
[52] *AE* 1983, 95; *CIL* VI 2028; cf. *AE* 1984, 0238, from Pompeii.
[53] Solin, 1989.

[54] A surviving Greek inscription where 'Cornelia Sisenna of (Statilius) Taurus' was honoured by the people (*demos*) of Thespiae in Boeotia. *IG* 7, 1854. Kajava, 1989, 139-149, examines the inscription and its background, and argues that Cornelia, here honoured by the people of Thespiae, one of the Boeotian cities in Greek East, is most likely identified as the wife of Taurus the new man and daughter of Cornelius Sisenna; in his view, Taurus as the triumphant general of the wars in Greek East (particularly in Actium), rather than Cornelia herself, was the direct benefactor of the city, and Cornelia was honoured only for the reason that she was a wife of Taurus. However, her nomenclature in the inscription is quite ambivalent, and as identified in *PIR*[1] S 623, Cornelia here might rather be the daughter or wife of Sisenna Statilius Taurus (*cos.* AD 16).
[55] Caldelli and Ricci, 1999, 46.

previously slaves of the Cornelii, were transferred to the ownership of the Statilii.[56]

On the other hand, the 'Cornelia' in two fragmentary inscriptions is considered to be a different individual from Cornelia the elder since the epitaphs are recovered from the newer structure (O) (A382 and A384). The information likely to be relevant here is known from another source, namely the inscription on the *fistula aquaria*, 'Cornelia Tauri f. T. Axi', transcribed as (Statilia) Cornelia as Taurus' daughter and wife of 'T. Axius' (*CIL* XV 7440). From other surviving inscriptions, T. Axius here is presumably the consul during the reign of Claudius.[57] Her name on the *fistula aquaria* would mean that she not only possessed her own servants but even her own household establishment,[58] though it is within speculation whether this Cornelia is identical to the one in the *columbarium*.[59]

There are also at least two different individuals for 'Statiliae' recorded in the *columbarium*; they are apparently sisters in an earlier generation, usually named on the epitaphs as 'Statilia Maior' (*PIR*[1] S 621) or 'Statilia Minor' (*PIR*[1] S 622), and other plain 'Statiliae' might perhaps be assumed as 'maior'. Pliny the Elder informs us that a certain Statilia lived in the reign of emperor Claudius to 99 years of age.[60] This Statilia mentioned by Pliny must have been born sometime in 50-40 BC, which is the generation of daughters or granddaughters of the Augustan general T. Statilius Taurus, and can be identical to either Statilia Maior or her younger sister Statilia Minor. Another separate piece of information is that a certain Statilia was married to L. Calpurnius Piso (*cos*. 1 BC).[61] There were two men called 'L. Calpurnius' from an epitaph in the *columbarium*, and they were perhaps originally the servants of Piso.[62]

As for the identities of 'Messalina', there are three possibilities: the elder 'Messalina', wife of Taurus (*cos*. AD 11), their daughter 'Messalina Tauri f(ilia)', and the granddaughter 'Messalina Neronis (uxor).' As for 'Messalina Tauri f(ilia)',[63] this daughter of Messallina and Taurus was married to L. Valerius Catullus (*PIR*[1] V 35-36).[64] It was probably this husband of Statilia Messalina (L. Valerius Catullus), rather than the father of (Valeria) Messalina (M. Valerius Messalla Corvinus), who was the original owner of C. Valerius C. f. Cosanus (A387) and his freedwoman Valeria Prima (A400), in the sense that both epitaphs originate from the newer structure (O).[65]

To sum up, it is clear that slaves in the *columbarium* belonged to different *familiae*, and some are obviously living under different roofs. In other words, admission to the *columbarium* was extensive, as it appears to have included the dependants of the whole or a larger part of the *gens*. A broader kinship unit of the aristocratic masters played an important role in establishment of the *columbarium* and burials of servile members. Such cohesion of the dependants of the *gens Statilia* in the *columbarium* may be actually an aspect of their everyday lives, as we find a number of individuals in quasi-marital or -filial ties and at the same time belonging to different aristocratic masters of the same *gens*.

The *columbarium* of L. Arruntius

The *columbarium* of L. Arruntius was situated in close proximity to the sepulchral complex of the Porta Maggiore, about 60m. north-west of the Statilian *columbarium*.[66] Those buried there are considered to be the slaves and freedmen of L. Arruntius (*cos*. AD 6) (*PIR*[2] A 1130) or/and his adopted son L. Arruntius

---

[56] Such were Scirtus the musician (*symphoniacus*) (A108), Flaccus the carpenter (*faber tignuarius*) (A289), and a Helenus (A409).
[57] The fragment of wax-tablet from Pompeii record 'T. Axius' as the consul with T. Mussidius Pollianus. The inscription is dated to no earlier than AD 38, and T. Mussidius Pollianus is known to have been active during the reign of Tiberius. Cornelia's alleged husband T. Axius was probably identical either with this consul sometime after AD 39 or a certain T. (?) Axius Naso, proconsul of Cyprus under Tiberius (AD 29); on the discussion of dating and prosopography, Eck, 1981, 252ff.
[58] A woman might establish her own household and live separate from her husband's, for instance, on the verge of divorce; cf. Plut. *Ant.* 54.
[59] *PIR*[2] A 1687 considers T. Axius' wife Cornelia as a daughter of Sisenna (*cos*. AD 16); cf. Kajava, 1989, 148-149.
[60] Plin. *HN.* 7, 158, *Statilia Claudio principe ex nobili domo LXXXXIX*; cf. Sen. *Ep.* 77, 20; *PIR*[1] S 620.
[61] L. Calpurnius Cn. f. Piso (*cos*. 1 BC) (*PIR*[2] C 290): the augur (esp. in distinction to his homonymous brother 'pontifex'), and proconsul of Asia. He was a senator of outspoken, obstinate character, and was nearly prosecuted for treason; Tac. *Ann.* 2, 34; 4.21; on Statilia, wife of the augur, Syme, 1986, 337, 376-7.
[62] A freedman L. Calpurnius Abascantus is commemorating his patron L. Calpurnius Nedymus (A361).

[63] Apart from one servant of Messalina (daughter of Taurus) certainly from the *columbarium*, that is her *paedagogus* (A211), we know two other epitaphs of her servants, but apparently from outside the *columbarium*. One is that of Agrimatio, who is oddly titled as '*pumilio*' (dwarf) of 'Statilia Tauri f. Messalina' (B009=VI 9842=*ILS* 7411). The other is Donatus the *dispensator* (financial manager) (B007=VI 9191), and in the same epitaph Cirratus the freedman and '*Germanus armiger*' of Taurus are commemorated.
[64] The children apparently from them are the son L. Valerius Catullus Messallinus (*cos*. AD 73) (*PIR*[1] V 41), and the daughter also called Statilia Messallina (*PIR*[1] S 626). An inscription of unknown find-spot records that this young Messallina, the daughter of Catullus and Messalina, died in infancy: (26789) *Statilia Catulli f. Messalina vixit mensib. duobus et dieb. X*: it strikes us as rather odd that Messalina inherited the maternal *gentilicium* instead of the father's. If illegitimate children usually took the nomen of their mother (Sandys, 1969, 216), could she be as such, and Catullus and Messallina were not in the *conubium*?
[65] Apart from these, there are two more servants in the *columbarium* which might indicate the connection with Valerius Catullus, husband of Statilia Messalina; one with the agnomen 'Catullianus' (A025), and the other with the designation 'Catulli l(ibertus)' (A420, from P). Although Caldelli and Ricci, 1999, 48, claim that 'Catullus' here was the aristocratic master Valerius Catullus, I think that 'Catulus' should rather be identified with the attested Taurus' ex-slave Catullus (A158).
[66] The *columbarium* of L. Arruntius (*CIL* VI 5931-5960); R. Volpe, *LTUR*, 1999, iv, 275; Nash, 1968, ii, 309f.; Platner, 1929, 477; Richardson, 1992, 352; Caldelli and Ricci, 1999, 65.

Fig. 2.6 The *columbarium* of the Arruntii viewed from outside
Extracted from Nash (1968), n.1072, originally by Jean Barbault,
Vues des plus beaux restes des antiquités romaines, 1775, pl.21

**Fig. 2.7 The *columbarium* of the Arruntii inside
(with vaulted ceiling and stucco decoration)**
Extracted from Nash (1968), n.1074, originally by Jean Barbault,
Vues des plus beaux restes des antiquités romaines, 1775, pl.22

Camillus Scribonianus (*cos.* AD 32) (*PIR*² A 1140).⁶⁷ The structure was found in 1733, and subsequently destroyed. Fortunately, the plan of the inside and outside is known to us from the drawings of contemporary artists (Fig. 2.6-7), and was said to have consisted of three chambers.

The Arruntii were the contemporaries of the owners of the major *columbaria*, Statilii, Volusii, Livia, and their social standing is in many ways similar to the former two families. The advancement of the family was recent, begun by the *homo novus* L. Arruntius (*cos.* 22 BC), who served first with Sex. Pompeius and later with Octavian fighting at Actium as a fleet commander in 31 BC.⁶⁸ His son L. Arruntius (*cos.* AD 6), the probable patron of the *columbarium*, was renowned for his culture and respected for his longevity. According to Tacitus, Augustus once referred to him as a potential ruler (Tac. *Ann.* 1, 13). He was also nearly prosecuted in AD 32 by Sejanus' henchmen, certain *delatores* Aruseius and Sangurius, but Tiberius intervened to rescue him (Tac. *Ann.* 6, 7; Dio 58, 8, 3), though the emperor himself was said to be suspicious of Arruntius for his celebrated wealth and talents. At the end of the reign of Tiberius, L. Arruntius committed suicide in his old age, disdainful of living as a 'slave' under the 'evil' new master Gaius Caligula (Dio 58, 27, 4).⁶⁹ Before his death, he had adopted the son of M. Furius Camillus, L. Arruntius Camillus Scribonianus (*cos.* AD 32), who turned out to be a major catastrophe for the family. Immediately following the uprising of Statilius Corvinus and Asinius Gallus, Arruntius Camillus, then the governor of Dalmatia, revolted against Claudius in AD 42. Camillus apparently had a strong claim for the throne, and many senators and *equites* joined him. In spite of its scale, the revolt was suppressed within only five days, and one of his freedmen is said to have been brought before the Senate for inquiry. Shortly before Camillus, Appius Iunius Silanus (*cos.* AD 28), one of the Iunii who owned the *columbarium* on the *via Appia*, was executed for his alleged conspiracy against Claudius. Annius Vinicianus (*PIR*² A 701), the son of C. Annius Pollio (*PIR*² A 677) and yet another *columbarium* owner on the *via Appia*, also plotted against the emperor, approaching Camillus for military backup in vain.⁷⁰ Incidentally, Statilius Corvinus, Camillus, Appius Silanus, conspirators against Claudius, were all powerful masters and patrons of slaves and freedmen who possessed the *columbaria* on the outskirts of the city. Another family which owned a *columbarium*, the Volusii, was something of an exception, as L. Volusius Saturninus (*cos. suff.* AD 3) earned an exceptional honour supposedly for his service as *praefectus urbi* under Claudius.

II. The *columbaria* on the *via Appia*: the Volusii and Livia

The *columbaria* of the Volusii and of Livia, along with others such as those of Iunius Silanus and Annius Pollio, were situated along the roadway on either side of the *via Appia*, leading from the *Porta Appia*. These were among the so-called 'roadside cemeteries' expanded along the ancient roads, a common feature of many cities in the Empire.⁷¹ Below, I will describe the *columbaria* of the Volusii and Livia, and their family history, and those of other minor *columbaria* whose inscriptions are known in *CIL* VI '*monumenta*' section.

The *columbarium* of the Volusii

The inscriptions of slaves and freedmen of the Volusii are collected under the heading *Monumentum Volusiorum*, in *CIL* VI 7281-7393 and elsewhere. A recent re-publication of the inscriptions of the *Monumentum Volusiorum* has been undertaken by Buonocore (1984), who has added 69 inscriptions omitted in *CIL*.⁷²

A number of inscriptions attributed to the slaves and freedmen of the Volusii were originally found *en masse* from the field near Vigna Ammendola. However, a report regarding the sepulchral structure itself is not known; the excavation undertaken in the early nineteenth century (first in 1825) apparently did not record any ground plan, and no structure remains at the site at present. Though without any archaeological information, however, circumstantial evidence points to the existence of the *columbarium* of the Volusii in the area of the Vigna Ammendola on the *via Appia*. First of all, a substantial number of inscriptions referring to the nomen 'Volusius' have been found on the spot. Secondly, numerous other fragments of stones with ornamental decoration (such as portions of friezes) were scattered around across the same area. From their architectural style they appear to belong to the same period as Volusius Saturninus, and are likely to be the materials used for the sepulchral building.⁷³ When the state archive called Camerlengato purchased the inscriptions found from the site in 1827, the collection of epitaphs were already labelled vaguely, in rather generic terms, as the '*Monumentum Volusiorum*' in the *vinea Ammendola*, although, to be precise, some of them

---

⁶⁷ We find two attestations of elite master and mistress from the *columbarium*, 'L. Arruntius L. f. Ter(etina tribu)' and 'filia Camilli Arruntii'. It is not clear whether the former refer to L. Arruntius (*cos.* AD 7) or L. Arruntius Camillus (*cos.* AD 32). In the sense that the *columbarium* yields comparatively small number of epitaphs, a total of only 30 inscriptions of 61 individuals, it may be more fitting to consider that the *columbarium* was in use briefly for only two generations (Camillus and his daughter) rather than for three generations. In any case, however, that the father and the adopted son successively met treason charges (*vd. infra*) might have resulted in significant deduction of the property including slaves.
⁶⁸ On L. Arruntius (*cos.* 22 BC), *PIR*² A 1129; Syme, 1939, 227, 282, 372, 434 et al.
⁶⁹ On L. Arruntius (*cos.* AD 6), Wiseman, 1971, 178; Crook, 1955, 152.
⁷⁰ Dio 60, 14-16; Suet. *Claud.* 13; 35; Routledge, 2001, 97 and 164-166.

⁷¹ Toynbee, 1971, 73f.
⁷² A review on Buonocore's work, Kepartová, 1986, 281-283.
⁷³ Buonocore, 1984, 23-25, which cites late nineteenth century accounts on the site of Canina, *La prima parte della via Appia dalla porta Capena a Boville*, Roma 1853, and other subsequent scholars.

were found from an estate neighbouring that of Ammendola.

Buonocore found a total of 191 inscriptions, in which 349 individuals are named as the deceased or commemorators or others relating to the *familia* of the Volusii, all of which supposedly derived from the *columbarium* on the *via Appia*. Mommsen in the *CIL* edition considered the period of use of the Volusian *columbarium* to be between AD 40 and 60, but it is now amended as the period between AD 20 and 97, according to the information from the 69 inscriptions newly attributed to the *monumentum*.[74]

The *gens Volusia*

The Volusii, an old praetorian family, had never reached consular rank before L. Volusius Saturninus (*suf. cos.* 12 BC). This first of the Volusii who rose to the consulship was then the governor of Syria in 5/4 BC under Augustus, and according to Tacitus, he was the founder of the family's vast fortunes.[75] The family had already been distantly related to Tiberius,[76] and Lucius further established the family connection with the Nonii Asprenates by marriage with Nonia Polla. It was probably during this generation that the family saw the first influx of slaves newly recruited. But Lucius died in AD 20, and as in the case of the Statilii, it was presumably the next generation that took up the establishment of the *columbarium* for the family's slaves and freedmen.

Tacitus reports that L. Volusius Saturninus (*cos. suff.* AD 3), the son of Lucius above, died in AD 56 at ninety-three years of age (born in 37 BC) with a distinguished reputation and leaving behind a great fortune. He was no less successful than his father; his career proceeded from the post of proconsul of Asia under Augustus, to that of the *legatus pro praetore* in Dalmatia under Tiberius and Gaius, and finally that of the *praefectus urbi* under Claudius.[77] The long-lived Lucius remained a prominent *amicus* of emperors throughout from Augustus to Nero.[78] The recent excavation of the family's villa in Lucus Feroniae (1962-1968) and the discovery of new inscriptions from there have shed new light on his distinguished career.[79] In particular, they inform us that L. Volusius Saturninus earned a remarkable honour upon his death; it was decreed by the Senate on the prompting of Nero to give a public funeral and dedicate nine statues, including three triumphal ones.[80] He married a certain Cornelia, daughter of a Scipio, as Pliny reports that the consul (Quintus) Volusius Saturninus was born from Cornelia when the father was 62 years old (i.e., AD 25).[81] The burial structure of slaves and freedmen was apparently established in his time as *paterfamilias*.

By the time of his son Q. Volusius Saturninus (*cos.* AD 56), the family entered the patrician rank. The epitaphs of servants attest to a Lucius, apparently an older brother of Quintus, who only reached the priesthood of *pontifex*. The *columbarium* was in use probably until the next generation, i.e. that of Lucius Volusius Saturninus (*cos.* AD 87) and Quintus Volusius Saturninus (*cos.* AD 92). Thereafter we do not hear of any remarkable name or family record. The *columbarium* appears to have been overridden by another group's sepulchral space as some epitaphs of alien nomen, including a freedwoman of an emperor, were found together in the same place.

The masters and mistresses of the *gens Volusia* in the *columbaria* inscriptions

As in the case of the Statilii, it appears that the Volusian *columbarium* did not restrict its admission to the servile dependants of one particular aristocratic master but included those of his brothers and sisters. It is rather more difficult, however, to know which Volusian masters correspond to the names in epitaphs, because of the conventional onomastic practice adopted by the family. Unlike the Statilii, the Volusii maintained the traditional use of *praenomina*: either 'Lucius' or 'Quintus' with unchanging 'Volusius Saturninus'. Apart from the names articulated as 'L. Volusius Saturninus pater' and 'L. Volusius Saturninus pontifex',[82] the identity of masters only designated as 'Lucius' and 'Quintus' is largely obscure (Table 2.3).

---

[74] Buonocore, 1984, 44; *CIL* VI, pp.1043-44.

[75] Tac. *Ann.* 3, 30; Tacitus' favourable accounts of the family, offering lengthy obituaries for L. Volusius Saturninus and then his son of the same name, Syme, 1970, 79-90.

[76] Q. Volusius who married Tiberius' ascendant was probably Lucius' father; Syme, 1939, 362, 424, 381 *et al.*; Levick, 1976, 52-53; Cic. *Att.* 5, 21, 6; Crook, 1955, n.359.

[77] Plin. *HN.* 7, 62; 7, 156; 11, 223; cf. Columela, 1, 7, 3; *ILS* 923, 923a, the governor of Dalmatia during the late period of Tiberius and early Caligula. On details of his career, Eck, 1972; Crook, 1955, no.360; Vogel-Wiedemann, 1982, 343-344.

[78] Tac. *Ann.* 13, 30, *inoffensa ei tot imperatorum amicitia fuit*.

[79] Eck, 1972; Boatwright, 1982.

[80] Eck, 1984, 143-145; 151-152; Boatwright, 1982, argues that the honour Volusius Saturninus received was only known for individuals who helped to suppress conspiracies; Saturninus, as *praefectus urbi* in AD 42, played a significant role in the trials of that year and earned Claudius' recognition. It is considered that the family's entrance to the patrician rank by the third generation of Q. Volusius (*cos. ord.* AD 92) was the result of the favour shown to him by Claudius for his meritorious service. Saturninus' funeral honour was also a declaration by the new emperor Nero of restoration of peace and harmony with the Senate; Talbert, 1984, 153; 380.

[81] Plin. *HN.* 7, 62; L. Saturninus also had a sister who was to be the mother of Lollia Paulina, of whom we know nothing otherwise; Tac. *Ann.* 12, 22.

[82] A certain Volusia Stratonice was the nurse (*nutrix*) of L. Volusius L. f. Saturninus pontifex (7393). Another epitaph that attests to the masters 'L. Volusius' and 'L(ucius) flius' appears to be L. Volusius (*cos. suff.* AD 3) and Lucius pontifex, respectively. Iphus the *cubicularius* of Lucius the father was commemorated by his nephew Carpos who 'had belonged' to Lucius the son (*Carpos qui fuit L. fili*) (7288). The phrase indicates that Lucius *pontifex* died young before his long-lived father (*PIR*[1] V662). He was probably born from the father Lucius' previous wife, therefore half-brother with Quintus (who was born from Cornelia).

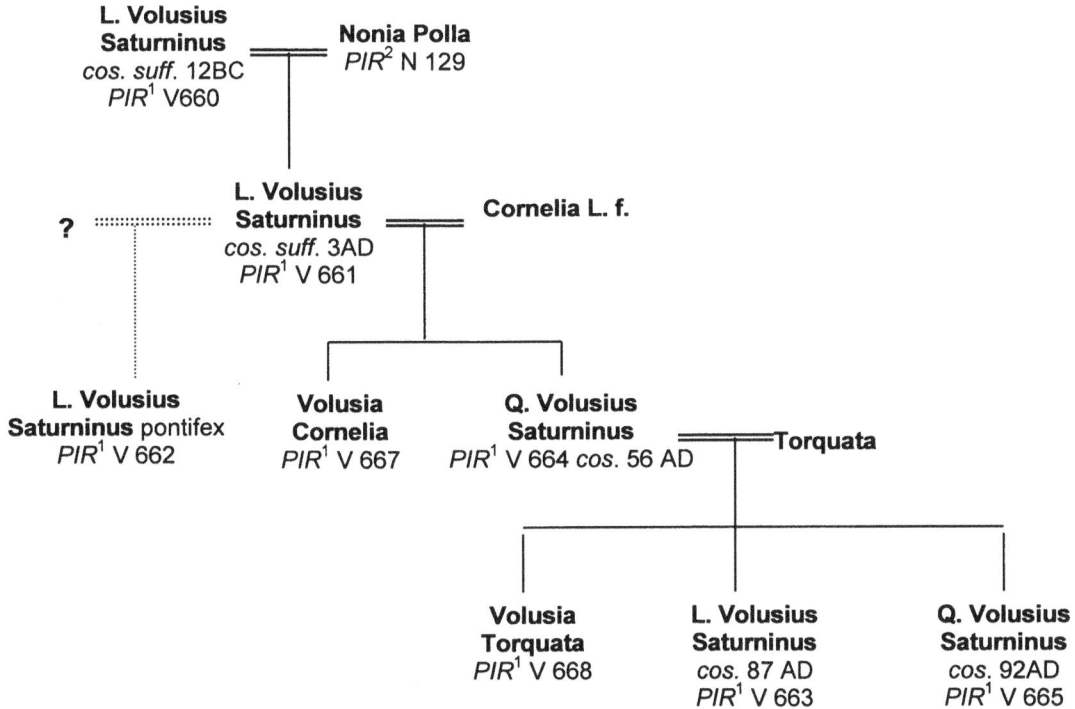

Fig. 2.8 The *gens Volusia*

Table 2.3 Named *domini* and *dominae* (the Volusii)

Name	Number	Percentage	
L. Volusius Satuninus pater (*PIR*[1] V 661)	3	1.0%	
Cornelia L. Volusi (wife of Lucius above)	2	0.7%	
L. Volusius Saturninus pontifex (*PIR*[1] V 662)	2	0.7%	
Volusia Cornelia (*PIR*[1] V 667)	2	0.7%	a. Total: 57 (19%)
Q(uintus) et Cornelia n(ostra)	1	0.3%	
Q(uintus) n(oster)	14	4.7%	
Torquata (wife of Quintus *cos.* AD 56)	3	1.0%	
Volusia Torquata (*PIR*[1] V 668)	3	1.0%	
L. Volusius Saturninus / L(ucius) n(oster)	19	6.3%	
Volusius / Volusius Saturninus	3	1.0%	
L(ucius)	5	1.7%	
b. Intermediate owners (owned by slaves/freedmen)	20	6.6%	
c. Unknown / others	224	74.4%	
Total (a, b, c)	301	100%	

The *columbarium* of Livia

The *columbarium* of Livia in the Vigna Benci on the *via Appia* was excavated in 1726 and published by F. Bianchini in 1727. We can see the marvellous inside structure of the *columbarium* through the drawings (Fig. 2.9-10). It consisted of two underground chambers. The major chamber was rectangular 10,66m × 6,22m, with two rectangular recesses and a semicircular one on each of the long sides, and with one semicircular recess on each of the short sides. It was connected to the smaller chamber (used as an entrance hall) on the same level and to the ground by stairs. The report of Bianchini is outlined by J. Kolendo as follows: "the pavement of the chamber was covered with mosaic, and the ceiling and the wall were ornamented with decoration of plaster (stucco). On the wall of the two chambers, constructed in bricks, we find niches, in each of them two urns were placed. The major chamber was equipped with seven rows of niches, while the smaller chamber with only one row of niches…On the pavement of the chamber we find a few sarcophagi and a few funeral altars". The *columbarium* of Livia was erected in the final year of the reign of Augustus and was in use until the end of the reign of Claudius.[83]

Apart from the *columbarium* of Livia's staff in the Vigna Benci, there were other *columbaria* for Imperial slaves and freedmen or household staff of those closely related to the Imperial family. For some reason a handful of epitaphs of Livia's servants ended up in such places. The so-called 'Colombari di Vigna Codini' were located between the *via Appia* and *via Latina* within the Aurelian Wall (Fig. 2.11-12). A great number of *columbaria* had been known in this area, but most of them were destroyed after the fifteenth century, and only three *columbaria* of the Vigna Codini are preserved today. One of them is called 'Monumentum Marcellae', occupied mainly by the staff of Marcella (*PIR*² C 1102), once the wife of Agrippa, and her sister Marcella the Younger (*PIR*² C 1103). Both are daughters of C. Claudius Marcellus (*cos.* 50 BC) and Octavia, the sister of Augustus.[84] The elder Marcella married M. Vipsanius Agrippa and was divorced, then married Iulius Valerius. The younger Marcella married first M. Valerius Messalla Barbatus (*cos.* 12 BC) and then Paullus Aemilius Lepidus (*cos. suff.* 34 BC). In their *columbarium*, we find at least seven slaves/freedmen who apparently once belonged to Livia.[85] Another *columbarium* which contained some of the servants of Livia and Tiberius is considered to be owned by Livia's son Nero Claudius Drusus and wife Antonia, located between the *via Appia* and *via Latina* near the city wall, which is not extant today.

Livia Augusta

Livia's origins were aristocratic, but her marriage to the later Princeps yet meant a significant elevation of her status. Her first marriage to Tiberius Nero was a hardship. He fought in an uprising against Octavian in Perusia in 41-40 BC and was defeated. Later they managed to join Sex. Pompeius in Sicily, but there was a temporary political reconciliation of Octavian and Sex. Pompeius, and the couple now set out for Antony in the East, who eventually dispatched them to Sparta. Due to the husband's political stance, the living condition of Livia and her children had been that of fugitives; the couple were constantly on the run from Octavian accompanied by young Tiberius and a few servants. Their lives were seriously threatened on several occasions during their flight by day and night.[86] Finally, Livia and her husband were able to return to Rome following the amnesty granted to the followers of Sex. Pompeius in 39 BC (the Treaty of Misenum), and Octavian fell for her. Livia married Octavian in 38 BC, though she was pregnant at this time with her younger son Drusus. She was only twenty at this time. Her marriage to Octavian secured her decent aristocratic life with a *domus* and servants waiting.[87]

In her second marriage, she was said to be an exemplary wife and a good advisor to her husband. She initiated important public constructions and religious ceremonies, and exercised not insignificant political power in the shadow of her husband and son. Dio claims that after Augustus' death Livia received the *salutatio* of the prominent people at her house.[88] In less than a decade since her marriage to Octavian, she had become the most powerful woman in Rome. Undoubtedly by the time of Augustus' death, Livia had her own household staff established under her command.[89] In his will, she was named as his heir together with Tiberius, and received the share of a vast inheritance. Her slaves and freedmen were again dramatically increased, and the *columbarium* was erected around this time. Livia had been granted the privileges of the mothers of three children in 9 BC, one of which was the right to administer their own property without a guardian.[90] In this regard, it is hardly surprising to find that, by sheer comparison of numbers in the

---

[83] Kolendo, 1991, p. xxii (in Bianchini, 1991); Caldelli and Ricci, 1999, 60-61.

[84] Toynbee, 1971, 113-115; Nash, 1968, ii, 333-339; Richardson, 1992, 356.

[85] (4448) C. *Iulius Eutyches, Fausti Iuliae Augustae a manu filius v. a. V, m. V*; (4636) *Philiae Iuliae / Alexio Caesaris ser. frater fecit*; (4608) *…Lycaetis Iuliaes*; (4601) *M. Livius Anteros*; (4602) *M. Livius Eros*; (4603) *Livia Chreste…*; (4581) *C. Iulius Heracleo / Livia Egloge*.

[86] Suet. *Tib.* 4-6; Dio, 48, 15, 3; Vell. 2, 75-76.

[87] Barrett, 2002, 16-27; 174-177.

[88] Dio, 57, 12, 2; on Livia's role and public activities as *princeps femina*, Purcell, 1986; Suet. *Tib.* 50, Tiberius' vexation on the mother's interference into the public business as if wanting to be co-ruler of the Empire; Tacitus' consistent view on Livia as the political intriguer and murderer of rivals to Tiberius, Tac. *Ann.* 1, 3, et al.; Syme, 1939, 229; 340f.; Levick, 1976, 13-15; on her character, Tac. *Ann.* 5, 1.

[89] cf. on Augustus' death, Livia blocked the house and roads with her guards; *acribus namque custodiis domum et vias saepserat Livia*, Tac. *Ann.* 1, 5; Bauman, 1992, 124-138.

[90] Dio, 55, 2, 5; (9 BC); her third child died prematurely: Suet. *Aug.* 63, 1; the right to administer the property without a guardian had already been granted to Livia in 35 BC: Dio 49, 38, 1; Rich, 1990, 220.

Fig. 2.9 The *columbarium* of Livia's staff on the via Appia (I)
Extracted from F. Bianchini (1991 reprint), *Camera ed inscrizioni sepulcrali de'liberti, servi, ed ufficiali della casa di Augusto scoperte nella via Appia*, Naples

Fig. 2.10 The *columbarium* of Livia's staff on the via Appia (II)
Extracted from F. Bianchini (1991 reprint), *Camera ed inscrizioni sepulcrali de'liberti, servi, ed ufficiali della casa di Augusto scoperte nella via Appia*, Naples

Fig. 2.11 The *columbarium* II of the Vigna Codini
Extracted from Nash (1968), n.1107

Fig. 2.12 The *columbarium* III of the Vigna Codini
Extracted from Nash (1968), n.1110

CHAPTER 2: THE *COLUMBARIA* AND THE ARISTOCRATIC FAMILIES

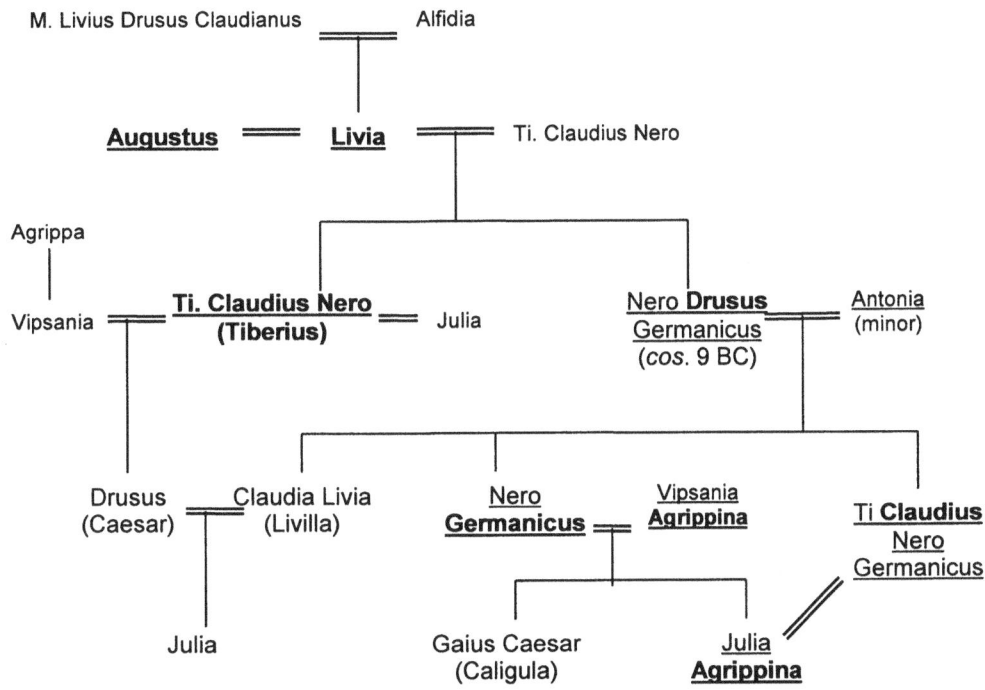

Fig. 2.13 Livia's family (simplified)
*Note: The persons with underline are the ones whose names were mentioned in Livia's *columbarium*.

Table 2.4 Named *domini* and *dominae* (Livia)

Name	Number	Percentage	
Livia	63	10.4%	Total (Livia): 111 (18.3%)
Aug(usta)	42	6.9%	
Ti. Caesaris maternus	3	0.5%	
Diva Augusta	3	0.5%	
Caesar Augustus	16	2.6%	a. Total: 145 (23.9%)
Ti. Caesaris / Neronis Aug. f / Neronis Caesar: (Tiberius)	7	1.2%	
C. Caesar	4	0.7%	
Antonia	2	0.3%	
Drusus	2	0.3%	
Iulia Germanici filia / Agrippina	2	0.3%	
Drusi Caesaris filiae	1	0.2%	
b. Intermediate owners (owned by slaves/freedmen)	70	11.6%	
c. Unknown	390	64.5%	
Total (a, b, c)	605	100.0%	

columbaria, Livia's personal servants excel those owned by any other single aristocratic master.

Livia died in AD 29, and was buried in the Mausoleum of Augustus; her son Drusus was already buried there and they were to be followed by Tiberius and other members of the imperial family.[91] In the meantime, the *columbarium* of her servants continued to be in use, at least until the reign of Claudius.

The masters and mistresses in Livia's *columbarium*

Like the *columbaria* of the Statilii and Volusii (Table 2.2-3), that of Livia (Fig. 2.13; Table 2.4) included not only the servants of Augustus and Tiberius, but also Drusus, his wife Antonia, and even a handful of servants of Livia's grandchildren and greatgrandchilden. Livia's son Nero Drusus Germanicus and his wife Antonia had their own *columbarium* of their servants situated near the city wall between *via Appia* and *via Latina* (*CIL* VI, pp.899-907), which also included several servants of the mother Livia, the brother Tiberius, and others. Some servants might have been buried in a different *columbarium*, as a result of change of ownership in the course of time (especially after Livia's death in AD 29) or because of their personal connections (marital union, etc) with those who belonged to different households.[92]

From the inscriptions, it appears that the *columbarium* continued to be in use beyond Livia's death in AD 29. Some servants survived until after the reign of Claudius, by whom she was officially deified in AD 42. The variation of the designation of Livia in servants' epitaphs attests to the chronological span of the use of the *columbarium*. Livia called herself 'Livia Caesaris Augusti' while Augustus was alive. Then, she took up the appellation of 'Iulia Augusta' after her adoption in AD 14 at the death of Augustus. As Mommsen observed, those who were manumitted before the death of Augustus, were called M. Livius, and those of later manumission were M. Iulius.[93]

The imperial residence of Augustus on the Palatine was supposedly the main workplace of most of Livia's staff.[94] As in the case of the Statilii and Volusii, servants worked in a circumstance where cohabitation or close association between Livia and her relatives was taking place.[95] Such would have led to a certain degree of shared use of their servile dependants, not strictly bound by legal ownership. Livia's household, as well as those of the Statilii, Volusii, and others, could not have existed on its own in complete isolation from her close relatives.[96]

The women as mistresses of slaves

The difference between Livia Augusta and the matrons of the Statilii and Volusii is unmistakable. The job-titles of Livia's slaves/freedmen confirm that she was virtually the head of the household; the range of her staff's occupations is meant to fully cover the necessities of a huge living unit (see Chap. 3), whereas the servants of the matrons of the Statilii or Volusii are found only in a very small number, usually of secondary personal service such as *ornatrix* (hair-dresser), *paedagogus*, or *nutrix*.

In Roman law, women were in principle assigned lifelong guardians for the management of property. Augustus relieved women of this disability if they were mothers of more than three children, and Livia was certainly one of those granted this right. Moreover, at Augustus' death, Livia received one-third of his estates as an heir, by which she must have also acquired slaves attached to the estates. Needless to say, in the course of marital life with an emperor, an increase in staff numbers was inevitable, but it appears that (Statilia) Messalina's marriage with Nero did not bring as much increase of servants as Livia's. The differences are firstly that Statilia Messalina's marriage with the emperor only lasted for two years, and also that we do not hear Statilia Messalina bear offsprings, and therefore that it is doubtful that she was ever conferred the title of 'Augusta'.[97] Other matrons in the Statilian family tree, such as Cornelia or Messalina, presumably had more than three offspring, but as far as the *columbaria* epitaphs are concerned, it is doubtful that they had ever received or exercised that privilege.

Aside from the otherwise routine lifelong guardianship for women, another practice that needs to be taken into consideration for women's slave-owning is the *dos* (dowry) attached to them at marriage. In custom, a woman of wealthy family brought her own slaves or even freedmen/women as attendants into the new household, and Roman law speaks frequently of dotal slaves transferred from one household to another at their mistress' marriage. The marriage of Roman nobles in this period became largely *sine manu*, namely, a woman even after marriage remained under her father's *potestas* or legally independent (*sui iuris*) under guardianship. Upon marriage *sine manu*, the distinction of the property of wife and husband had to be more strictly observed in case

---

[91] Barret, 2002, 216-8.
[92] Some of her servants had been bequeathed to Livia by other prominent figures, such as Vergil, Agrippa, Maecenas etc.: Barrett, 2002, 175-6; 374, n.7.
[93] Mommsen, *CIL* VI p.878; Treggiari, 1975a, 49; Barret, 2002, 307-8.
[94] Augustus' house on the Palatine once burned down, Suet. *Aug.* 57, 2; on the so-called Casa di Livia (house of Livia) on the Palatine, identified as such from the inscription on the lead pipe found there bearing the name of Iulia Augusta (*CIL* XV, 7264), Richardson, 1992, 73-74; Treggiari, 1975a, 48-49; Barret, 2002, 177-8.
[95] For instance, the emperor Gaius Caligula, the son of Germanicus, had lived with his great-grandmother Livia after his mother's exile, and then came to live with his grandmother Antonia until the age of eighteen: Suet. *Gaius*, 10; Tac. *Ann.* 3, 3.

[96] We might recall that Cicero in his letter frequently mentions and make use of his brother Quintus' slaves and freedmen.
[97] One surviving inscription from the Greek East (Boeotia) refers to Statilia Messalina as '*Sebastê*' (*ILS* 8794=E. M. Smallwood, *Documents illustrating the principates of Gaius, Claudius and Nero*, 1967, no.64). However, ruler cult and use of regal titles were very common in the Greek East, and it remains doubtful if Statilia Messalina was ever conferred the title; on the title *Augusta*, Flory, 1988, 126; cf. Kienast, 1990, 100; Barret, 2002, 322-323.

of restitution. The dowry that she brought with her was officially her husband's property during the duration of marriage, but when the marriage ended in divorce, or the death of either partner, all or a large part of the dowry could be claimed back by the wife or by her family. The husband could manumit dotal slaves or take the profits from them (by receiving their service or collecting their earnings),[98] but the gift of the property between the husband and wife was prohibited so that there might not be any substantial increase or decrease in the property of each partner. The principle of return of dowry made women less at a disadvantage for remarriage in the event of divorce or the death of a husband.[99] This was a basic principle that would have been equally applied to Livia and Statilia Messalina; the former went through divorce with Ti. Claudius Nero and second marriage with Octavian, the latter the death of her first husband Vestinus Atticus and remarriage with Nero. In that process, the dotal slaves moved back and forth following their mistresses.

In the form of dowry, marriage activated the traffic of servants from a wife's father's household to the husband's. But at the same time, a wife received service provided by husband's slaves as well as by her own,[100] and naturally in a household, slaves of wife and husband lived together.[101] As we have seen above, some slaves who ended up buried in the *columbaria* might have originated from the wife's family.

The *columbarium* of Iunii Silani and others

The Iunii Silani owned the *columbarium* on the *via Appia* (*vigna Randanini*). Though epitaphs known there are not many, it appears to have accommodated the slaves and freedmen of several masters from the two main branches of Iunii Silani: these probably include M. Iunius Silanus (*cos.* AD 19) (*PIR²* I 839), who married Aemilia Lepida, a great granddaughter of Augustus, and two of their five children, M. Iunius Silanus (*cos.* AD 46) and D. Iunius Silanus Torquatus (*cos.* AD 53), and the former's son L. Iunius Silanus Torquatus, and from the other branch, C. Appius Iunius Silanus (*cos.* AD 28) and the son M. Iunius Silanus. As is characteristic of that period, many of these masters were either executed or committed suicide for disreputable allegations. Noteworthy in particular is D. Iunius Silanus Torquatus (*cos.* AD 53), who according to Tacitus was accused by Nero of copying the titles of imperial offices for his freedmen. It was considered as an act challenging imperial authority that Silanus let freedmen in his personal service hold the same titles in imperial court, *ab epistulis, ab libellis, ab rationibus* (in charge of correspondence, documents, and accounts), though naturally such titles are not known from the epitaphs of the *columbarium*. The building is considered to be in use during the reigns of Claudius and Nero and later.[102] Though it was probably before the establishment of the *columbarium*, slaves of C. Iunius Silanus (*cos.* AD 10), father of C. Appius Iunius Silanus (*cos.* AD 28), were sold to a public treasury-agent and interrogated for the master's *maiestas* charges with torture,[103] which may perhaps have resulted in a diminished number of his descendants' servants known from the *columbarium*. Incidentally, an important legislation regarding slavery and domestic security, the *senatusconsultum Silanianum* in AD 10, which notoriously put slaves whose master was murdered in or outside the *domus* and who were with him into torture and possibly execution,[104] was passed by this master in consulship.

In the same Vigna Randanini as that of the Iunii Silani, was the *columbarium* of the family of the Carvilii, though its specific aristocratic patrons (if any) are not clear from the small number of epitaphs of the Carvilian freedmen there. In the area of Vigna Amendola there was the *columbarium* related to the family of the Caecilii but specific aristocratic patrons are again not known. The patrons of one *columbarium*, located in the same Vigna Amendola as those of the Volusii and the Caecilii, are considered to be C. Annius Pollio (*PIR²* A 677) or his father (*PIR²* A 679), and the former's son L. Annius Vinicianus (his plot against Claudius, Dio, 60, 15; Sen. De. Benef. 4, 31). A sizable number of epitaphs of the servile dependants of the Passienii were found in Vigna Moroni, with the indications of the patrons L. Passienus Rufus (*cos.* AD 4) and his immediate descendants. Those of the Bruttii, located between the via Appia and via Ardeatina, are apparently of a later date, belonging to C. Bruttius Praesens (*PIR²* B 165) (*cos.* II AD 180) and his son L. Bruttius Quintius Crispinus (*PIR²* B 169) (*cos.* AD 187). To be precise, the epitaphs of the Passieni and Bruttii were merely reported as '*monumentum*', and it is not clear whether they were in fact accommodated in the '*columbaria*' or '*columbaria*-like' structures. On the *via Salaria*, there was the *columbarium* of the servile dependants of L. Caninius Gallus (*cos. suf.* 2BC) (*PIR²* C 390), though only a small number of epitaphs are

---

[98] In Cicero's letter to his wife Terentia, he explains his intention to manumit the slaves attached to the estates, in case his property was to be confiscated in the crisis of 58 BC. Nonetheless, in manumitting her slaves, Cicero was effectively asking Terentia for permission: Cic. *Fam.* 14, 4, 4; Treggiari, 1991, 349.
[99] Crook, 1967, 103-106; Treggiari, 1991, 327-364; distinctions between the property of wife and husband were so scrupulously observed that in principle, the husband could claim back the money he spent on the upkeep of his wife's dotal slaves from her family (*onera matrimonii*).
[100] Plaut. *Menaechmi*, 120-2; *Aul.* 475f.; Treggiari, 1991, 339-340, 354-356.
[101] *Dig.* 29, 5, 1, 15 (Ulpian) states that if either wife or husband was murdered, slaves who belonged to either might be tortured, because they were mingled together in the one and same household; Treggiari, 1991, 374-378, slaves were by practice shared by the couple in receiving their service or product, for instance, spinning maids might produce clothes both for master and mistress; on Augustus' will, Suet. *Aug.* 101.

[102] *CIL* VI, p.1066-1067; Decimus' freedmen with imperial job-titles: Tac. *Ann.* 15, 35; 16, 8; Appius Silanus (*cos.* AD 28) accused of treason and acquitted: Tac. *Ann.* 6, 9.
[103] Tac. *Ann.* 3, 67; cf. 2, 30.
[104] *Dig.* 29, 5 (Ulpian); cf. Tac. *Ann.* 14, 42.

known.[105] We also find two groups of epitaphs, each from the families of L. Abuccii and Q. Sallustii, but we neither know the reports on the structures or the sites nor the specific aristocratic patrons they might have been subordinate to. There were a number of other *columbaria* which are not discussed here, since they were occupied by miscellaneous groups of people, not belonging to a single family (*gens*) or patron.

III. The inscriptions

The epitaph types

The types of epitaphs from the *columbaria* of the Statilii and Volusii can be classified largely in four types: plaque (*lastra*), pillar (*stele*), altar (*ara*), and urn (*urna*) (vd. Appendix).[106] Most of the inscriptions are found on plaques (94% for the Statilii, 76% for the Volusii), and more precisely these are usually flat 'wall-plaques' (79% for the Statilii, 57% for the Volusii), which would have been inserted in the walls just below the loculi. Another type of plaque was to be placed over the loculi to close the aperture (8% for the Statilii, 14% for the Volusii). One could say that the wall-plaque or aperture type of epitaph is specifically intended to fit into the *colubmaria* structure. Other more lavish forms of epitaph, namely pillars, altars, and urns, are also found in a small number (4% for the Statilii, 25% for the Volusii). As a whole, the Volusian *columbarium*, by comparison, had fewer wall-plaques and more differing forms of epitaphs (non-plaque types) that were not designed particularly for the *columbarium* structure. Most of the pillars, altars, and urns in the Statilian *columbarium* were found in the newer sepulchral structures (O) and (P). When juxtaposed with the archaeological information discussed above, this would suggest that these new structures had very few loculi and more space for religious rites. One may further speculate as to the capacity and function of the unknown Volusian *columbarium*, perhaps a combined form of the Statilian old structure (N) and new structures (O, P).[107]

Numbering of inscriptions

Throughout this book I cite the inscriptions relating to the household of the Statilii using the numeration of the recent edition by Caldelli and Ricci, 1999, 83-134. They present two different number sequences, one for the inscriptions from the *columbarium* and one for the inscriptions relating to slaves and freedmen of the Statilii found outside the *columbarium*. I have here prefaced the *columbarium* sequence by the letter 'A' and the extra-columbarian sequence by the letter 'B'. Each inscription's number thus consists of 'A' or 'B' followed by three digits. For convenience the texts are reproduced following Caldelli and Ricci's edition and with this numeration in Appendix below. A concordance with the numeration of *CIL* VI is supplied at the end.

Caldelli and Ricci arrange the inscriptions from the *columbarium* according to what can be known about their findspots and material type. The inscriptions are classified first by the structure in which they were found (N, O, or P), and then by the type of epitaph - plaque (*lastra*), pillar (*stele*), altar (*ara*) or urn (*urna*). Inscriptions A001-381 are from the structure (N), A382-407 from (O), and A408-427 from (P). I have added as A428-9 two inscriptions attributed to the *columbarium* by *CIL* VI but omitted by Caldelli and Ricci.

Inscriptions from other *columbaria* are cited below by their numeration in *CIL* VI. Inscriptions cited simply by four- or five-digit numbers, without other specifications, are thus from *CIL* VI.

The sample body of inscriptions

The statistical analysis made in this thesis is either by the number of epitaphs or by the number of persons, depending on the aim. We find 429 epitaphs from the Statilian *columbarium* (from the three structures N, O, P), and 657 names of individuals – of slave, freedman, and free-born status – either as the deceased or commemorators in these inscriptions. Additionally, 48 Statilian inscriptions from 'outside' the *columbarium* will also be taken into consideration from time to time, excluding the illegible materials. As for the Volusian *columbarium*, of Buonocore's total of 191 inscriptions mentioning 349 individuals, I have excluded 33 inscriptions because of their extremely damaged condition and, consequently, a total of 158 inscriptions and 301 individuals are within my scope here. As for Livia, we find 401 inscriptions published in *CIL* (though I find only 322 inscriptions legible enough to make any sense as an epitaph), and 608 names of individuals from them.

---

[105] cf. Vell. 2, 100, 2; Tac. Ann. 6, 12; the mistress of 'Caninia (Gaiae) l(iberta) Fausta' (*CIL* VI 7995) is probably the daughter of Gallus, Caninia Galla, as an epitaph (14327) records 'L. Canini Gallae l. Anchiali, Caninia Gallae l. Philemationis'.

[106] The Statilian *columbarium* also contained non-epigraphic materials (*instrumentum*), such as amphora, lamps, vases, or cups. These vessels were supposedly used for libation, and lamps for illumination during commemorative rituals: Caldelli and Ricci, 1999, 25-39; though not from the Statilian *columbarium* but from a sepulchral building on the north side of the complex, a series of friezes with illustrations from scenes of *Aeneid* and the early Roman history were found depicted on the walls; Nash, 1968, ii, 359-369.

[107] As for the *columbarium* of Livia, among 222 inscriptions published by Bianchini, six (2.7%) are considered to be either sarcophagi or altars, while the rest are mostly wall-plaques. It is pointed out that the quality of the cuttings of the epitaphs is particularly poor in this *columbarium*: Caldelli and Ricci, 1999, 61; Nielsen, 1995, 44-45.

Conclusion

The establishment of great *columbaria* for servile dependants, we have seen, should be considered as part of household management, directed by thriving aristocratic families during the Julio-Claudian period. They are the cream of the social hierarchy, ranked among the most powerful and the wealthiest in Rome. In particular, the Statilii, Arruntii, and Volusii were families of recent advancement, achieving their first consulship during the reign of Augustus, and enormously increased family property in a few generations. As for Livia Drusilla, her marriage with Octavian in 38 BC, later Princeps, eventually elevated her status to the top of all Roman matrons. With political and social advancement, as well as with the general stability brought about by the end of civil wars, these masters must have come to recruit a large number of slaves in a short period of time, and as a result, their households were faced with an increasing need to secure sufficient burial facilities for their swollen *familiae*. Masters had a moral obligation to provide slaves with the basic necessities of life, which included the provision of food, clothes and burials. But burial was not a 'need' in a real sense. Many poor people in Rome, slaves or free, were buried in the common unroofed graveyards on the Esquiline Hill, or merely dumped in the pits instantly dug (*puticuli*), unable to afford an epitaph. The slaves and freedmen who could receive decent burials in the *columbaria* were by comparison privileged in this respect. The construction of the *columbaria* and preservation of the memorials of their dependants was not from stingy economy, to compress the place of their afterlife, but was rather a lavish form of welfare for the dependants, and in this sense, it was also to satisfy the ostentation of the aristocratic masters. While the *columbaria* of the Statilii, Arruntii, Volusii, Livia, and others differ in various respects such as size, location, range of members admitted, and period of use, these *domus* saw the utility of this particular sepulchral structure and came to share a trend in the early first century AD.

It must be also noted that each *columbarium* was fairly extensively intended for servants of more than one master. It included servile dependants of the collateral families as well as those of the mainstream. An upper-class family of this period was a dynamic and complex entity. The household was in custom rarely the pure nuclear family unit of modern conception. Marriage, divorce (or death of the partner), and remarriage were frequent occurrences, which often resulted in cohabitation of those who were not blood relations (e.g. stepmother and children).[108] The *columbaria* inscriptions certainly attest to this aspect of the family structure of Roman nobles, and the cohesion, not of nuclear family but of extended family or even clan (*gens*), is the background, in which our subjects were located. The use of the *columbaria* lasted only for a few generations, and the closure of the *columbaria* marked the conclusion of the *domus* or *gens*.

As is seen in the attempts of Caldelli and Ricci and other scholars to reconstruct the archaeological information, a series of excavations of the *columbaria* were undertaken rather poorly, and subsequent reports are found obscure on some important details. Such general neglect may have resulted from, as they point out, an underlying lack of interest by the scholars in the *columbaria*, or in the epitaphs of the historically 'insignificant' slaves and freedmen.[109] It is certainly spectacular for us now to imagine a number of such burial structures scattered in the outskirts of the city.

---

[108] On complex family structure of the Roman nobles caused by frequent remarriage, Bradley, 1991.

[109] Caldelli and Ricci, 1999, 50.

Chapter 3

The occupations of slaves and freedmen

I. Self-sufficient households

For the Romans, the ideal household was like a community.[1] A large household comprised masters and a number of dependants, and there was a long-standing aspiration among Roman aristocrats, that the household should be able to satisfy their material needs from its own resources.

Petronius' rich freedman Trimalchio, at his dinner party, boasted of the common desire for independence and security, '*omnia domi nascuntur*' ('everything is home-grown'). As he tells his audience, "under the gods' providence, I do not have to buy. Anything here which makes your mouths water is grown on a country estate of mine".[2] The idea of self-sufficiency goes back to the Greek philosophers' argument as to ideal ways of life. Aristotle stated that pastoralism, agriculture, fishing, or hunting are the "ways which do not depend for a food-supply on exchange or trade", and that men could live happily with combining them.[3] The universally shared esteem for agriculture, as Cicero declared agriculture was the most gentlemanly labour among all occupations,[4] was closely linked with awareness of the realistic necessity of obtaining food and other living requirements. Most Roman aristocratic families were great landowners in the country, and their wealth and social status ultimately derived from land, which produced food, materials of clothes, and timber for building.[5] Thus, traditionally, the ideal of the self-sufficient household was primarily concerned with the management of rural estates.[6]

In reality, however, simply following the old traditional style based on cultivation of land would hardly bring satisfactory living conditions. One would also need economic strategy and the means to accumulate enough resources to obtain an advanced level of self-sufficiency, and in that process, the exchange of resources is inevitable. The motivation of self-sufficiency was economic as well as moral. Cato the Elder, the exemplar of conservatism, ploughed the farm himself and was highly admired for the *autourgia* (self-work), but he could neither dispense with slaves nor live self-sufficiently; indeed, the farm management, of which Cato gave instructions in his book *De agricultura*, was primarily for producing wine or olive oil for sale. His traditional lifestyle was blended with an extreme and innovative economic sense. He bought slaves, food, and clothes at the market, though always at the cheapest price possible.[7]

Naturally, for wealthy Romans under the early Empire, possession of land and agricultural slaves was hardly enough; hence, while urban property becomes an equal or even greater source of income,[8] specialised human resources arise as luxurious but crucial to have in order to achieve aristocratic ways of living. In other words, the quality and range of the *familia urbana*, the staff of the urban household, become a more and more conspicuous indicator for the degree of independence of a household. The wealthy household bought or invested in training slaves with special skills. The trend was already evident in the former period. Cicero's friend Atticus was praised for possessing specially educated staff of home-born slaves; Crassus was also acclaimed for the high quality of his slaves, including architects, readers, secretaries, silversmiths, stewards, and waiters, to whom he gave education and instruction himself.[9] On the other hand,

---

[1] see Chap.1.
[2] Petr. 38; 48, *deorum beneficio non emo, sec nunc quicquid ad salivam facit, in suburbano nascitur meo*.
[3] Arist. *Pol.* 1256a40.
[4] Cic. *Off.* 1, 42, 151; *omnium autem rerum, ex quibus aliquid acquiritur, nihil est agri cultura melius, nihil uberius, nihil dulcius, nihil homine libero dignius*.
[5] Caecilius Isidorus who died in 8 BC left the enormous fortune of 4116 slaves and 3600 yoke of oxen, 257,000 head of other cattle, and 60 million sesterces in cash (Plin. *HN.* 33, 134f): this inventory undoubtedly attests to his fortune based on agricultural estates.
[6] On ideal of self-sufficiency (*autarkeia*) on land, Veyne, 1979; Finley, 1973, 109-110; D'Arms, 1981, 82-84, 99; Treggiari, 1973, 245-250; Wiedemann, 1981, 97-98.

[7] Plut. *Cat. Mai.*, 3-4; 21; on self-sufficiency in Cato's farms, Astin, 1978, 243ff. Cato was a contradictory figure in terms of his attitudes towards agriculture, trades, and money-making.
[8] Elite Romans preferred to emphasise the foundation of their property on rural estates, and in contrast, profits from their urban possessions are not much talked about. Garnsey, 1976, 126-127, examined the scale of urban investment of elite Romans, and argued that urban property was as important as rural estates as the source of income. Garnsey suggests that Cicero's urban property, mainly renting out of the apartment blocks (*insulae*), brought almost as much income as that from rural estates.
[9] Nepos, *Att.* 13; Plut. *Crassus*, 2.

Cicero made it the subject of contempt against L. Calpurnius Piso that he possessed neither a baker (*pistor*) nor a wine-cellar (*cella*), but instead, had bread bought from the shop (*propola*) and wine from the tavern (*cupa*). Piso's failure to keep a sufficient number of slaves and other essential products in his household was considered vulgar and inadequate for his social standing and wealth.[10]

The point I would like to make here is that the range of occupational activities performed by dependants of a large family indicate an 'advanced' – I do not mean 'more perfect' – level of self-sufficiency of the household. With this in mind, the current chapter will examine the job-titles recorded by the servile dependants in the *columbaria*. The range of job-titles known from each *columbarium* were first of all the service and skills that benefitted the household, while they might also be part of the society outside at the same time, doing business with ordinary customers. Certainly, we must carefully note that it is misleading to judge the wealth or scale of the household simply by the number and range of their occupations obtained from the *columbaria* epitaphs: each *columbarium* stood under varying conditions in terms of time span and range of membership. Nonetheless, apart from the scope of non-surviving data to the whole (which haunts every historical source), the information is reliable as individual and as a whole, and deserves systematic analysis as it will be indicative of certain characteristics of each household establishment as a living unit.

II. The evidence of occupational activities

Slaves and freedmen without job titles

Before I set out to the detailed discussion of job-titles, I must first draw attention to the nature of the information handled here. Table 3.1 shows the proportions of servants with job-titles in the *columbaria* of the Statilii, Volusii, Livia, and Iunii Silani. As is clear from the figure, there was a large proportion of staff 'without job titles'; overall 72% did not record their occupations. There is a reason not to be too pessimistic over this figure: by comparison, the percentage in the *columbaria* is higher than those of most other social groups known to us. For instance, in Huttunen's sample, which is every fifth epitaph in CIL VI (N=10523), less than 8% of individuals are found recording their occupations (9.5% of the deceased, 4.4% of the dedicators had record of occupations).[11] Certainly, however, the large number of servile dependants whose occupation is unknown is admittedly a problem to be acknowledged.

Part of the reason for not recording occupation would be purely epigraphic, namely simple selection and omission of certain personal information based on convention or accident.[12] It might also be possible to speculate about personal identity as a motive. It has been remarked by scholars that a main motive in choosing to record (or not to record) job-titles was the matter of 'pride'; those who recorded job-titles were proud of their job, while those who remain silent were ashamed of them because they did menial, undefined, or denigrating work.[13] This type of reasoning, however, seems to be a highly prejudicial and judgmental simplification, uncritically applying Cicero's snobbish comments on occupations to those who actually performed such jobs. The elite might have observed the jobs of the dependants with contempt, but whether or not a slave feels ashamed of his job would totally depend on the person. If pride and shame were the 'rule' in (not-)recording one's job, such a household must have been an unbearable world to live in, full of envy and resentment.

Rather than the psychology of (not-)recording, I think that it is more important to note the point that households, like society, necessitated the coexistence of specialists and established posts with a non-specialised casual workforce. For instance, it was only three or four individuals of the Statilii at most who held the title *quasillariae*, *textores*, or *fabri* at a time, and they would have been highly skilled or intensively trained to do so. However, projects such as production of clothes or construction or the repairing of buildings were probably too labour-intensive to be done only by a few of these specialists. In other words, these types of work necessitate unskilled casual labour to work under the supervision of professionals. I suppose that, for the needs of such casual labour, those servants without job-titles were flexibly available. Nobody in our *columbaria* recorded the title *ministri* (waiter-slaves), though it would have been an undoubtedly essential task as frequent references to them are found in literary sources. While servants with job-titles were in regular 'posts' or 'occupations', there were numerous untitled 'tasks', in which other slaves had to engage.[14]

In fact, the evidence shows that one starts finding their established profession (i.e. a job-title) only after certain ages. The earliest age of death with a record of job-title was for the Statilii the age of sixteen (as a *pedisequa*), and for other *columbaria* after the age of twenty.[15] In other words, no one in our *columbaria* below sixteen years old is recorded with a job-title. These late teens and early twenties are considered as a period of transition for many, from an apprentice to a professional, yet constituting an important source of the labour force for a

---

[10] Cic. *Pis.* 27; a 'poor plebeian' friend of M. Antonius, grandfather of Mark Antony, goes to a tavern to buy wine (Plut. *Mar.* 44).
[11] Huttunen, 1974, 16-22, 47-49.
[12] The *columbarium* of L. Abuccius, from which 99 individuals are known, contained no record of job titles.
[13] Joshel, 1992, 86-87; Treggiari, 1975a, 57; Flory, 1978, 80; methodological problems of interpreting occupational activities of the society or household are summarised by Dixon, 2001, 113-132.
[14] Sen. *Ben.* 3, 28, 5.
[15] In the Volusian *columbarium*, the earliest age with job-title is twenty, as a *citharoedus*, a *cantrix*, and an *ornatrix*.

number of unspecific tasks, for instance, as waiters or general cleaners.

Another important point to be noted is a significant gender imbalance in job-titles. It is evident that only a very few females recorded job-titles; 89% of all Statilian job-title holders, and similarly, 90% of the Volusii and Livia, and 87% of Iunius Silanus were male. It appears that females were largely excluded from professional posts; women are about 10% of the total of individuals with job-titles in the *columbaria* and all the major jobs were almost exclusively held by men, and only a few job-titles such as *quasillariae* or *nutrices* etc. were predominantly held by females.[16] Females, especially as children, seem to be much less regarded in their potential to serve as professionals for the large households. It has been well observed that women in epigraphic sources were addressed more for their family roles than for their job-titles.[17] However, this does not mean that females generally stayed at home as housewives. Females in servile status or of lower class had to participate in some kind of productive work other than pure housekeeping, even though secondary to male labour (vd. Chap. 5).[18]

In sum, as far as can be judged from the comparison of four *columbaria*, the proportion of those with and without job-titles is largely similar, which makes us suspect that they may reflect a certain reality. It is clear that a household needed to maintain a work force for unspecialised ordinary labour as well as for specialised posts. What the *columbaria* epitaphs offer us as tangible evidence is probably only the latter kind, and the examination of occupations is inevitably that of job-titles as they appear in epitaphs. Since it is often difficult and most likely futile to attempt to pin down precise job descriptions from job-titles alone, in the following, the subject will be discussed more broadly in terms of the self-sufficiency of the household, largely in three divisions of working sectors, namely, private service, production, and property management, though, needless to say, the divisions are to an extent artificial ones.

Table 3.1 The proportion of job-title holders in the *columbaria*

	Statilii (N=657)	Volusii (N=301)	Livia (N=608)	Iunii (N=58)
Without job titles	72%	80%	76%	68%
With job-titles (male)	25%	18%	19%	28%
With job-titles (female)	3%	2%	3%	4%
With job-titles (gender unknown)	0%	0%	2%	0%

III. Private service

The bodyguards and servants of transport

As we have seen in the previous chapter, the *gens Statilia* established their place of influence almost dramatically through the military role played by the new man Taurus (*suf. cos.* 37, *cos.* 26 BC) as the Augustan marshal. Despite the significance of this prominent figure for the family's establishment, it is considered that the *columbarium* was not constructed until the time of his grandson Taurus (*cos.* AD 11), and therefore did not include any of his direct servants.[19] However, although the *columbarium* might not have existed during Taurus' lifetime, his renown as an important military figure is reflected in the job titles of the slaves/freedmen in the *columbarium*. Uniquely in the Statilian *columbarium* a sizable number of job-titles of a paramilitary nature are found, that is *Germani* (Germanic bodyguards), and also *lecticarii* (litter-bearers) (Table 3.2).

The corps of *Germani* is famously known as the special armed forces of emperors from the time of Augustus until Galba finally discharged them.[20] The use of Germanic bodyguards was extensive, from everyday personal bodyguards or armed police forces in the city to soldiers in the field. Tiberius sent his son Drusus with the army augmented by the best of the Germanic bodyguards to deal with the mutiny of the legions in Germany in AD 14.[21] In principle, slaves of private individuals, unlike the *Germani* of emperors, could not be enrolled for fighting in the fields, unless in auxiliary regiments or strictly as armour-bears. Suetonius reports that Augustus had kept the *Germani* among the *armigeri*,[22] and among the total eleven *Germani* known from the Statilian *columbarium*, two of them are followed by the title '*armiger*' (armour-bearer). A precedent is found in Octavian's enemy Brutus in Philippi who, as mentioned by Plutarch, possessed a

---

[16] This seems to be the least unfamiliar situation when compared with that in our own times (or even deteriorating?): According to the survey from FTSE leading share index, "men fill 98% of senior executive posts" within the UK's largest 100 listed companies, reported in the *Guardian*, October 5, 2002. "Out of the 600-plus senior executive jobs in Britain's boardrooms, only 10 are filled by women," the proportion that has barely changed over the last 10 years.
[17] Dixon, 2001, 115.
[18] Female participation in the agricultural labour was discussed by Scheidel, 1995; id. 1996; on visual images of working women from the Isola Sacra Necropolis in Ostia, Kampen, 1981; women and children as business managers, Aubert, 1994, 419-420. But it must be emphasised that all these evidence attest to far more working men than women.

[19] Caldelli and Ricci, 1999, 43-48; see Chap. 2.
[20] Suet. *Galba*, 12, 2; on the *Germani corporis custodes*, Bellen, 1981; Speidel, 1984.
[21] Tac. *Ann.* 1, 24.
[22] Suet. *Aug.* 49.

CHAPTER 3: THE OCCUPATIONS OF SLAVES AND FREEDMEN

group of his own slaves as military servants, specially called 'Briges'.[23]

The private upkeep of armed forces, usually slaves, marked lawlessness during the late Republic. Earlier, Gaius Marius was reported to have taken command of a ferocious group of personal bodyguards - no less than four thousand - called 'Bardyiae' during the time of terror, which went about slaughtering a number of his political enemies.[24] This kind of excessive liberty of private individuals would become impossible after Augustus' time in power, but possession of paramilitary slaves could be tolerated under the pretext of public benefit. During the reign of Augustus, M. Egnatius Rufus helped to put out a fire in Rome with a group of his own slaves, as the office of the aedile that Rufus held was responsible for fire fighting in the city, and with this act gained much popularity: he was rewarded by the people with reimbursement for costs spent during his aedileship and then elected praetor.[25] In terms of Taurus' career, then, his possession of paramilitary forces might have been justified in his presiding over Rome with the responsibility of Prefect of the City between 16 and 13 BC. This was in fact before the establishment of the 'official' *praefectus urbi* in AD 13 that held the command of the urban cohorts (*cohortes urbanae*).[26] Taurus might have felt the necessity of such police forces to carry out the duty entrusted by Augustus and formed quasi-urban-cohorts composed of his own private slaves/freedmen. Taurus' predecessor assigned to this post, M. Valerius Messalla Corvinus, with whom the Statilii established family connection through the marriage of Taurus (*cos.* AD 11) and Messalina, resigned the post after only a few days, because he did not know how to exercise its powers (*primusque Messala Corvinus eam potestatem et paucos intra dies finem accepit, quasi nescius exercendi*). This probably means that he confronted a lack of appropriate forces under his command necessary for governing the city, especially, in Tacitus' words, for keeping order among the slaves and troublesome citizens (*qui coerceret servitia et quod civium audacia turbidum, nisi vim metuat*). By contrast to his predecessor, Taurus succeeded in fulfilling the responsibilities of the post (*tum Taurus Statilius, quamquam provecta aetate, egregie toleravit*).[27] Though we can only speculate, if his bodyguard slaves contributed to keeping order in the city in this way (unlike the fate of Egnatius Rufus), the family might have been able to gain the approval of the Senate or the people to receive the honour of retaining the *Germani*, a privilege otherwise reserved for the imperial family.

According to Bellen's study of Germanic bodyguards of emperors, some of the *Germani* attested in inscriptions belonged to members of the imperial family, especially the emperors' sons such as Drusus or his son Germanicus.[28] But from a sheer comparison of the number known by inscriptions, Taurus' *Germani* outnumbered those of the princes. Augustus might have confided his trusted marshal Taurus to take a share of the security forces as a mark of honour, but it is peculiar that even his subsequent generations could retain the licence. The paramilitary connotation of Taurus' *Germani* strikes us as no longer appropriate for private individuals under the Empire: not least if we think of D. Iunius Silanus Torquatus (*cos.* AD 53), one of the Iunii whose slaves and freedmen were buried in the *columbarium* on the via Appia. He was accused by Nero of letting his freedmen hold the same job titles as those of imperial service and was forced to commit suicide.[29]

The members of the imperial *Germani* were apparently genuine Germans by birth. But the Romans seem to have been accustomed to bestowing fictive titles to special armed forces of slaves, as in the case of Brutus' 'Briges' or Marius' 'Bardyiae'. As both titles indicated old names of minor tribes on the periphery of the empire, the titles did not necessarily correspond to the real nationalities of the title-holders. As to the *Germani* of the emperors and of Taurus, it is not clear whether they were all Germans, but there seems to have been no reason to limit recruitment to real Germans from the west.[30] In particular, since the Statilian *Germani* appear to be well integrated as members of the *familia*, some of them were perhaps recruited from among the home-born slaves, rather than mere *mercenarii*.

Another occupational group in the *columbarium* which needs to be considered alongside the *Germani* is that of *lecticarii* (litter-bearers). The Statilii owned at least fourteen *lecticarii*, among whom a freedman T. Statilius Spinther stood as *supra lect(icarios)* (over the litter-bearers, i.e., supervisor of the litter-bearers) (A210). In contrast, the same occupation is almost completely absent

---

[23] Plut. *Brut.* 45; according to Herodotus (7, 73), 'Briges' was the name of a Thracian tribe.
[24] Plut. *Mar.* 43-44; id. *Sert.* 5; the word 'Bardyaei' might be derived from 'Bardyetae', the name of a tribe in northern Spain (*TLG*); Sulla's bodyfuard 'Cornelii', consisting of more than 10,000 slaves of the prescribed, whom he freed with Roman citizenship: Appian, *B Civ*, 1, 11. 100; cf. Plut. *Ti. Gracch.* 18; armed gang of slaves for political violence, Cic. *Dom.* 3, 5-6; armed friends, gladiators, and household slaves of Metellus, Plut. *Cat. Min.* 27, 1; Lintott, 1968, 83-85.
[25] Rufus was later executed for conspiracy; Dio, 53, 24, 4-5; Rich, 1990, 159; another reference to the private fire brigade is in Juv. 14, 305f.; Augustus in 22 BC, to deal with frequent fires in the city, established a corps of 600 public slaves for fire fighting under aediles' command: Dio, 54, 2, 4; 53, 33, 5: on the Vigiles, Reynolds, 1926, 19-21 *et al.*
[26] Kienast, 1982, 272-273.
[27] Tac. *Ann.* 6, 11.

[28] Bellen, 1981, 22-33; the empresses were also entitled to have Germanic bodyguards. In AD 55, Nero confiscated the *Germani* that had been given to Agrippina: Tac. *Ann.* 13, 18, 3; Suet. *Nero*, 34; Nippel, 1995, 92-93.
[29] Tac. *Ann.* 15, 35; 16, 8.
[30] As for the Germanic bodyguard of emperors, they do not seem to be strictly Germans: when the wars in Germany brought the disaster of Varus in AD 9, Augustus sent away '*Galatai kai Keltoi*' who were serving among his bodyguards to certain islands, fearing their rebellion at home (Dio, 56, 23, 4). Galba dismissed the *Germani* and sent them off to their native country (unspecified *patria*) without rewards (Suet. *Galba*, 12); cf. Suet. *Gaius*, 55, *Thraeces quosdam Germanis corporis custodibus praeposuit*.

from the *columbaria* of the Volusii (only one instance) and Livia (none).[31]

The use of litters might signify the luxury and laziness of the masters, as there was much commercial use of litter-carriers (hiring) and the ostentatious procession of litters or carriages. Elite Romans usually walked in the city, and the idea of being carried by slaves instead of using their own foot could invoke mockery as a mark of corruption. The emperor Domitian disliked any physical exertion; he rarely walked on foot in the city, let alone riding on horse, but was regularly on a litter (*lectica*).[32] The motives of these reports are essentially satirical. Seneca the Younger describes the *geruli* ('bearers', here meant as 'litter-bearers') in military costume, which attest to the original 'masculine' nature of the corps of *lecticarii*, while Seneca was criticising the less 'militaristic' master's luxury and laziness in being carried around by them.[33] At the same time, the procession of litters or carriages connotes the image of a triumphal march, and the *lecticarii* resemble military forces or personal bodyguards. It is noted that the staff surrounding the grand carriages such as the rider (*rector*), forerunner (*cursor*), or *lecticarii*, are often emphatically foreign and 'masculine' slaves. Seneca twice mentions Numidian horsemen, and in Martial appears a black horseman on a Libyan horse (*rector Libyci niger caballi*) and Cappadocian *lecticarii*.[34] According to Suetonius, when the emperor Caligula was attacked by the assassins, the first group of slaves who could defend him from the enemy were *lecticarii* who were carrying him in a litter, before his proper corps of bodyguard *Germani* arrived to fight back.[35] Working as a prominent individual's litter carrier could be a privileged post, serving close to the master; Seneca the Elder mentions a former slave Timagenes, who was enslaved in war as a captive, but achieved successive promotion from a cook to a litter-bearer, and finally entered friendship (*amicitia*) with Augustus.[36]

In terms of cost, the group of professional *lecticarii* is cosidered to be among the most expensive items to maintain privately, just as keeping private bodyguards placed a heavy burden on household finance.[37] For this reason, the litter-carriers and other kinds of carriages were probably a usual item for rental between friends, or for hiring by wage.[38] As long as the road conditions permit, a carriage with wheels would have been more economical because it was led by animals (horses or asses) which spared hard labour of human *lecticarii*. Carriages were often used for transporting a quantity of agricultural products and other commodities.[39]

Considering the costs it required, the motivation of the Statilii's upkeep of *Germani* and *lecticarii* could hardly be mere convenience or impulse, but was the result of a certain conscious decision. The organised set of *Germani* and *lecticarii* characterises the Statilii's military-oriented household scheme following the custom of the *Familia Caesaris*. We also find the group of Statilian staff managing the amphitheatre built by Taurus (*vd. infra*). and all these were the visible legacy and family tradition from Augustan marshal Taurus the new man.

Table 3.2 List of Job titles: bodyguards and servants of transport

Job-titles	Statilii	Volusii	Livia	Iunii
Germanus (Germanic bodyguard)	11	-	-	-
lecticarius (litter-carrier)	14	1	-	1
strator / *equiso* (groom)	1	-	1	1
ad impedimenta (in charge of travelling luggage)	1	-	-	-

---

[31] The appearance of only one *lecticarius* of the Volusii is perplexing. The *columbarium* of Iunii Silani also included one *lecticarius* (7608), and that of L. Caninius Gallus two (7988, 7989). Because of the nature of the job, *lecticarii* must constitute a substantial group. The number of *lecticarii* for carrying a litter seems to have been usually eight or six, according to Catullus (10, 29-32), Cicero (*Verr.* II, 5, 27, *ut mos fuit Bithyniae regibus, lectica octaphoro ferebatur*), Martial (2, 81; 6, 77, *vd. infra*), and Suetonius (*Gaius*, 43, *ut octaphoro veheretur*); the group of *lecticarii* bequeathed as a set: *Dig.* 31, 65 (Papinianus); *Dig.* 45, 1, 29 (Ulpian); Maxey, 1938, 63.

[32] Suet. *Dom.* 19, *laboris impatiens pedibus per urbem non temere ambulavit, in expeditione et agmine equo rarius, lectica assidue vectus est*; Juvenal and Petronius make a connection between litters and the masters suffering obesity or arthritis: Juv. *Sat.* 1, 32-33; Petr. 96; sickly Augustus had to turn up in a litter at the battle of Philippi, or that quaestor Marcus Lollius, though he was ill, begged by a friend to throw a vote at the trial, was carried in a litter to the court to fullfil the duty: Plut. *Cato minor*, 16, 9-10; Cic. *Verr.* II, 5, 27; Ulpian (*Dig.* 32, 49, pr.) refers to *lecticarii, qui solam matrem familias portabant*.

[33] Sen. *Ben.* 3, 28, 5, *quo tandem ab istis gerulis raperis cubile istud tuum circumferentibus? quo te penulati in militum quidem non vulgarem cultum subornati, quo, inquam, te isti efferunt?*

[34] Sen. *Ep.* 87, 9, *cursores et Numidae*; 123, 7, *omnes iam sic peregrinantur, ut illos Numidarum praecurrat equitatus, ut agmen cursorum antecedat*; Mart. 12, 24, 2; 6, 77, *quid te Cappadocum sex onus esse iuvat?*; cf. Juv. 6, 474; 3, 240.

[35] Suet. *Caligula*, 58, 3, *ad primum tumultum lecticarii cum asseribus in auxilium accucurrerunt, mox Germani corporis custodes, ac nonnullos ex percussoribus, quosdam etiam senatores innoxios interemerunt*; cf. Gell. 10, 3, 5.

[36] Sen. *Controv.* 10, 5, 22, *ex captivo cocus, ex coco lecticarius, ex lecticario usque in amicitiam Caesaris enixus*.

[37] Shatzman, 1975, 91-94; according to Cicero (*Q Fr.* 2, 4, 5), C. Cato (*tr. pl.* 56) had to sell off his private bodyguard consisting of gladiators because of the high cost of maintenance: *nam ille vindex gladiatorum et bestiariorum emerat de Cosconio et Pomponio bestiarios, nec sine iis armatis umquam in publico fuerat; hos alere non poterat, itaque vix tenebat*.

[38] In Catullus' poem (10, 29-32), he claimed to have 'eight' litter-carriers. When a girl he desires requests their loan for a small journey, however, it is revealed that they are actually lent from his friend Gaius Cinna for a while; cf. Sen. *Ben.* 7, 5, 2, hiring a carriage; Cic. *Fam.* 4, 12, 3, *coactus sum in eadem illa lectica, qua ipse delatus eram, meisque lecticariis in urbem eum referre*.

[39] Use of wheeled-vehecles: Mart. 3, 47, 13, for carrying vegetables and other products from farm; cf. *Dig.* 17, 2, 52, 15 (Ulpian) *iumentorum carrulorum uecturae uel sui uel sarciarum suarum*; *Dig.* 19, 2, 13 (Ulpian).

CHAPTER 3: THE OCCUPATIONS OF SLAVES AND FREEDMEN

Table 3.3 List of Job titles: personal servants

Job-titles	Statilii	Volusii	Livia	Iunii
cubicularius / supra cubicularios / a cubiculo (bedchamber servants)	13	10	8	4
pedisequa/-us (foot attendants)	6	-	9	-
silentiarius (confidant)	1	-	-	-
eunuchus (eunuch)	-	-	1	-
ab hospitis (on reception of guests)	-	1	-	-
ornatrix (dresser)	-	3	5	-
tonsor (barbar)	3	-	-	-
specularius / a speculum / a specularibus (mirror-holder or -maker?)	-	2	1	-
citharoedus / cantrix (singer)	-	2	-	-
comoedus (comic actor)	-	-	1	-
lector (reader)	-	-	1	-

Personal attendance: *cubicularius, pedisequa/-us, silentiarius*

The *cubicularius* (bed-chamber servant) emerges as the most attested personal attendant in the *columbaria*. This group of servants was often hierarchically ordered, as we find from supervisory titles, such as the freedman T. Statilius Synistor as *supra cubicularios* (B008), L. Volusius Paris and L. Volusius Heracla as *a cubiculo* (7370, 7368), and Livia's servant Myrtilus as *supra cubicularios* (3954).[40] It seems that such an influential post was restricted to males - even for a mistress -[41] and possibly with preference to home-born slaves.[42] While the *cubicularii* were in principle attendants in the bedroom, the *pedisequi/-ae* escorted the master outside the household, as the word *pedis-sequor* ('follow by foot') indicates.[43]

An unusual title known from the Statilian columbarium deserves mention: a freedman called Chius with the title '*silentiarius*' (A255). The word supposedly derived from *silentium* (silence), from which we might speculate that the original responsibility of the silentiarius was perhaps disciplining the rest of the slaves into 'silence', namely discouraging them from leaking private household information. One might recall the literary authors who speak of masters who demanded the silentium of his surrounding domestic slaves; masters were anxious that their secrets or disreputable qualities might be observed by slaves and then disclosed to others without their notice.[44] Cato the elder instructed slaves never to divulge to neighbours what their master was up to (Plut. *Cat. Mai.* 21). These masters' worries were not easily dismissed as paranoia, since tip-offs by domestic slaves not infrequently brought fatal damage to the masters throughout Roman history. As this same title was to become a powerful post in the imperial court of the late Empire, here it probably meant a trusted slave/freedman as a master's confidant. It is noteworthy that the title *silentiarius*, otherwise only known to be associated with the *familia Caesaris*, was given to one of the staff of the Statilii (apart from this Statilian Chius, only two imperial freedmen are known as the holders of the title during the early Empire).[45]

Other than these, the *tonsores* (barbars) or *ornatrices* (dressers) were kept to take good care of shaving the masters' beard and the daily arrangement of the mistresses' hair. The title specularius or *a specularibus* is not clear, but perhaps related to working with a mirror (*speculum*). The Volusii's citharoedus and *cantrix* (singers), and Livia's *comoedus* (comic actor) might have entertained the guests at the banquets; the former's *ab hospitis* selected the guests or received visitors. One lector attested in Livia's *columbarium* could be one of those readers who used to tell sleep-story to the insommniac princeps.[46]

---

[40] (7370) *a cubiculo et procurator*; (7368) *capsarius idem a cubiculo*; (3954) *Myrtilus supra cubicul.*; (8766) *M. Livius Augustae l. Amarantus supra cubicularios*; cf. (33842) *Alexae Eburnaes ser. supra cubicul.*

[41] Petr. 132, *matrona... vocat cubicularios et me iubet catomidiari*; Apul. *Met.* 10, 28, *cubicularii mulieris*; by contrast, in the Greek novel of Achilles Tatius (2, 19), the maid Cleo was a bedchamber-maid of the heroine Leucippe who slept in the room next to hers.

[42] Hermann-Otto (1994, 341-343) lists *vernae* (home-born slaves) who became *cubicularii*, in the *familia Caesaris* and in private households, though the evidence is not enough to prove any clear connection of *verna* and *cubicularius*.

[43] e.g., *Dig.* 31, 65, *pr.* (Papinianus); Plaut. *Poen.* 41; *Aul.* 501; Nepos, *Att.* 13.

[44] Fitzgerald, 2000, 18-21; cf. master's uneasiness over the noise of slaves: Sen. *Ep.* 47, 2, silence at the dinner; Sen. *Ep.* 56, 7, silence during sleep; Plin. *Ep.* 2, 17, silence in the *cubiculum* in Pliny's villa.

[45] (9401) *P. Aelius Aug. lib. Telesphor selentiarius* (sic); (9402) *T. Aelius Theon Aug. lib. silentiarius*; Seeck, *RE*, iiia, 1929, 57-58.

[46] *Suet. Aug. 78.2: si interruptum somnum reciperare, ut evenit, non posset, lectoribus aut fabulatoribus arcessitis resumebat.*

Attendance for children: *nutrix, paedagogus, capsarius*

As is shown in the Table, the set of *paedagogi* and *nutrices* was commonplace in the *columbaria* of the top aristocratic families, and even other minor *columbaria*, those of Iunius Silanus (7618) and of L. Arruntius (5939), had at least one *nutrix*.

Servile dependants literally took care of the aristocratic master from cradle to grave. As a rule, a baby delivered by an *obstetrix* (midwife) was then handed over to the care of a *nutrix* (nurse, child-minder).[47] After a while, a *paedagogus* was employed to accompany a boy to school as a guard, and sometimes even entrusted to discipline him as a supervisor or impart education as a teacher.[48] The Volusii had two '*grammatici*' apart from three *paedagogi*. We hear from Suetonius that some of the most prominent grammarians of servile origin cost even 400,000 – 700,000 sesterces, though the *grammatici* in the Volusian *columbarium* were perhaps rather modestly involved in an advanced level of education for the young master as private tutors.[49]

The title '*capsarius*' is ambiguous in its job descriptions. It is speculated that, like *paedagogus*, it engaged in attending and taking care of children,[50] but what difference was there between the two? Oddly enough, there was one *capsarius* as well as several *paedagogi* in each *columbarium* (Statilii, Volusii, Livia).[51] The word, derived from '*capsa*' ('box'), is usually translated as an attendant-porter, carrying or keeping a master's satchel.[52] In the domestic context, a *capsarius* here seems to be a satchel-carrier for the boy whom he accompanied to school like a *paedagogus*. In Roman law, the *capsarius* was included into an exceptional category of slaves who, along with the *nutrix* and *paedagogus*, could be formally manumitted even by a master under twenty years old (*Dig.* 40, 2, 13, Ulpian). The distinction between *paedagogus* and *capsarius* was perhaps not so much in job descrption as in the qualifications held by the title-holders, that the former, with some education, taught and disciplined a young boy while the latter primarily attended him in the same way as a *pedisequus* for adult masters.

One aspect of the paradox of slavery is revealed in the mind of some fathers who were alarmed by the degenerate influence of a *nutrix* or *paedagogus* of servile birth over a child. Suetonius' account that Nero was brought up by two paedagogi, a dancer (*saltator*) and a hairdresser (*tonsor*), seems to be a conscious allusion to his notorious character that becomes clear in later age.[53] Traditional Roman values encouraged 'model' fathers and mothers to take part in the nurture and education of their own children. Such anachronism was attempted most famously by Cato the elder and Augustus, who were known as exemplary supporters of traditional values.[54] However, the ready availability of a slave workforce gave most masters little reason to resist employing slave nannies or tutors, which relieved them from the time-consuming, hard work of child upbringing.[55]

Table 3.4 List of job-titles: child care

Job-titles	Statilii	Volusii	Livia	Iunii
nutrix (nurse, childminder)	2	4	1	1
paedagogus (tutor)	5	3	3	-
grammaticus (grammarian)	-	2	-	-
capsarius (satchel-carrier?)	1	1	1	-

Financial manager, accountant

The position of *dispensator* is generally understood as a prestigious one, standing at the top of the hierarchy of household slaves. His job of taking charge of household accounts (*rationes*) involved far-reaching effects on the

---

[47] The Latin word *nutrix* for 'childminder' or 'wet nurse' does not contain the meaning 'the person who nurses the sick'. Though slaves certainly cared ailing masters, they are not called '*nutrix*'.

[48] Not only to school, a *paedagogus* walked with a young master for the *salutatio*. Sarpedon, the *paedagogus* of Cato the younger, used to lead Cato along to Sulla's house to foster friendship with him. At least until fourteen years of age, Cato was being accompanied by Sarpedon in this way (Plut. *Cat. Min.* 1, 10; 3, 3f.); cf. a slave of L. Volusius Saturninus who was a *paedagogus* and at the same time (or more likely promoted to) the *ab hospitis* (in charge of reception of guests) (7290): see Table 3.3.

[49] *Grammatici* as private tutors; Treggiari, 1969, 110-128; Joshel, 1992, 86.

[50] In Suetonius' description (*Nero*, 36), children of the noble families attending the banquet were slaughtered by Nero's assassins together 'with their *paedagogi* and *capsarii*.'

[51] (A374) *Epaphra, puer capsarius*; (7368) *a cubiculo idem capsarius*; (3952) *Eutactus Liviae capsar(ius), Asia Liviae Cascelliana*; cf. comments on the reading of this inscription, *CIL* VI, p.880.

[52] The *capsarius* is found in various different contexts: it might be a wage-labourer in public baths looking after one's clothes while bathing: *Dig.* 1, 15, 3, 5 (Paulus): *capsarii, qui mercede seruanda in balineis uestimenta suscipiunt*; a slave *capsarius de Antonianas* (sic) (9232=*ILS* 7621) is considered to be a clothes-keeper at the famous bath (*thermae*) of Antoniana; There is an alternative view that, taking *capsa* as clothes-chest, the *capsarius* in private houses might have been a bedroom attendant employed to keep clothes in storage chests, like *ad vestem* or *cubicularius*: Treggiari, 1975a, 53.

[53] Suet. *Nero*, 6, 3; cf. Plaut. *Pseud.* 446, *hic mihi corrumpit filium, scelerum caput; hic dux, hic illi est paedagogus, hunc ego cupio excruciari*.

[54] Cato taught his son himself, even though he had an educated slave tutor Chilo in his household: Plut. *Cat. Mai.* 20; Suet. *Aug.* 64; 73; Gell. 12, 1; Tac. *Dial.* 28; Cic. *Tusc.* 3, 1, *cum lacte nutricis errorem suxisse videamur;* instruction to choose a good nurse and a *paedagogus*, Quint. 1, 1, 4-9; Soranus, *Gynaecology*, 2, 19.

[55] On the effect of use of slave nurses, Dixon, 1988, 120-9, 145-6 et al.; Bradley, 1986, 201-229; Evans, 1991, 195-199.

CHAPTER 3: THE OCCUPATIONS OF SLAVES AND FREEDMEN

Table 3.5 List of Job titles: on finance

Job-titles	Statilii	Volusii	Livia	Iunii
dispensator (financial manager, steward)	12	4	4	-
tabularius / a tabulario (record-keeper;)	4	1	4	-
arcarius (in charge of money-box; treasurer)	-	-	3	-
sumptuarius (accountant?)	1	1	-	-
procurator (accountant?)	-	1	-	-
ad hereditates / custos rationis patrimoni (on inheritance, or transfer of properties?)	1	-	1	-
argentarius / ab argento (in charge of silver; money-changer? silver-smith?)	-	-	4	1

responsible, trusted post requiring substantial training that it might be preferably held by a *verna* (home-born); but again we have no tangible evidence that proves the case.[56] According to Weaver, the manumission of the *dispensatores* of the Familia Caesaris was often delayed until about the age of forty or even later because of their responsibilities; for administrative reason, they might have been required to remain slaves until they rendered accounts or were promoted.[57] From the *columbaria* evidence, it is not clear whether protracted manumission was particularly characteristic for the *dispensatores*, compared to those in other posts. Other posts such as *tabularius*, *arcarius*, or *procurator*, in a domestic context, are considered to be financial secretaries working under *dispensator*;[58] they needed to deal with increasingly more complex household finance with divisions of responsibilities.[59]

The unusually numerous *dispensatores* are known from the Statilii (twelve in total). Four of them were related to a certain Posidippus, the most prominent freedman of the Statilii.[60] Perhaps Posidippus himself was a *dispensator*, and had them as his apprentices. The Volusii had the *sumptuarius* and the *procurator* as well as *dispensator*, though the specific difference between their job descriptions, in a domestic context, is not clear.[61] The *ad hereditates* of the Statilii (A209) and the *custos ration(is) patrimoni* of Livia (3962) would be the financial managers specifically keeping register of the items received by inheritance and the transfer of the property; it was also a sensible way to deal with the newly introduced 5% inheritance tax that Augustus imposed on Roman citizens. The title *argentarius* usually refers to the banker or money-changer of large and small scales, and Livia's diverse properties would have been run by the group of professionals for each specialised area.

Apart from one *argentarius*, the title of financial manager is not found in the *columbarium* of Iunius Silanus, but a certain L. Iunius Paris, a *dispensator* and freedman of a Silanus, is known from elsewhere outside the *columbarium*; since this freedman attained the office of '*calator augurum*' (a servant of an augural priest), he was supposedly fairly independent and detached from the rest of the servile dependants.[62]

Secretaries and other clerical staff

In a society without a postal service system for private individuals, one means of communication was to entrust someone reliable with the delivery of letters. The professional title for this job is *tabellarius* (courier), and though the title itself is only found in the Statilian *columbarium*, other households must have made similar and frequent use of their trusted servants if not always working full-time for this purpose.[63] Better still, in composing a letter, wealthy men did not need to write themselves. The *librarii* or *a manu*, as scribes, assisted

---

[56] Herrmann-Otto, 1997, 369ff.; cf. Volusius Torquatus, probably the grandson of Q. Volusius Saturninus (*cos.* AD 56), entrusted this job to a person with an alien nomen M. Licinius Eutychus, who married a Volusia Olympias (9327).
[57] Weaver, 1972, 104; Treggiari, 1975a, 49-50; *Dig.* 35, 1, 32 (Africanus), *quamuis rationes reddere nihil aliud sit quam reliqua soluere, tamen si et statuliberi et heredis culpa, sine fraude tamen serui minus solutum sit et bona fide redditas esse rationes existimatum fuerit, liberum fore*; *Dig.* 35, 1, 82 (Callistratus), *cum seruus ita liber esse iussus sit 'si rationes reddiderit' eique fundum heres dare damnas sit...*
[58] Duff, 1928, 90; Treggiari, 1975a, 49-50; on *tabularius* of the *patrimonium* (inherited property), Sen. *Ep.* 88, 10, *patrimonium tabularios lassat*.
[59] The *familia rustica* given a separate *dispensator* from that of *familia urbana*: *Dig.* 50, 16, 166 (Pomponius), *potest enim aliquis dispensator non esse seruorum urbanorum numero: ueluti is, qui rusticarum rerum rationes dispenset ibique habitet*.
[60] (A021) *Philomo Posidippi dispensator, vixit an. XX*; (A053) *Gratus Posidippi disp.*; (A058) *Eros, T. Statili Posidippi ser. disp.*; (A268) *Stablio, Posidipi l., disp.*; about Posidippus, see Chap.4; one *dispensator* in the Statilian *columbarium* was a slave of an emperor (A426).

[61] (7370) L. Volusius Paris *a cubiculo et procurator*; cf. Petr. 30, apart from a *dispensator*, Trimalchio had a *procurator* who was receiving accounts (*procurator rationes accipiebat*); on Trimalchio's staff, especially the *dispensator* and the *procurator*, Baldwin, 1978, 90-91.
[62] *CIL* VI 2187=7445, *L. Iunius Silani l. Paris dispesator calator augur(um) vix. annos XXXII*.
[63] Cic. *Att.* 11, 2, 4; 8, 14, *tabellarios ad te cum inanibus epistulis mitterem*; *Dig.* 41, 1, 65, pr. (Labeo); cf. T. Statilius Heracla had the title 'viat(or)' (A346): while the *viator* (summoner) was the post in civil service held by public servants, Petronius' Trimalchio kept *decuria viatorum* (messengers' *decuria*) among his staff (Petr. 47).

the master by taking down the words as he dictated.[64] A Statilian '*actarius*' (A203) might perhaps be a misspelling of '*actuarius*', a short-hand writer.[65]

Cicero is well known for his employment of specialised clerical or secretarial staff; *a manu* Tiro, an *actuarius*, *librarii*, *tabellarii*, and the notorious slave Dionysius in charge of Cicero's library (*bibliotheca*), who ran away stealing a plentiful quantity of books. For Cicero, these secretaries and scribes were retained to help him in composing and eventually publishing his works. In other specialised areas not covered by Cicero's own slaves, his friendship with Atticus met the need. As a powerful supporter of his literary career, Atticus used his copiers and bookmakers to publish and circulate Cicero's writings.[66]

One may notice that, particularly in this area of service (financial and secretarial), the distinction between public and private is highly obscure. After Augustus held supreme power in 31 BC, his own *familia*, his personal slaves and freedmen, comes to share the burden of governing the Empire, which would later emerge more visibly as Imperial court. Naturally, Livia, as the wife of the princeps, possessed a range of servants whose job titles cannot be judged either as clearly personal or as of a more public administrative nature. That was the situation of the government and the *domus* of this period, continuing from the times of the Republic. Cato the younger, though he ceased to be quaestor after the term of office, from his excessive sense of justice, ordered his slaves to go to the public treasury every day and copy down the record of transactions, so that everything would continue to be under his watch.[67] Since employment of assistance of slaves/freedmen in one's public business was commonplace, as in the case of Pompey's father Strabo, when a master was accused of misappropriation of public funds, he might be able to say that it was actually his freedman who had done wrong.[68] It is a natural consequence that such servile staff, coming to be acquainted with the state-business as the secretaries of prominent public figures, might be able to aim higher up after manumission. T. Statilius Epaphra, a freedman of Corvinus, officially held the post of 'calator XVvir(orum)' (A274), a servant of a priesthood: this ex-slave was perhaps selected as one of fifteen *calatores* during his patron Corvinus' augural priesthood.[69]

Table 3.6 List of Job titles: secretaries

Job-titles	Statilii	Volusii	Livia	Iunii
a manu (scribe)	2	5	5	-
librarius / librarius a manu (copyist of book)	2	2	-	-
actarius=actuarius? (short-hand writer)	1	-	-	-
a bibliotheca (in charge of library)	-	-	1	-
tabellarius (letter-carrier)	2	-	-	-

Medical and therapeutic service: *medicus*, *obstetrix*, and *unctor*

In a society without any system of public health service, the poor did not have easy access to doctors, let alone have their own 'GP' or home doctors, as we might today. The very wealthy, ancient or modern, could retain privileged access to private and sometimes their own exclusive *medicus* (doctor).[70] In particular, Livia's *columbarium* is impressive in the sub-division of their specialities; a female and a male slave in charge of a domestic infirmary (*ad valetudinarium*) supposedly for slaves (9084, 9085),[71] and the specialists *medicus ocularis* (eye-doctor) and *medicus chirurgicus* (surgical doctor), as well as *supra medicos* (the chief doctor). The *obstetrices* (midwives), which the Statilii, Volusii, Livia, possessed, were called upon for the pregnant *dominae*, but perhaps more often when the *ancillae* gave birth to slave children within the household. Not only for the household, both *medici* and *obstetrices* are likely to have been accessible if necessary by ordinary people for a substantial fee.[72] Apart from the doctors and midwives, the role of a nurse was performed by ordinary slaves in ancient Rome. Seneca refers to slaves in charge of

---

[64] Augustus is reported to have broken the legs of his secretary (Thallus a manu) because he accepted a bribe for falsifying the contents of a letter: Suet. *Aug.* 67; Cic. *Q Fr.* 3, 3, *occupationum mearum tibi signum sit librari manus*; cf. *amanuensis*, Suet. *Nero*, 44; Suet. *Caes.* 74, Caesar put his secretary (*Philemo a manu servus*) to death after he tried to poison him.

[65] *TLL*, vol.1, 448-449; Suet. *Caes.* 55; Sen. *Ep.* 33, 9; cf. Trimalchio's *actuarius* was responsible for making a report on the household management (Petr. 53); in the later empire, the *actuarius* in the army kept accounts and took in charge of the assignment of military provisions: Amm. 15, 5, 3; 20, 5, 9; 25, 10, 7.

[66] *CIL* VI 4233, Livia's *a bybliotheca* [sic]; Cic. *Fam.* 13, 77, 3; id. *Att.* 4, 4a; 13, 44; 5, 20; Garland, 1992, 168; other than clerical staff, Cicero is known to have had a *dispensator* Philotimus, *cubicularius*, *coci* (cooks), *anagnosta* (reader), *operarius* (mechanic?), and *atriensis* (hall-porter); Nepos, *Att.* 13, 3.

[67] Plut. *Cat. Min.* 18, 9; he also had his accounts of administration in Cyprus written down in two copies of a book and preserved, so that it could be solicited by others as an example of scrupulous administration; though he carefully kept one copy himself and entrusted the other to his freedman called Philargyros, both copies were lost in the course of the journey home (Plut. *Cat. Min.* 38).

[68] Plut. *Pomp.* 4; cf. Cic. *ad Q. fr.* 1, 1, 11-18, *ac si quis est ex servis egregie fidelis, sit in domesticis rebus et privatis: quae res ad officium imperi tui atque ad aliquam partem rei publicae pertinebunt, de his rebus ne quid attingat*; Schumacher, 1982, 135, n.140.

[69] Suet. *Gram.* 12, mentions that Sulla's freedman Epicadus served as a *calator* in Sulla's augural priesthood: *Cornelius Epicadus, L. Cornelii Sullae dictatoris libertus calatorque in sacerdotio augurali*.

[70] Trimalchio's *medicus*, Petr. 47; 54; Suet. *Aug.* 9; id. *Nero*, 2; cf. the *paterfamilias* Cato the elder despising Greek physicians and playing the role of doctor himself for the family, Plut. *Cat. Mai.* 23; suspicion towards the profession, Tac. *Ann.* 6, 46.

[71] The *valetudinaria*, infirmaries for slaves in the *familia rustica*, are mentioned by Columella (11, 1, 18; 12, 3, 7-8).

[72] A mistress giving her *medicus* a shop to practice his profession is known in Cic. *Clu.* 178, *instructam ei continuo et ornatam Larini medicinae exercendae causa tabernam dedit*; cf. Plin. *HN.* 28, 18, 67; Tac. *Ann.* 6, 50.

keeping control of the sick and the insane in a large household, in contrast to a professional *medicus*.[73] As a solution to the shortage of doctors and nurses, which many societies face today as they increasingly relying on foreign recruitment, wealthy households trained slaves (though 'outsiders', likewise) to do the job.

The *unctores* were specialist masseurs, usually available in public baths. The number of *unctores* kept by the Statilii is outstanding. Since the Statilii had a *balneator*, they presumably had the bath in the house and possibly, next to the bath, they might have an *unctorium* (anointing-room) built, like the one Pliny had in his villa. If not totally for private use, the Statilii's *unctores* might be connected to the Statilii's amphitheatre business, or perhaps that the family owned a bath and rented out *unctores* attached to it for public use.[74] Aside from the luxury they connoted, the *unctores'* association with physical exercises at the *gymnasium* or *area* is often passed over without much notice in literary sources.[75] This may again indicate the military-oriented household of the Statilii, alongisde the set of *Germani* and *lecticarii*.[76] Livia had an *unctrix* (female masseur), and an *ad unguenta* who took in chage of Livia's perfumes or/and an *unguentarius* who purchased or sold the *ungentum* (ointment, perfumes).[77]

Table 3.7 List of Job titles: medical service

Job-titles	Statilii	Volusii	Livia	Iunii
medicus (physician)	2	2	8	2
obstetrix (midwife)	1	1	2	-
ad valetudinarium (in charge of infirmary)	-	-	2	-
unctor (masseur; anointer)	8	-	1	-
ad unguenta / unguentarius (on perfume)	-	-	2	-

IV. Production and Provision

Clothes provision

Clothes provision, as represented by the possession of a group of clothes makers and maintenance professionals, is an important measure of the self-sufficiency of households. Clothes had to be provided not only for a master, but for the *familia* as well. The provision of clothes (*uestiarium*), as well as foods (*cibaria*), was considered to be the obligation of a master.[78] In Cato's opinion, agricultural slaves should be provided with a tunic and a blanket (*sagum*) and a pair of wooden shoes (*sculponiae*) every two years.[79] Slave women in the *familia rustica* were strongly encouraged to do spinning and weaving, by which they could procure their own clothes with a minimum cost.[80] Clothes specialists and a sort of production line from the job-titles in the *columbaria* epitaphs are shown in Fig. 3.1-3 and Table 3.8.

The Statilian clothes production, maintenance, and management

The Statilian specialists appear to be highly organised in a line of production, maintenance, and management; its system of clothes provision might be drawn as in Fig. 3.1. First, the yarns of wool or cotton processed by a *lanipendius* and *quasillariae* were passed on to the *textores* (weavers) to transform them into cloth. Then, newly woven cloth might be handed over for dyeing or processing into finer fabric (by removing lanolin, grease on the wool),[81] a job which could be done either by well-equipped fullers or the group of *coloratores*.[82] There was also one shoemaker (*sutor*) (A107).[83] The fabric for home slippers could be provided from the same Statilian *quasillariae* or *textores*, but leathers, the usual material

---

[73] Sen. *Constant.* 13, 1-3, *in magna familia cura optigit aegros insanosque compescere.*

[74] Agrippa built a bath in the Campus Martius and it became public on his death (Dio, 53, 27, 1): Strong, 1968, 103; Aubert, 1994, 348-352.

[75] Plin. *Ep.* 2, 17, 11; Quint. 11, 3, 26; Mart. 7, 32, 6; three *iatraliptae* (physician who cures by anointing; masseurs) of Trimalchio, Petr. 28; Plut. *Cat. Mai.* 50, 1; anointing of both Trimalchio and Cato is described together with their playing ball-games; cf. Mart. 12, 70, 3.

[76] Note the Statilii's connection to the Greek town Thespiae, especially that a certain Polycratides of a rich local family made a dedication in honour of T. Statilius Taurus (either the new man or cos. AD 11) as his patron, and allegedly the same Polycratides was honoured by the people at Thespia for having built gymnasium and supplied it with oil: Kajava, 1989, 143-145.

[77] Two Helicones with the occupations concerning the *unguenta* (perfumes) might be either the same person, or father and son: (4046) Helico ad ung(uenta); (4252) Helico Liviae un[g]u[en]ta[rius]; cf. Plaut. *Trin.* 251, an *unctor* is included among a mistress' *familia tota*.

[78] Clothes and food for slaves: Sen. *Ben.* 3, 21, *est aliquid, quod dominus praestare servo debeat, ut cibaria, ut vestiarium; nemo hoc dixit beneficium*; Columella, *Rust.* 1, 8, 17, *servi, ne aut in vestiariis aut in ceteris praebitis iniuriose tractentur;* Juv. 1, 93; Sen. *Tranq.* 8, 8, *familia petit vestiarium victumque; tot ventres avidissimorum animalium tuendi sunt, emenda vestis...*; Dig. 7, 1, 15, 2 (Ulpian), *sufficienter autem alere et uestire debet secundum ordinem et dignitatem mancipiorum*; cf. Dig. 33, 7, 12, 5 (Ulpian, citing Trebatius), *lanificae quae familiam rusticam uestiunt.*

[79] Cato, *Rust.* 59, *vestimenta familiae. Tunicam P. III S, saga alternis annis. Quotiens cuique tunicam aut sagum dabis, prius veterem accipito, unde centones fiant. Sculponias bonas alternis annis dare oportet.*

[80] Columella, *Rust.* 12, 3, 6, *nihil enim nocebit, si sibi atque actoribus et aliis in honore servulis vestis domi confecta fuerit, quo minus patrisfamilias rationes onerentur.*

[81] The job-title '*colorator*' is often ambiguously translated as 'polisher' or 'painter', connected to the builders' group. But I do not find ancient sources attesting to such a job, and here I follow A. H. M. Jones in reference to Diocletian's Edict, which set two prices for a *colorator* whether he dyed newly woven cloth or old clothes: Jones, 1973, 361; cf. Vout, 1996.

[82] Juvenal (9, 28-30) implies that dyeing might have been done by a *textor*: *pingues aliquando lacernas, munimenta togae, duri crassique coloris et male percussas textoris pectine Galli accipimus.*

[83] Cf. a slave Zena without job-title held the agnomen 'Sutorianus' (A026, A357), which might indicate his connection to the shoe-maker.

for shoes, might have to be bought at the tanners' workshops in the city.[84]

Once the clothes were produced and provided to the masters and *familia*, they still required constant maintenance. For the cleaning of clothes, a group of fullers (*fullones*) were at work.[85] The fullers' specialty went beyong the simple washing of dirty clothes. They used special chemicals to rub off stains, to dye or bleach in white, and might use special press machines to take off creases on the clothes,[86] though it is not known how advanced were the tools with which the Statilian fullers were provided. Sometimes fullers gave a finishing touch to newly woven clothes by smoothing or cutting the nap, to a refined effect.[87]

Clothes recycling, that is the mending of worn clothes with patchwork, was an essential part of clothes provision in a household. The *sarcinatrix* (masc. *sarcinator*) specialised in this area. As in Fig.3.1, producing new clothes from raw materials involved a costly, time-consuming process. Naturally, the clothes industry of ancient Rome relied to a great degree on the circulation of mended clothes, particularly for less wealthy people, as numerous *sarcinatores* are known from inscriptions in Rome.

It was supposedly the servants with the job-titles *ad vestem* and *vestiarius*, which indicate concern with *vestis* (clothes) or *vestiarium* (clothes-chest), who took charge of provision and wardrobe of aristocratic masters.[88] Their supposedly higher status is indicated in that all three *ad vestem/vestiarii* are freedmen with *tria nomina*, and each mentions the particular name of the Statilian masters he worked for.[89] The same or similar titles are found in Livia's, as *a veste* and *ad vestem*,[90] and the only clothing-related reference in the *columbarium* of the Iunii Silani, '*cistarius*', probably also specialised in the management of a 'chest' or wardrobe.[91] They were entrusted to procure and make ready a range of clothes for the master. Keeping clothes in order and ready to wear was important for masters who were members of the senatorial class, since particular types of clothing and shoes signified their distinct status, and a particular occasion required particular dress. There were strict guidelines of appropriate types and colours of clothes according to age, social standing, and occasions.[92] Even a clothes-manager, however, might have to consult a *dispensator* (financial manager) concerning budget and expenditure, or entrust everyday clothes fitting to the *cubicularii*. Purchase of clothes for the *familia* was probably presided over by the *dispensator* who gave orders to each segment of specialists according to need. At the discretion of either *ad vestem* or *dispensator*, the workers (*quasillaria, lanipendius, textor, sutor*) produced clothes for the household, and the *fullo* and *sarcinatrix* were always accessible for regular cleaning and mending.

The actual labour of spinning and weaving, however, would not have been conducted exclusively by full-time professionals with job-titles. Columella recommended a *vilica* and other female members of *familia rustica* to do spinning and weaving in extra time or rainy days, whether or not it was one's speciality. In the same way, female slaves of our *columbarium* who did not claim such job titles would have been routinely called for *ad hoc* work.

The household of the Statilii seems to have possessed an ideal system of clothes production and maintenance. Although it is not known whether the family could procure raw materials such as wool or cotton on their rural estates or had to purchase from the dealers, the Statilian masters and *familia* could receive produced clothes and shoes and be given constant maintenance by their staff.

---

[84] On tanners (*coriarii*), Loane, 1938, 77-79; cf. Mart. 6, 93, 1-4; Juv. 14, 203.
[85] Plin. *HN*. 7, 196; cf. id. ibid., 18, 28, §107; Pomeroy, 1975, 200.
[86] Plin. *HN*. 28, 18, §66; 35, 50 §175; 35, 57, §197-198; 19, 2, §13; 17, 4, §46; Sen. *Q nat*. 1, 3, 2-3; Apul. *Met*. 9, 25ff.; Mart. 6, 93, 1; 14, 51; Plaut. *Pseud*. 782; cf. Petr. 42; their use of unusual chemicals and devices (especially, urines) facilitated mocking references to the fullers' workshop.
[87] Plin. *HN*. 16, 92, §244; 27, 66, §111; 27, 66, §92; Croom, 2000, 23-28; Jones, 1973, 361; Loane, 1938, 71-73, fullers in the city formed guilds and were ordered to pay rent for the use of *locus publicus;* the compensation on the part of fullers for lost clothes, *Dig*. 12, 7, 2 (Ulpian); the business of fulling was discussed in connection with the Roman conception of 'cleanness', by M. Bradley, 2002; on archaeology, Thompson, 2003, 198-209.
[88] We also find two '*velarii*' in the Statilian *columbarium*, though the interpretation of the title *velarius* is unclear: (A144) *velarius Zena*; (A080) *velarius Aphrodisius*. This title supposedly comes from the *velum*, any kind of curtain or cloth. As a domestic post, '*velarius*' has been variously translated as a curtain-drawer of chamber, as a synonym to *cubicularius*, or it might be the occupation of a curtain-maker or curtain-dealer; cf. Joshel, 1992, 182.
[89] The *vestiarius* was often understood as a 'clothes-dealer' who bought and sold clothes either as a peddler (*Dig*. 14, 3, 5, 4, Ulpian) or as a trader of a larger scale (*Dig*. 38, 1, 45, Scaevola).
[90] Cf. *CIL* VI 5197=*ILS* 1514: a *vicarius* with the title *ab veste* who belonged to the imperial slave Musicus, the *dispensator* of the imperial treasury of the Gallic province in Lyon.

[91] *CIL* VI 7601; cf. *CIL* VI 5193 *Anteros Ti. Caesaris cistarius a veste foren. vixit ann. XXV.*
[92] According to Plutarch (*Pomp*. 53), a servant with a change of clothes followed Pompey during election campaign; on the importance of the clothing and shoes distinctive to the senatorial status, such as the *latus clavus* (tunic with broad purple stripe), or *toga praetexta* (bordered with purple) for the higher magistrates, Talbert, 1984, 216-220; Croom, 2000, 30-72 *et al*.; Dio, 60, 24, 6, when Umbonius Silio was expelled from the senate, he put on sale for auction his senatorial dress; *Dig*. 34, 2, 23, 1-2 (Ulpian), on appropriate dress for male, female, children, and slaves; Croom, 2000, 28; Apul. *Florida*, 8, *sed ut loquar de solo honore, non licet insignia eius vestitu vel calceatu temere usurpare.*

Table 3.8 List of Job titles: on clothes and accessories

Job-titles	Statilii	Volusii	Livia	Iunii
lanipendius (wool worker, wool producer)	1	-	2	-
quasillaria (spinner)	8	-	-	-
textor (weaver)	3	-	-	-
colorator (dyer?)	2	-	1	-
a purpura (dyer of purple)	-	-	1	-
fullo (fuller)	4	1	-	-
cistarius (in charge of 'chest' or wardrobe)	-	-	-	1
margaritarius (in charge of pearl/jewellry?)	-	-	1	-
ab ornamentis / ab ornamentis sacerdotalibus (in charge of [ceremonial] garments/accessaries)	1	-	2	-
sarcinatrix/-tor (clothes-mender)	5	-	8	-
sutor / calceator (shoemaker)	1	-	1	-
velarius (in charge of cloth?)	2	-	-	-
ad vestem (in charge of fine clothes)	2	-	5	-
vestiarius / vestiarius de horreis Volusianis (clothes dealer?)	1	1	-	-
vestiplicus (ironer, presser)	-	1	-	-

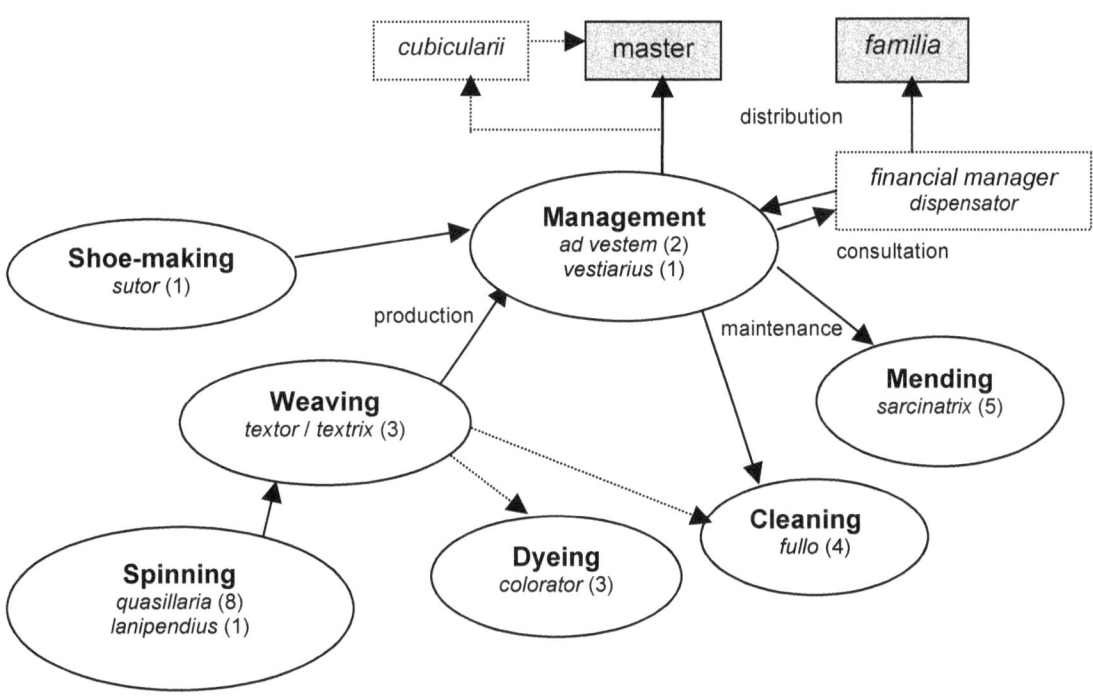

Fig. 3.1: Provision of clothes: the Statilii
Note: ( ) is the number of title-holders in each *columbarium*

Comparison: clothes provision of the Volusii

In contrast to that of the Statilii, the *columbarium* of the Volusii is marked by its absence of clothes makers. Whereas they possessed a manager and workers on the maintenance side – *vestiplicus* (for clothes-folding, pressing, ironing) and *fullo* (fuller) –, we do not find any trace of those involved in production such as *quasillaria*, *lanipendius*, or *textor*.[93] But this absence in the *columbarium* only suggests that they may not have had specialists 'in the urban household'. From the viewpoint of supply of raw materials, when a household possessed a clothes-manufacturing team, it might be convenient to have them in the *familia rustica*. Certainly, such was the case for Atticus' household: clothes were produced by the *familia rustica* of his estate in Epirus in a larger scale, so that he could send some to his friend Cicero.[94] As the Volusii are known to have owned the villa in Lucus Feroniae, which was excavated in 1962-1968,[95] it is possible that the clothes were mainly produced there. It is noted that the Volusii had a *vestiarius de horreis Volusianis* (clothes-dealer of the *horrea Volusiana*). Although the title was held by a freedman of an alien nomen 'T. Aquilius Pelorus', if Buonocore's inclusion of his epitaph in the Volusian *columbarium* was correct, T. Aquilius Pelorus' close connection to the family indicates that the Volusii could either procure clothes through this clothes-dealer, or even sell clothes produced in the rural household through him. It is possible that T. Aquilius Pelorus did not work for the Volusii, merely renting the space of the *horrea* for his trade, as an independent shopkeeper (*vd. infra*). But even so, the Volusii were the owner of the *horrea* which stored commodities including clothes, which would mean that the Volusii never lacked in the provision of such items for their own household.

Comparison: clothes provision of Livia's household

Likewise, as far as the columbarium epitaphs are concerned, Livia's household appears to have had workers on the maintenance side of clothes provision but very few producers. Although she had the *lanipendii* (wool-producer), their small number (only two) and the total absence of a spinning maid (*quasillaria*) or weaver (*textrix*) make it unlikely that we are seeing a body of manufacturers here.

However, in her case, we have Suetonius' account that her husband Augustus, the supporter of traditional family values, had his daughters and granddaughters brought up acquiring skills of spinning and weaving (*lanificium*); moreover, he himself used to wear the clothes made by his sister, wife, daughter, and granddaughters.[96] If we believe this report, the very absence of professional weavers and spinners here perhaps means that Livia herself actually performed and took the initiative in domestic *lanificium* with the help of her ordinary *ancillae*, probably in their spare time, and they did not consider themselves as full-time professional weavers or spinners. Spinning and weaving symbolised the virtue of Roman matrons,[97] and every woman, noble or servile, used to perform this job in the household. It was now largely the girls or even boys of low birth who were expected to learn this skill, and many noble women at this period abandoned engaging in the labour.[98] Certainly, in some households, probably those such as Livia's, the clothes production continued to be worked by the *materfamilias* "in collaboration with the slave-women of her establishment."[99] Realistically, however, there was a limit to the involvement of a *materfamilias* in the operation, and the employment of some full-time specialists was unavoidable in an elite household like Livia's. Incidentally, Suetonius gives more information about Augustus' domestic clothing: he instructed that his purple stripe should be neither narrow nor broad, and his shoes somewhat high-soled, to make him look taller than he really was, and his shoes and clothing to wear in public be always kept ready in his *cubiculum* for any unexpected occasions.[100] The presence of a shoe-maker (*calceator*), clothes managers (*a veste/ad vestem*), and a purple dyer (*a purpuris*) in Livia's *columbarium*, seems to perfectly match Suetonius' account.

Unlike the Statilii and Livia, probably many other families (even aristocratic ones) could not produce clothes at home. Some might be able to receive clothes from households which did possess such facilities by way of *amicitia* (friendship), as Cicero from Atticus. But others would have had to buy ready-made clothes from shops, or to rely on external manufacturers by way of contracts or order. There were markets for such have-

---

[93] The Volusii had two male '*librarii*' (9516, 7293), which could mean 'spinners' equivalent to '*lanipendii*', like a female *libraria* attested in Juv. 6, 475; but in absense of *quasillaria* or *textor* in the *columbarium*, here I attributed the *librarii* to 'scribe' or 'bookmaker' (see Table 3.7).
[94] Cic. *Att.* 11, 2, 4, *a tuis et nummorum accepi HS XX et vestimentorum quod opus fuit.*
[95] On the successful career and wealth established by the new man L. Volusius L. f. Q. n. Saturninus, Boatwright, 1982, 7-16, especially on the family's property, 12-15.
[96] Suet. *Aug.* 64, *filiam et neptes ita instituit, ut etiam lanificio assuefaceret;* Suet. *Aug.* 73, *veste non temere alia quam domestica usus est, ab sorore ut uxore et filia neptibusque confecta.*
[97] e.g., Livy, 1, 57, 9: *nocte sera deditam lanae inter lucubrantes ancillas in medio aedium sedentem inueniunt. muliebris certaminis laus penes Lucretiam fuit.*
[98] Columella, *Rust.* 12, pr. 9, *pleraeque sic luxu et inertia diffluant, ut ne lanificii quidem curam suscipere dignentur, sed domi confectae vestes fastidio sint, perversaque cupidine maxime placeant, quae grandi pecunia et totis paene censibus redimuntur*; Juv. 6, 287-91; Plaut. *Merc.* 520, *de lanificio neminem metuo, una aetate quae sit*; Petr. 132, *mulier... convocat omnes quasillarias familiaeque sordidissimam partem.*
[99] Dixon, 2001, 118-9; Asconius, *Pro Milone*, 43, *deinde omni vi ianua expugnata et imagines maiorum deiecerunt et lectulum adversum uxoris eius Corneliae, cuius castitas pro exemplo habita est, fregerunt, iterumque telas quae ex vetere more in atrio texebantur diruerunt*; Dig. 24, 1, 31, pr.-1 (Pomponius).
[100] Suet. *Aug.* 73, *togis neque restrictis neque fusis, clavo nec lato nec angusto, calciamentis altiusculis, ut procerior quam erat videretur. Et forensia autem et calceos numquam non intra cubiculum habuit ad subitos repentinosque casus parata.*

CHAPTER 3: THE OCCUPATIONS OF SLAVES AND FREEDMEN

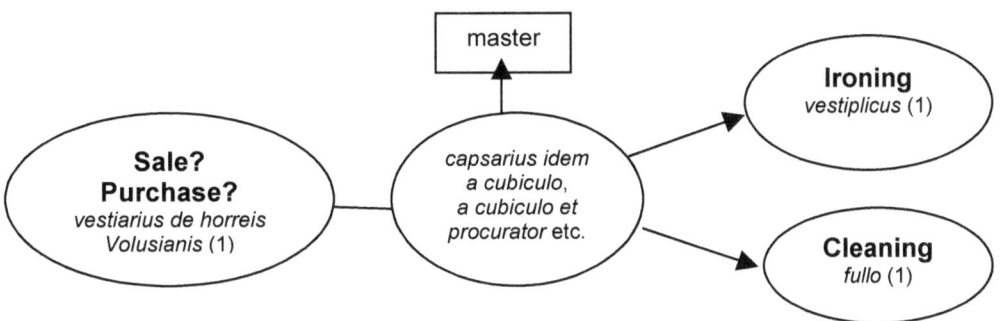

Fig. 3.2: Provision of clothes: the Volusii

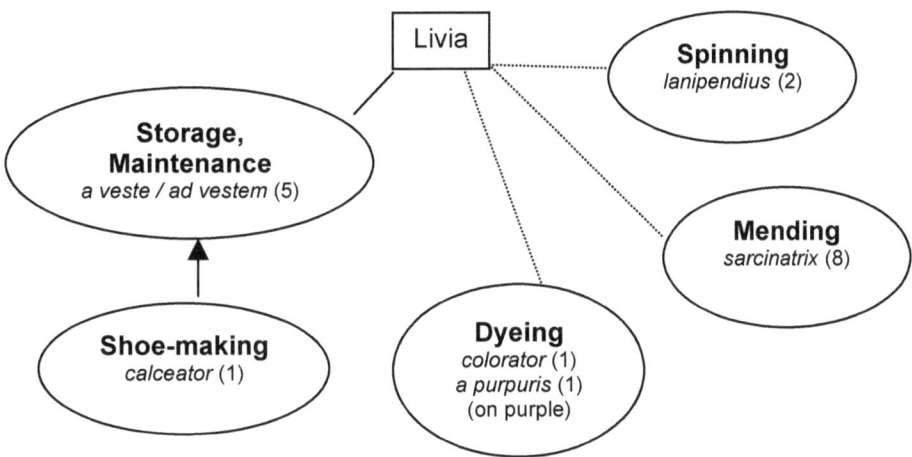

Fig. 3.3: Provision of clothes: Livia

nots.[101] Nero forbade the people to wear purple, and closed all the shops of dealers of purple dyes.[102] A celebrated grammarian Q. Remmius Palaemon, as a *verna* (home-born slave), was originally trained for weaving (*textrinum*), before he took up the job of accompanying his master's son to school (probably as *paedagogus*). He subsequently acquired an education and was set free, and he achieved the status of a leading grammarian at Rome. Even after this, Suetonius says that he retained a shop selling clothes (*officinas promercalium vestium exerceret*) and a vineyard with the purpose to increase his property, alongside the regular income from his school.[103] It is likely that the clothes makers of the Statilii received orders from other households and made profit, and perhaps had shops established in the city under the patronage of the Statilii.

Food provision and catering

Pliny talks about the general practice in Plautus' days, that is towards the end of the third century BC, when people did not have cooks in the household and hired *mercenarii* cooks at the market for special occasions.[104] Though this situation might not have changed much down to the end of the late Republic, we find here very wealthy households possessing not only professional cooks (*coci*) but also separate pastry-cooks (*pistores*).[105]

With *coci* and *pistores*, the Statilian household could provide bread on their own, and cater for special banquets. Messallina, who became Nero's wife, had her own *opsonator* (caterer).[106] The *fartor* (sausage-maker) (A264) and the *salarius* (a dealer in salted fish) (A103) are also known to have been associated with the Statilii.

In addition to the *coci* and *pistores*, an important role in the food provision of an urban household was played by a *cellarius*, who supervised the storeroom.[107] As Cato claims, products produced on the land would become profitable after a period of storage in *cella* and are to be sold for a good price. Such a strategy brought the head of the household, according to Cato, *res* (profit), *virtus*, and *gloria*.[108] If not for commercial purposes, the stock in the *cella* enhances the degree of self-sufficiency of the household. Wine, grain, or vegetables were usual items kept in the *cella*.[109]

In the *columbarium* of the Volusii, though we do not find any *coci* or *pistores*, there were posts called *a frumento* ('on grain'), *cellarius*, and *a cella*. As for the *a frumento*, they might be working primarily for feeding the household, by purchasing the grain from the wholesale dealers (*frumentarii*) who transported from Egypt or Africa to the city. At the same time, they could also make profit by selling the stock grain, especially at times of grain shortage:[110] most conveniently, the family owned a warehouse (*horrea Volusiana*) for storage and retail.[111] The Volusii are also known as the producers of wine or oil on a large scale; the inscriptions on the amphorae found in the Praetorian Camp in Rome bear the name 'L. Volusius Saturninus'.[112] Beside commercial purposes, some of the wine produced on their country estates would be brought into the urban household and stored under the supervision of *a cella* (7368) and *cellarius* (7281), and consumed there.[113]

Livia had three pistores and one *opsonator*. The absence of a cocus in Livia's as well as in the Volusii might be explained by assuming that everyday catering and procuring of foods were performed by ordinary servants.

As for the household of Iunius Silanus, we only know a cocus from its *columbarium*, but a family tomb of a baker

---

[101] On the clothes industry on a much broader scale across the Empire, Jones, 1974, 350-364.

[102] Suet. *Nero*, 32, 3.

[103] Suet. *Gram.* 23, and the commentary of Kaster, 1995, 233-4; cf. Juv. 1, 105, a rich freedman who ran five shops; cf. Treggiari, 1979, 67-71.

[104] Plin. *HN.* 18, 28, §107, *nec cocos vero habebant in servitiis, eosque ex macello conducebant*; freelance cooks, who worked for wage or by contract, are described as boastful of their skills or kleptomaniac in a series of Plautine comedies, Plaut. *Pseud.* 801f; *Aul.* 408f; *Merc.* 779f.; Livy, 39, 6, 9 (187 BC), *tum coquus, vilissimum antiquis mancipium et aestimatione et usu, in pretio esse, et quod ministerium fuerat, ars haberi coepta.*

[105] Cato the younger was even accompanied by his cook and baker on his trip and used to send them ahead to the town, so that they could arrange lodging for him: Plut. *Cat. Min.* 12, 3; Sen. *Ep.* 95, 23-24, *cocos numera...pistorum turba*; Mart. 14, 220, *cocus domini debet habere gulam* (a cook ought to know the taste of his master); Apuleius, 10, 13 (slave brothers of *pistor* and *cocus*); Mart. 11, 31; 14, 222; Suet. *Caes.* 48; *Vit.* 16; *pistor* as an independent profession: Mart. 14, 223; Petr. 47; 60; Julius Caesar punished his *pistor* for serving different kinds of bread to him and to his guests: Suet. *Caes.* 48, *pistorem alium quam sibi panem convivis subicientem compedibus vinxerit*; Varro cited by Aulus Gellius, 15, 19, 2, *quantum operae sumpsisti tuus pistor bonum faceret panem.*

[106] Cf. Sen. *Ep.* 47, 8.

[107] *Cocus, pistor, cellarius* as a set of caterers in a household: Mart. 11, 31; Columella, *Rust.* 12, 4, 2, *pistoris et coci nec minus cellarii diligentia*; cf. Sen. *Ep.* 122, 16, *pueri* (=*ministri*), *cellarii, coqui*, for dinner.

[108] Cato, *Rust.* 3, 2, *patrem familiae villam rusticam bene aedificatam habere expedit, cellam oleariam, vinariam, dolia multa, uti lubeat caritatem expectare: et rei et virtuti et gloriae erit.*

[109] Plin. *HN.* 19, 188, a *cellarius* getting rid of stinks from wine; *Dig.* 33, 9, 3, 8 (Ulpian), *frumentum sive quid leguminis in cella penuaria habuit*; in Plautus' *Captivi* (894) Hegio rewards the parasite Ergasilus by giving him free access to the store-room (*tu intus cura quod opus est. sume, posce, prome quid vis. te facio cellarium*).

[110] Rickmann, 1980, 143; Loane, 1938, 121-123; Suet. *Aug.* 42, 3; Tac. *Ann.* 2, 87; there was the shortage of grain in AD 32 and 51: Tac. *Ann.* 6, 13; 12, 43.

[111] see Table 3.11.

[112] Boatwright, 1982, 13; *CIL* XV 4559; 4571; 4646; 4784.

[113] An *exactor* with a *vicaria* attested in the Volusian *columbarium* (7371) (Table 3.11), might be an agricultural overseer, either from the villa rustica or suburban gardens; Col. 3, 13, 10, *peritus ac vigilans exactor*; Plin. *Ep.* 9, 37, 3, *ex meis aliquos operis exactores, custodes fructibus ponam.*

Marcus Iunius Pudens outside the columbarium (9810) is considered to be the descendant of a slave of the Iunii.[114]

Table 3.9 List of Job titles: on foods

Job-titles	Statilii	Volusii	Livia	Iunii
cocus (cook)	4	-	-	1
pistor (baker)	4	-	3	-
fartor (sausage maker)	1	-	-	-
a frumento (grain supplier)	-	3	-	-
opsonator (caterer)	1	-	1	-
salarius (dealer of salted-fish)	1	-	-	-
cellarius / a cella /cellaria libraria (storeroom keeper)	1	2	1	-

V. Management of urban property

Horrea

Of the *horrea*, storehouses, that stood in large numbers across the city, we know about twenty by name. The *horrea* might be a granary, which stored and distributed grain under the state's supervision, or a warehouse for other sorts of commercial products, often combined with retail shops. The owners also gained income by renting them out, and the *horrearii*, who took charge of a *horreum*, are known from the *columbaria*.[115] Their roles were like the *insularius*, making contracts with commercial tenants, or alternatively, depending on the scale and nature of the *horreum*, they might merely be acting as *ostiarius* (porter).

For the advantage of transport, the great *horrea* had been constructed along the Tiber bank in the Regio XIII; most famously the *Horrea Galbana*, and others such as *Horrea Lolliana, Agrippiana, Seiana*, or *Petroniana*. The *Horrea Piperataria* of the emperor Domitian stood in the north part of the Neronian Sacra Via, and were intended for the sale of pepper and spices from the East in this busy commercial street. As the names tell us, some of the *horrea* were built originally by private individuals, but later, in one way or another, the majority seems to have become state-owned property. For instance, the *Horrea Lolliana* apparently first belonged to the gens Lollia (probably first established by M. Lollius Palicanus, the tribune of plebs in 71 BC) but then one of the staff in Livia's *columbarium* is found to be in charge (4239; 4226), and it continued to be supervised by the imperial slaves.[116]

We are not informed of the precise location of the *horrea Volusiana* or how long the *horrea* were under the control of the Volusii.[117] As the *horrea* were usually rented out section by section to individual private dealers,[118] we cannot deny the possibility that a clothes-dealer T. Aquilius Pelorus in the *horrea Volusiana* might be such a private contractor (9973).

Apart from such celebrated *horrea*, there would have been a number of anonymous ones which were more for private use (i.e., *horrea privata* in contrast to the *horrea publica* described above). The *horrea* allegedly owned by the Statilii, or that of the Furii (9469, *Thalamis M. Furi Camilli ab horr.*), the names or locations of which are not known to us, might have been ones that merely functioned for private use, as a sort of extension of the *cella* (storeroom) in the household.[119]

Architects and carpenters

The building of houses in imperial Rome was conducted, probably mearly exclusively, by agents of the wealthy, while the poor could only rent or possibly purchase portions from them. The art of architecture in Rome had been fast growing, as conveyed by Pliny, to the extent that the house considered as the city's finest in 78 BC would no longer rank among the first hundred within thirty-five years.[120] According to Vitruvius, in his *De architectura*, architects need genuine training, which would be attained with the protection of a patron. While disapproving of some amateur architects and builders who have no special training or experience, Vitruvius refers in praise to those who successfully built their own houses from their own means with slave/freedman builders trained as architects.[121] The catastrophe of building collapse is reported at Fidena, close to Rome, in AD 27: a certain local freedman Atilius, who embarked on constructing an amphitheatre for profit (*in sordidam*

---

[114] Joshel, 1992, 96-97, suggested that his wife Claudia Eurine who commemorated Pudens probably originated from the family of Appius Claudius, who was connected to Iunius Silanus by marriage. Provided that Joshel's speculation is right, i.e., either Pudens or his close ascendant (patron or father etc.) was the slave/freedman of the Iunii, this would be an example of the transformation of the skill of a household slave into a family business of an independent nature over generations.
[115] Statilii, A045, A087, A319, A349; Volusii, 7289; Livia, 4239, 4226.
[116] (9467) *Q. Lollius Lolliae l. Hilarus horrear.*; (4226) ...*Calamus Ti. Claudii Caesaris Augusti Germanici Pamphilianus, vilicus ex horreis Lollianis...* (cf. 4226a); (4239) *Eros Caesaris horr. Lollianis...*; (4226=ILS 1620); *Calamus Ti. Claudii Caesaris Augusti Germanici Pamphilianus vilicus ex horreis Lollianis*; D'Arms, 1981, 66.
[117] As Tacitus says that the new man L. Volusius Saturninus (*cos.* 12 BC) first amassed the family's wealth (*Ann.* 3, 30, 1), the construction of the *horrea* might be ascribed to him or his son Lucius (*cos.* AD 3): D'Arms, 1981, 69-71; Rickman, 1971, 169.
[118] Leasing of space of *horrea* for storage and retail, Rickman, 1971, 164-180; id. 1980, 138-143; cf. individual contractors of imperial *horrea* from inscriptions: (10026) [...]*us de horreis Agrippianis*; (9972) *C. Iulius Lucifer vestiarius de horreis Agrippianis*; (9801) *Aurelia C. l. Nais, piscatrix de horreis Galbae*.
[119] Apul. *Met.* 4, 18, *horreum ubi vespera sagaciter argentum copiosum recondi viderat*; id. 5, 2; cf. Sen. *Ep.* 45, 2, *ego vero quoscumque habeo, mittere paratus sum et totum horreum excutere*; on *horrea* in general, Fiechter, *RE*, viii, 1913, 2458-2464; Rickman, 1971, 87-122; Loane, 1938, 114-116.
[120] Plin. *HN.* 36, 109.
[121] Vitr. 6, pr. 6-7.

mercedem), failed to establish a sufficiently solid foundation or adequate wooden framework. The result was the structure, packed with spectators, collapsing to the ground with a great number of casualties.[122]

The most notable builders in private ownership are Crassus' five hundred strong slave gang. The anecdote goes that his entrepreneurial talent took notice of the frequent collapse of buildings in Rome because of fire or poor construction; Crassus first bought up slave architects and builders, and after they reached 500, he started buying houses on the verge of collapse or those located close to such houses at a very cheap price. Plutarch does not exactly tell us about what Crassus did with these houses and his 500 slave architects and builders, but he merely remarks that the result was that "most of Rome came into his possession" (Plut. *Crass.* 2). Undoubtedly, Crassus made an enormous profit by this project. He probably ran a business of renting out or reselling houses, after his slave gang had rebuilt or refurbished them.[123]

Cicero relied on external contractors to build and refurbish town houses, keeping a watchful eye over every process of their work. While Cicero does not seem to have had his own specialist slave builders, building or refurbishment of less demanding kinds could be performed by those who were not specifically called *fabri*. Cicero mentions that his brother Quintus' *vilicus* Nicephorus, the steward of the country estate, was himself contracted to refurbish a house in Laterium but eventually dropped it because of disagreement as to the cost.[124]

Though not profit-pursuing, Agrippa organised 240 slaves for repairing and building the aqueducts, who were later bequeathed to Augustus at his death and formally organised as public slaves.[125] Livia's two *aquarii* might be technicians in the same line, but if in a domestic context, they were perhaps closer to 'plumbers'.

Among eight *fabri* of the Statilii, four of them were specifically called *faber tignuarius*, and one *faber structor parietarius*, with the emphasis on carving timber (*tignum*) and constructing walls (*paries*), respectively.[126] There were other specialists called *structor*,[127] *marmorarius*,[128] *mensor*, and *ad aedificia* ('in charge of building'). The actual workforce probably numbered a lot more than these title-holders, possibly not far away from Crassus' or Agrippa's slave gangs. P. A. Brunt argued that a certain number of wage labourers had to be hired by professional architects or builders for constructing public buildings. A bulk of poor free citizens in the city only found employment in unskilled casual work.[129] In the same way, the Statilii's professional and skilled builders would have had to hire a number of ordinary unskilled workers to work under their direction.

Though it was not included in the Statilian *columbarium*, one epitaph is known from Rome, which records 'T. Statilius Vol (tinia tribu) Aper mensor aedificiorum', commemorated by his parents T. Statilius Proculus and Argentaria Eutychia and his wife Orcivia Anthis (*ILS* 7737).[130] The father Proculus is titled *accensus velatus*, a designation for unarmed reserve troops which were also mobilised for the construction of public roads. Their nomen 'T. Statilius' indicates the family's origin as a slave of the Statilii possibly not many generations ago.

It is tempting to connect the original establishment of these builders with T. Statilius Taurus' public enterprise of the construction of the stone amphitheatre in Rome. D'Arms suggested that Taurus imported timber from Dyrrachium for the construction, from a rather bold conjecture of two facts, namely Taurus' connection with Dyrrachium and that timber was the town's most important product.[131] While the sources only tell us that it was built from the spoils of Taurus' African campaign,[132] this grand project is the most likely occasion when the family's slave gang of builders was first organised and undertook the construction work with the family's private resources, probably supplemented by individual contractors (*redemptores* or *mancipes*).

---

[122] Tac. *Ann.* 4, 62-63; Suet. *Tib.* 40.
[123] On Crassus' building activities, Loane, 1938, 81-82; Gummerus, 1920.
[124] Cic. *Q fr.* 2, 4, 2-3, *domus utriusque nostrum aedificatur strenue. redemptori tuo dimidium pecuniae curavi... etiam nunc tribus locis aedifico, reliqua reconcinno;* cf. Cicero refering to Quintus' *topiarius* doing a good job for his gardens, Cic. *Q.fr.* 3, 1.
[125] Frontin. *Aq.* 2, 98, *habuit et familiam propriam aquarum, quae tueretur ductus atque castella et lacus. Hanc Augustus hereditate ab eo sibi relictam publicavit;* id. 2, 116; Loane, 1938, 80-85.
[126] *Dig.* 50, 16, 235, 1: *fabros tignarios dicimus non eos dumtaxat, qui tigna dolarent, sed omnes qui aedificarent.*
[127] Apart from 'carpenter', the *structor* might mean the carver of the decorative food at a banquet, as in Petr. 35.

[128] Imported marbles were used in many public buildings in Rome from the late Republican period: Loane, 1938, 41-42; cf. Sen. *Ep.* 90, 15, *marmorarius ac faber;* Vitr. 7, 6.
[129] Brunt, 1980, 83-100; apart from nameable occupations, there were people who earned livelihood by casual employment. Cic. *Off.* 1, 42, 150, *illiberales autem et sordidi quaestus mercennariorum omnium, quorum operae, non quorum artes emuntur; est enim in illis ipsa merces auctoramentum servitutis.*
[130] *T. Statilio Vol. Apro mensori aedificior., vixit ann. XXII m. VIII d. XV, T. Statilius Vol. Proculus accensus velatus et Argentaria Eutychia parentes filio optumo et Orciviae Anthidi uxori eius, sibiq. et suis, libertis libertabus posterisque eorum...;* According to Salomies, 2001, 84, 'Voltinia' was tribe name of many cities in Narbonese Gaul.
[131] D'Arms, 1981, 155.
[132] Taurus' victories in wars entitled him to a share of booty, and as the general, he used the *manubiae* for the public as he was expected to. On *manubiae*, as the general's personal share of the booty, Shatzman, 1972, 177-205.

CHAPTER 3: THE OCCUPATIONS OF SLAVES AND FREEDMEN

Table 3.10 List of Job titles: builders

Job-titles	Statilii	Volusii	Livia	Iunii
faber (carpenter)	8	-	1	-
marmorarius (worker/dealer of marble)	1	-	-	-
mensor (surveyor? architect?)	1	1	3	-
structor (carpenter? cook?)	1	-	3	-
ad aedificia (in charge of building)	1	-	-	-
topiarius (landscape gardener)	1	-	-	-
aquarius (water-pipe worker)	-	-	2	-

De amphitheatro of the Statilii

As I have mentioned above, the new man T. Statilius Taurus is known to have built the stone amphitheatre for the people of Rome. It is no less remarkable to find servile dependants of subsequent generations holding job-titles concerning this 'public' building, which means that the Statilii were virtually entrusted with its management and maintenance as well.[133] Whereas occasional expensive public benefactions such as gladiatorial games were presided over by the emperors or magistrates,[134] running the amphitheatre also required everyday custodians. A question that arises here is whether or for how long the Statilii retained responsibility for the amphitheatre after Taurus. Although only three examples are known from the *columbaria* epitaphs, the words of the title are similar but subtly changed, as *custos de ampitheatro* (A009), *ostiarius ab amphitheatro* (A068), and *de amphiteatro* (sic) (A313). To judge from the slight differentiation in the titles of these ambiguously same or similar jobs, I think that the three titles were developed over a sequence of time, rather than existing in parallel. Any major difference is hardly recognisable in the job descriptions of a *custos* and an *ostiarius*, and the *de amphitheatro* vaguely refers to the general role as a custodian. The titles appear to show a chronological decline in elaboration, from the '*custos* (guard) of the amphitheatre', then '*ostiarius* (door-keeper) of amphitheatre', and finally, simply called 'concerning the amphitheatre' which was now delegated to a *vicarius* of a slave of the Statilii. As Taurus' amphitheatre was soon regarded too small by Caligula and Nero, who subsequently built their own (Dio, 62, 18, 2), it perhaps became increasingly ignored by the public.

The amphitheatre of Taurus was destroyed by the fire in AD 64, shortly before Nero married Statilia Messalina, the last of the Statilii. But probably the family had already withdrawn from the management of amphitheatre before that, at the time of Taurus' suicide in AD 53.[135]

Insularius

In parallel to the profit from country estates, urban property could bring a considerable income, especially the rents of *insulae* from tenants. A certain Afer in Martial (4, 37) made as much as 3,000,000 sesterces' profit from his *insulae* and *fundi* altogether, and 600,000 sesterces from grazing (*pecus*), and at the same time he was the creditor of 3,200,000 sesterces on loan. Whether the figure whom Martial refers to as Afer is factual or not, the numbers were probably exaggerated. However, the point that can be drawn from the passage is that profit from urban property was as important as that from traditional agriculture or horticulture. Cicero had at least two of his shops and other *insulae* rented out, some of which Cicero complains about as collapsing or suffering from cracks. Such was a common problem for the owners of urban buildings; while renting out *insulae*, *tabernae*, or *horrea*, etc. instantly brought large sums of money, frequent fires in the city or poor construction rendered the business 'high profit, high risk'.[136]

The tenants of *insulae* were not only poorer people in the city, but those from noble families short of capital. We hear from Plutarch of the dictator Sulla's disreputable past, when he used to live in a cheap apartment house, sharing it with a former slave; while Sulla rented the lower rooms for 3,000 sesterces (yearly?), his fellow tenant occupied the upper rooms for 2,000 sesterces (Plut. *Sull.* 1). In other cases, those who decided to stand for election to the magistracies temporarily rented houses close to the forum for the convenience of campaign activities (Plut. *Pomp.* 66). Also, rented houses were acquired by office-holders particularly of the equestrian

---

[133] It appears that repairment of public buildings was felt to be the obligation of the descendants of the original buiders: Eck, 1984, 141; Tac. *Ann.* 3, 72: in AD 22, M. Aemilius Lepidus asked the senate's permission to refurbish the basilica built by L. Aemilius Paullus (*cos.* 50 BC).

[134] Tiberius and Caligula gave gladiatorial shows in the amphitheatre of Taurus: Suet. *Tib.* 7; id. *Calig.* 18, *munera gladiatoria partim in amphitheatro Tauri...edidit....neque spectaculis semper ipse praesedit, sed interdum aut magistratibus aut amicis praesidendi munus iniunxit*; cf. Dio, 59, 10, 5; the *columbarium* of Iunius Silanus contained an epitaph of a *palaestrita* (either wrestler or manager of wrestling school) (see Table 3.11).

[135] There is an epitaph that records a certain Hyacinthus, 'the supervisor of the amphitheatre', commemorating his wife, an imperial freedwoman, and a daughter: (10163=*ILS* 5155) *Claudiae Thallusae Aug. lib. et Thalliae f., eius Hyacinthus vilicus [am]phitheatri coniugi suae et filiae eius et sibi et suis*. From Thallusa's *nomen* (*Claudia, Aug. l*), she was a freedwoman of either Claudius or Nero. His title '*vilicus amphitheatri*' and the date of the inscription make us suspect that this Hyacinthus was one of the last amphitheatre managers after the death of Taurus (*cos.* AD 44), though the original location of the inscription is not known and it remains unclear whether the 'amphitheatre' here was precisely that of Taurus.

[136] For the threat of fire and collapse of buildings in the city: Gell. 15, 1; Juv. 3, 6-9; cf. 3, 164-167, high rents at Rome; Cicero occasionally discussed with Atticus the matters of the rent of his property: Cic. *Att.* 14, 9, 1; 16, 1, 5, *fructus insularum*; 12, 32, 2; Garnsey, 1976, 126-128.

Table 3.11 List of Job titles: property managers / keepers

Job-titles	Statilii	Volusii	Livia	Iunii
insularius (rent-collector)	7	1	2	-
horrearius (store-house manager)	4	1	-	-
ex hortis ('from gardens')	5	-	-	-
custos de ampitheatro / ostiarius ab amphitheatro / de amphiteatro (custodian of amphitheatre)	3	-	-	-
palaestrita (wrestler, director of wrestling school)	-	-	-	1
balneator (bath-keeper)	1	-	-	1
atriensis (hall-manager)	5	2	1	-
ostiarius/-a (door-keeper)	3	-	4	-
ab suppellectile (in charge of household furniture)	-	-	3	-
ad possessions (in charge of properties?)	-	-	1	-
exactor (overseer? rent collector?)	-	1	-	-
a monumento (in charge of tomb?)	1	-	-	-

order coming from outside Rome, who were to return home after their term of office.[137]

To handle the business of renting property, one could appoint slaves/freedmen as *insularii* whose duty was to collect rent, make contracts, or launch repair operations.[138] We know of seven *insularii* from the Statilian *columbarium*, as well as one from the Volusii's (7291/17454) and two from Livia's (3973, 3974). One of the Statilian *insularii* was specifically called *insularius ex horteis Pompeia(na)* (rent-collector from the Pompeian gardens), which indicates that the Statilii were in possession of these famous gardens on the Campus Martius after the deaths of the original owner Pompey and his succeeding owner M. Antony, and rented out the whole or part of it.[139] Since it is known that the Statilii owned at least three other *horti*, it would have been the wise decision to rent them out instead of leaving them idle. The relatively large number of *insularii* of the Statilii gives us an impression that the family was running its urban property as a large-scale business. It was, furthermore, advantageous that the Statilii also possessed a substantial group of builders (*fabri*) as discussed above: the *insularii* could work in close collaboration with these builders, for constructing rentable *insulae*.

Horti

The urban property owned by the Statilii included the *horti*, 'pleasure gardens' located in the suburbs of the city.[140] The Statilii were supposedly the owners of at least four *horti*. First of all, the *horti Tauriani* on the Esquiline hill, in the neighbourhood of the *columbarium*, known from the *cippi* designating the boundary against the *horti Calyclani* (*CIL* VI 29772). Other names we find from the epitaphs of their slaves/freedmen, the *horti Pompeiani* (on the Campus Martius), the *horti Scatoniani* (unknown locality), and the (*horti*) *Albani* (or perhaps rather '*villa*' *Albana*, country estates located in Alba?).[141] It is not clear what the duty of the staff was exactly – the title takes the form of *ex hortis*, rather than *hortulanii* (gardeners) –, while three of them specified their role concerning the *horti* as *atriensis* (hall-manager), *insularius* (rent collector), and *topiarius* (decorative gardener).[142]

The question that interests us here would be the role of the *horti* rather than the job descriptions of their staff. What was the use of the *horti* in terms of the achievement of a self-sufficient household? What did masters gain from possession of suburban property?

First of all, *horti* were classified as one of those *voluptuariae possessiones* of the wealthy.[143] In other

---

[137] Eck, 1997, 76-77, so that they do not need to purchase a house and water-supply (*fistulae aquariae*) for a huge sum of money.
[138] Sen. *Ben.* 7, 5, 2; *Dig.* 50, 16, 166 (Pomponius), *non multum abest a uilico insularius: autem urbanorum numero est.*
[139] Gall, *RE*, viii, 1913, 2482-2488; Plut. *Pomp.* 44; id. *Cat. Min.* 48; Cic. *Phil.* 2, 27, 67.
[140] On *horti*, Gall, *RE*, viii, 1913, 2482-2488; Grimal, 1969, 148-149; Farrar, 1998.
[141] (A090) *insularius ex horteis Pompeia(nis)*; (A082) *ex Albano*; (A262) *ex horteis atriensis*; (A280) *ex hortis Scatonianis*; (A276) *ex hortis topiarius*; (A263) *ex ortis*.
[142] The *atriensis* as a highly responsible post in a household is mainly in Plautus' comedies: Plaut. *Poen.* 1283; *Pseud.* 608f; *Asin.* 333ff; an *atriensis* giving orders to the other slaves, *Asin.* 406; otherwise, the post appears to be no more than a hall manager: Petr. 29-30; Cic. *Paradoxa stoicorum*, 5, 36-37, *atrienses ac topiarii*; Plin. 15, 29, 37, § 122; Treggiari, 1975a, 51; *atriensis* was employed both in *familia urbana* and *familia rustica*: in country estates, *Dig.* 33, 7, 8, 1 (Ulpian); Col. 12, 3, 9; Plin. *Ep.* 3, 19, 3.
[143] Cic. *Att.* 12, 25, 1; cf. 13, 25, 1; Plin. *HN.* 19, 50, *iam quidem hortorum nomine in ipsa urbe delicias agros villasque possident*; Garnsey, 1976, 126.

words, men aspired to get hold of them for mental and physical enjoyment rather than necessity. We know a number of *horti* by name built in the suburbs of the city, and the sources unanimously refer to their lavishness. *Horti* included gardens and houses, and they were decorated with colonnades, artistic statues, or paintings. Possession of the *horti* essentially signified the wealth and leisure (*otium*) of their owner.[144]

Such lavishly decorated *horti* often attracted other people's envy. The *Horti Lucullani*, originally built around 60 BC by L. Licinius Lucullus (*cos*. 74 BC), came into the possession of Decimus Valerius Asiaticus (*cos*. II, AD 46) during the reign of Claudius. As Asiaticus was refurbishing them, Tacitus reports that Messalina plotted to prosecute him since she coveted the garden in addition to her personal enmity against him (Tac. *Ann*. 11). It is noted that the same reason was given as the catalyst for the prosecution of T. Statilius Taurus (*cos*. AD 44) that ended in his suicide, leaving his gorgeous garden in Agrippina's hand.

Aside from leisure or ostentatious wealth, the *horti* offered other functions for the master's lifestyle. Above all, the suburban houses with spacious gardens would have felt more like 'home' for the aristocrats, than the houses of a rather cramped neighbourhood in the city. Eck (1997, 78-79) argued that after Augustus ended their struggles to influence public opinion by appearing in the forum or other public space at the centre of the city, such suburban houses and parks became a more integral part of the lives of the senatorial elite under the Empire; the conferment of public honour or display of one's importance, which used to take place in public space, then shifted location to the private space of the suburban garden or villa. In another respect, the *horti* could offer secluded private space for the retired; after his return from Rhodes, Tiberius lived a retired life in the *Horti Maecenatiani* on the Esquiline.[145] In the newly obtained *Horti Lucullani*, Messalina celebrated her 'marriage' to her lover C. Silius, behind her husband Claudius' back, and when she was condemned by Claudius, she ran into the *horti* to hide, and was eventually found dead there.[146] Indeed, the *horti* were often the places where their owners were buried. Nero's ashes were brought by his *nutrices* (nurses) into the family tomb (*monumentum*) of the Domitii, which was located next to their *horti* (*horti Domitiorum*) on Mons Pincius. Galba's head, mutilated and cut off from his body, was collected by his *dispensator* Argivus and carried into the tomb (*sepultura*) at Galba's private garden, *Horti Galbae*, situated on the Via Aurelia. Domitian's corpse was cremated by his nurse Phyllis at her suburban estate (*suburbanum*) on the *via Latina*.[147] Burial in the *horti* or in its precinct may have been preferable not only for its privacy, but also for its location (suburb of the city) convenient to procure a funeral pyre and a suitable place in which to conduct cremation. Gaius Caligula's body was conveyed to the *Horti Lamiani* on the Esquiline, and cremated and buried in the grounds of the *horti*. An additional story went that the poorly erected funeral pyre did not perfectly incinerate the body, and according to Suetonius, because of this inadequate burial, caretakers of the *horti* were haunted by ghosts, and later the remains were dug up by his sisters to be cremated properly and consigned to the tomb.[148]

Such usages of *horti* attested in the literary sources may allow us to speculate on a possible scenario as to the end of our T. Statilius Taurus. Envied by Agrippina for his possession of no less than four gardens, it is possible that Taurus' suicide took place in the eponymous gardens of the family, the *horti Tauriani*, and that he was buried there, as it was also at a close distance to the *columbarium* of his family's dependants.[149]

Furthermore, importantly for the self-sufficiency of the household, the *horti* might contain fertile ground for cultivation to produce food and other materials for living. Suetonius' account of Nero's garden on the Esquiline is striking; the estate included "tracts of country, varied by tilled fields, vineyards, pastures and woods, with great numbers of wild and domestic animals."[150] Imperial slaves with the title *vilicus hortorum*, or *supra hortos*, are known from epigraphic evidence, and these supervisory titles also indicate the presence of ordinary field workers under their command.[151] The *ex hortis* (A280) in the Statilian *columbarium* might be the cultivators of the garden, while '*topiarius ex hortis*' (A276) was a design-

---

[144] e.g., Nero's *horti Maiani* on the Esquiline, with a huge portrait of himself, though soon it was struck by thunder and damaged by the fire: Plin. *HN*. 35, 51; cf. (8668) *proc(urator) hortorum Maianorum et Lamianor(um)*; (6152) *ex hortis Maianis*; (8669) *vilicus hortor(um) Maianor(um)*; Plin. *Ep*. 4, 2, 5, the *horti M. Reguli*, on the right Tiber bank; Plut. *Pompey*, 40, the gardens of Pompey's freedman Demetrius; cf. Sen. *Ben*. 3, 28, 5.
[145] *Horti Maecenatiani* had gone into imperial possession after the death of Maecenas: Suet. *Tib*. 15, *Romam reversus... in hortos Maecenatianos transmigravit totumque se ad quietem contulit*. Hor. *Sat*. 1, 8, 8-16; Tac. *Ann*. 15, 38.
[146] Tac. *Ann*. 11, 1, *pariterque hortis inhians, quos ille a Lucullo coeptos insigni magnificentia extollebat, Suillium accusandis utrisque immittit*; 11, 32 and 37; Juv. 10, 334; Plut. *Luc*. 39.

[147] Suet. *Nero*, 50; *Galba*, 20, 2; Tac. *Hist*. 1, 49; Suet. *Dom*. 17, 3.
[148] Suet. *Calig*. 59; on funerary gardens, i.e., the tombs surrounded by the gardens, Toynbee, 1971, 94-100; Purcell, 1985, 30-31.
[149] A master might not be able to achieve suicide without the support of their slaves. Tacitus' description of the suicide of Seneca in 65 AD, forced by Nero, in view to what it might have been like for Taurus; when Seneca failed to injure himself fatally, slave secretaries were summoned to write down his last speech, and other slaves were ordered by Nero's soldiers to bandage the wife's bleeding (and she survives). Seneca then asks his *medicus* to procure poison but again he could not die from it, and was carried by his slaves to the bath of warm water, closely attended by his slaves, and finally he was put into the vapour-bath and suffocated to death: Tac. *Ann*. 15, 63-64; cf. 4, 22, 3.
[150] Suet. *Nero*, 31.
[151] Cf. (9991=*ILS* 7374) *d. m. Hermeroti vicario suo, Lupercus subvillicus hortorum Antonianorum bene merenti fecit*; the epitaph (4346) from the *columbarium* of Nero Claudius Drusus and his son Germanicus: *Cydnus, Ti. Germanici supra hortos, Narcissus fratri merent. f.*; (*ILS* 3521), *Tychicus Glabrionis n. ser. vilicus hortorum*; (8669=*ILS* 1617) *Felici Caesaris ser. vilico hortor. Maianor*; (9472=*ILS* 7373) *vilicus supra hortos*; (8670=*ILS* 1619) *Dama C[aesaris] ex hortis Salusti ab hortu nov.*

gardener, '*ex hortis atriensis*' a steward of the garden-house (A262), and '*insularius ex hortis*' (A090) a renting agent. If so, it leads us to suppose that the Statilii were assured of the supply of products grown in their suburban estate (such as vegetables or fowl).

Conclusion

Of the four *columbaria* examined here, the Statilian *columbarium* presents the richest catalogue of job titles. Of course, we cannot say that the households lacked those professions that are not attested in epitaphs. The Volusii and Iunii Silanii and other notable aristocratic families surely had a more complete variety of skilled staff available at hand than presented here. The case of the Statilii is a specimen of how the aristocratic ideal way of life developed in accordance with the reality of the contemporary society that actually made it possible. Apart from personal servants, the Statilii had under their patronage groups of clothes-makers and builders, and managers of urban property, *insulae* (building blocks), *horrea* (storehouses), and *horti* (gardens). The question remains, what did it mean to have slaves and freedmen with such a variety of occupations?

There were barbers (*tonsores*), bakers (*pistores*), doctors (*medici*) in the city. The workshops (*tabernae*) of *textores, fullo,* and *sutor*, were all available for the people in Rome.[152] People could hire even *mercenarii* as servants for personal service.[153] They might buy luxurious clothes, jewellery, or receive special medical treatment from expensive freelance professionals or craftsmen. But in principle, it was not the way the wealthy Romans like the Statilii preferred to satisfy their needs. The elite Romans despised and were reluctant to associate with immediately unknown petty merchants and craftsmen. They instead tried to keep a number of professional slaves/freedmen to provide them with necessary products and services. When a household lacked certain specialists, these were actively exchanged between circles of friends.[154] Since they contained (and to a degree monopolised) the skills and products that were usually not easily accessible to the ordinary public, in times of emergency, as it is reported, it was legitimate for the *domus* with resources to come out to the public and offer a share of their privileges; when an amphitheatre at Fidena collapsed in AD 27 and a number of people (twenty to fifty thousand) were injured or died at the incident, large households were said to have supplied the victims with clothing and doctors.[155]

What, then, were the social conditions that made this form of household self-sufficiency praiseworthy? For one reason, Roman nobles had to rely on themselves because the government scarcely provided public services or facilities. But I think that the insistence of the wealthy and powerful on self-reliance would not be altered whether there was public service or not. Lack of public services and facilities is more significant for the poor. True, even the wealthy Roman elite went to the public baths, like Petronius' fictive freedman Trimalchio, but he also had his own bath in the house, where he could bathe with his guests after dinner (Petr. 73). From the Statilian *columbarium*, it is known that Taurus had his own bath-keeper (*balneator*) slave Neo (A049), which might mean that he also had his own bath in the house. So did the household of Iunius Silanus (7601). Public baths were not necessarily a basic need for the wealthy.

It was in part for ostentation, and in part in pursuit of security. In fact, more than security, to organise a household production system could bring enormous economic and social advantage, shared by friends as favour. The number of slaves one owned was not immediately the measure of one's wealth or political influence,[156] but it certainly indicated the competence of the *pater familias* as a household manager.

It must be noted that some of the occupations discussed above might not have been for the exclusive use of the masters who owned them. While servants such as the *cubicularii, pedisequi, dispensatores, paedagogi,* or *nutrices*, were more personal to the master, others, especially the craftsmen, were likely to have established a shop in the city and made business with customers other than their original patrons. Such professionals might be those appointed as the master's business agents, or, as freedmen, they might run their business more independently.

A general impression, as has been pointed out by many scholars, is that a dominant proportion of craftsmen or other skilled workers in the city appear to be freedmen. Put otherwise, even some prominent political figures are rumoured (with some reason at least for the

---

[152] Mart. 12, 59; Hor. *Epist.* 1, 7, 46 (*tonsor*).
[153] The porter and *tonsor* Corax who accompanied Eumolpus on a journey was a poor free-born *mercenarius*: Petr. 99, *Eumolpus quidem mercennarium suum iam olim dormientem exire cum sarcinis iubet*; Petr. 103, *mercennarius meus, ut ex novacula comperistis, tonsor est*; Petr. 117, "*Quid vos*" *inquit* "*iumentum me putatis esse aut lapidariam navem? Hominis operas locavi, non caballi. Nec minus liber sum quam vos, etiam si pauperem pater me reliquit*"; Volanerius hired a *mercenarius* to assist him for his disabled fingers: Hor. *Sat.* 2, 7, 15-18, *scurra Volanerius, postquam illi iusta cheragra contudit articulos, qui pro se tolleret atque mitteret in phimum talos, mercede diurna conductum pavit*: a hair-plucker of arm-pit (*alipilus*) at bath, Sen. *Ep.* 56, 2; on wage-labourers in general, Finley, 1985, 62-94; Treggiari, 1980; Garnsey, 1980b.
[154] *Dig.* 38, 1, 27 (Iulianus), *si libertus artem pantomimi exerceat, uerum est debere eum non solum ipsi patrono, sed etiam amicorum ludis gratuitam operam praebere: sicut eum quoque libertum, qui medicinam exerceat, uerum est uoluntate patroni curaturum gratis amicos eius.*

[155] Tac. *Ann.* 4, 62-63, *ceterum sub recentem cladem patuere procerum domus, fomenta et medici passim praebiti*; Suet. *Tib.* 40.
[156] Some households had fewer slaves than others. Apuleius (*Apologia*, 17), a writer and philosopher of the second century AD, defended himself from a reproach of prosecutors, insisting that he had had more than one slave, since he had already manumitted three freedmen. In the same line of discussion, he cites examples of prominent figures who owned few slaves; Marcus Antonius only had eight slaves at home, Carbo only seven slaves, Manius Curius two camp followers.

contemporaries) to have had freedman ancestors with 'mean' occupations.[157] This pattern of social mobility undoubtedly existed: slaves given training as an investment by large households come to practise their occupations of slavery in public. The outward flow, the dissemination of skilled professions from a household into society, represents an important feature of ancient vocational education and advancement. The professionals in the *columbaria* received training at the cost of the aristocratic families and were protected by their patronage, but at a certain point they were to be manumitted and their descendants might no longer retain strong connections with the patron family, as the ties with their original patrons gradually weaken in the course of time. In this way, supposedly a great deal of craftsmanship and associated business was nurtured, and their successors would find their place in society as independents. The elite's aspiration for a self-sufficient household gave their slaves and freedmen a source of learning skills and protection under its patronage, and ultimately left skilled resources as by-products in society.

In the light of self-sufficiency, the other important commodities, slaves, were also 'home-produced'. In Petronius' Satyricon, it is boastfully reported that thirty boy and forty girl vernae were born on Trimalchio's estate on one single day.[158] An ideally self-sufficient household could reproduce and maintain slaves within the household. The basis and result of such a reproduction system will constitute a key question of subsequent chapters.

---

[157] There was a popular allegation on the emperor Vitellius' ancestry that the family was founded by a freedman or a cobbler (*sutor veteramentarius*), Suet. *Vit.* 2, 1; Augustus' great-grandfather was alleged to have been a freedman ropemaker in Thurii, Suet. *Aug.* 2.
[158] Petr. 53.

Chapter 4

Legal status and ownership structure in elite Roman households

Pliny the Elder reports that upon his death in 8 BC the rich freedman C. Caecilius Isidorus left the extraordinary number of 4,116 slaves. During the reign of Nero, when a senator L. Pedanius Secundus was murdered by one of his slaves, it is claimed that there were a total of 400 slaves and freedmen living in his household. We are also familiar with the image of the fictitious freedman Trimalchio in Petronius' novel; the total body of slaves he owned was so massive that only a tenth of them actually knew their master Trimalchio by sight.[1] In this prominent slave society, it was not unusual to find a single master owning a large number of slaves, and consequently complex subdivisions and hierarchisation arose among the personnel since, obviously, such a great number of servants could not function under a single master's direct command; a master would otherwise hardly be able to sleep at night for fear and the pressures of excessive attention and responsibility. Despite this practical unfeasibility, however, a simplistic image of slave ownership, namely a master against a mass of slaves, seems pervasive among modern scholars. Such a dichotomy, which lurks in a range of scholarly discussions concerning slavery is, I think, inaccurate and rather misleading. This conception has exercised so strong an influence that it allowed us to overlook the other reality, namely, the existence of internal hierarchy and small-scale ownership within the servant body. The presence of separate ownership units in a household is glimpsed in an incident described by Petronius: Trimalchio's *dispensator* (financial manager) threatens a slave boy with flogging as punishment (*poena*) for having his valuable clothes stolen at the bath - one of the tasks of this slave boy was to accompany the *dispensator* to the bath and keep an eye on his clothes. Trimalchio's *dispensator* (we do not know whether he was a slave or freedman), demonstrates dominance over his subordinate slave, in a way identical to the master-slave relationship. Further light is shed on these issues by the *columbaria* inscriptions, which reveal some detailed information about the membership of the *familiae* in terms of structure of ownership and hierarchy at a personal level. This chapter thus asks what constituted membership in the *columbaria*, and how they as a workforce were being deployed to serve the *domus*.

I. The composition of legal status

The first issue that requires clarification would be the legal status of those who were buried in the *columbaria*. The criteria of determining one's legal status (whether *ingenuus* or *libertus* or *servus*) are firstly the formal designation within nomenclature, such as 'T(iti) l(ibertus)', 'T(iti) f(ilius)', or less frequently 'T(iti) ser(vus)'. Those in the Volusian *columbarium* tend to include 'L(uci) n(ostri)' (of our Lucius) in nomenclature, but by itself this is an obscure designation, since the person could be either slave or freedman of Lucius.[2] Instead of these formulae as part of formal nomenclature, people might use certain terms to identify their social status in a more casual manner, such as *servus, vicarius, ancilla, verna, libertus, patronus* etc. Some of them immediately show their legal status (*servus, vicarius, libertus*), but others, such as *ancilla, verna,* or *patronus*, do not define their legal status (*ancilla* and *verna* could be either slave or freed, *patronus* freed or free-born): for this reason, without any other clue, the latter group will be categorised as *incerti* (uncertain). The same is the case for the word used for those in informal marital union '*contubernalis*', which indicates at most the servile origin of one or both of them. Likewise, where we find the *tria nomina* (or *duo nomina*), the individual concerned will be at least a freedman or freeborn (and cannot be a slave) since only if you were a freedman could you adopt the *nomen* and *praenomen* of your patron.[3] On the other hand, those persons with a single name are most likely to be slaves as is usually supposed, but the possibility that they might be freedmen or freeborn who abbreviated the *nomina* cannot be entirely excluded.[4] Sometimes the commemorators designate themselves as *conservus*, or *vicarius* of the deceased, in which case we can determine the status of the deceased as slave. Results based on these principles are shown in Table 4.1:

---

[1] Pliny *HN*. 33, 135; Tac. *Ann*. 14, 42f; Petr. 37: *familia vero babae babae, non mehercules puto decumam partem esse quae dominum suum noverit;* Trimalchio, alongside the *classis* where his *ministri* (slave waiters) were organised to work in shifts, had more than forty *decuriae* (units of ten each) of slaves; Petr. 47; 74; cf. id. 57, a freedman guest of Trimalchio had 20 slaves to feed (*viginti ventres pasco et canem*).

[2] Weaver, 1972, 54-55.

[3] The crime of assuming a false identity was to be severely punished: Crook, 1967, 48: *Dig.* 48, 10, 13, pr. (Papinianus), *falsi nominis uel cognominis adseueratio poena falsi coercetur*; Suet. *Claud.* 25, 3, *civitatem R. usurpantes in campo Esquilino securi percussit.*

[4] On the methods and criteria of determining one's legal status, Rawson, 1974, 383ff.; Weaver, 1972, 43ff.

CHAPTER 4: LEGAL STATUS AND OWNERSHIP STRUCTURE IN ELITE ROMAN HOUSEHOLDS

Table 4.1 Legal status of individuals in the *columbaria*

	STATILII (N=657)	VOLUSII (N=301)	LIVIA (N=608)	ARRUNTII (N=61)	ABUCCII (N=99)	IUNII (N=58)
Slave	8%	6%	1%	0%	0%	7%
uncertain slave (single name)	57%	36%	51%	53%	5%	34%
Freed	17%	7%	22%	13%	22%	21%
uncertain freedmen / free-born (*tria nomina*)	17%	50%	26%	34%	71%	38%
free-born	1%	1%	0%	0%	2%	0%

The result is unfortunately not as revealing as might be expected, since only 13-28% of the people left clear evidence as to their legal status. Otherwise, surprisingly often, we cannot determine whether a person is a slave or free(d), and presumably this silence was partly due to the familiar environment of people under the same aristocratic family. It appears that the identification *servus / serva* was felt rather too strong a term to be used on epitaphs, and in fact, the designation *libertus / liberta* emerges much more often than '*servus*'. In the case of the Statilian *columbarium* in particular, '*vicarius/-a*' (under-slave) is found even more than '*servus*' itself.[5] A tacit understanding that slaves comprised the majority of individuals buried in the *columbarium* seems to have been operating here. In this sense, the absence of the designation '*servus*' does not immediately undermine our understanding of the membership of the *columbaria*.

But the problem remains as to how we can make sense of the disorderly, obscure mixture of records of legal statuses represented in the *columbara*. First of all, we must note that when we say 'freed status', two different status groups of freedmen are possible, namely, Roman citizens and Junian Latins.[6] The latter, formally created during the time of Augustus as the status of those who failed to satisfy criteria of formal manumission (usually those manumitted under the age of thirty), was the freedman imperfect. They did not have the right of inheritance – therefore, when a Junian Latin died, his property did not go to his heirs, but to the patron as if it were a slave's *peculium*[7] –, although they could claim citizenship relatively easily, particularly if they had a family with children. In other words, Junian Latins were denied family and kinship like a slave,[8] while paradoxically, marriage and begetting children become important for their application to Roman citizenship.[9] The lack of inheritance rights was the very defect that a slave with family suffered most, and that was equally carried by Junian Latins.[10] The problem is that while those enjoying this imperfect freed status were supposedly numerous, as abundant references in legal sources indicate, we can hardly distinguish Junian Latins from proper freed Roman citizens (or from slaves) in individual cases; the designation of Junian Latin is not recognisable on epitaphs.[11] The lack of designation for Junian Latins perhaps indicates the essentially temporary nature of the status in the process of a slave becoming independent, namely, the period of 'moratorium' spared for establishing his own basis in society, family and means of livelihood. The emergence of such an intermediate status might be one possible factor that led to obscure or confuse individual's own conceptions of freed / slave status.[12]

---

[5] The word *servus/-a* or *conservus/-a* was used 22 times, *vicarius/-a* 27 times, *libertus/-a* 98 times in the Statilian *columbarium*. The *servus* or *vicarius* status is rarely found in Livia's *columbarium*, though there are many *liberti/-ae*.

[6] In fact, there was a third group of freed status, defined in the *lex Aelia Sentia* enacted during Augustus' reign, the *peregrini dediticii* ("subject foreigners" or "surrendered enemies"). Those who entered this category were former slaves who had been serious criminals, namely, those who as a slave had received specific punishments (either by their master or by the public authority) such as being chained, branded, imprisoned, tortured for interrogation, or forced to fight in the arena as gladiators. The creation of such an extreme category of freedmen reflects the trauma experienced during the late Republic when a number of slaves and freedmen in the city participated in the civil disturbances led by popular leaders or political opponents. Because of previous crimes, the *dediticii* were forever excluded from Roman citizenship and denied the right to make a will or to inherit property, and even banned from entering the city of Rome or anywhere within the hundredth milestone from Rome. Therefore, obviously, no freedmen in the *columbaria* should fall into this category; Gaius, *Institutes*, 1, 13; 1, 27; cf. Dion. Hal. *Ant. Rom.* 4, 24; Crook, 1967, 45-46; Duff, 1928, 72-75.

[7] Weaver, 1997, 62-63.
[8] Junian Latins did not have the right of marriage (*conubium*): Crook, 1967, 44.
[9] Gaius, *Inst.* 1, 29: "If they beget a son, then, when that son reaches the age of one year, they are empowered by the Act to go to the praetor, and to prove that they have, a prescribed in the Act (*Lex Sentia Aelia*), married a wife and had by her a child of the age of one year. If the magistrate before whom the proof is brought pronounces that it is so, it is laid down that the Latin himself, and his wife and son, if they are of his status, are Roman citizens."; this procedure of *iteratio*, was discussed by Weaver, 1997, 60-72.
[10] Pliny's benevolent policy was that he would try to manumit slaves on their death as much as possible, and he also allows those who remain slaves to make wills to distribute their property as they like: Plin. *Ep.* 8, 16.
[11] Weaver, 1990; id. 1997; As Weaver revealed in his studies of Junian Latins, in spite of abundant references in the legal sources, we do not know how numerous they actually were in proportion to Roman citizens, or whether the majority of them eventually managed to gain citizenship or remained Junian Latins.
[12] One of the freedman friends of Trimalchio, who had originally sold himself into slavery in order to be a freed Roman citizen, claims, '*annis*

Moreover, lack of attention to one's formal status might also be attributed to the fact that there was no apparent discrimination by legal status in the sorts of vocations one could hold, at least in the context of the *columbaria*. It is often found that both freedman, slave, and even *vicarius* (under-slave), were assigned in the same occupations, and presumably it was not unusual for them to be working side by side together. For various reasons, some ex-slaves remained living in the master's household after manumission as servants (in particular as steward, nurse, financial manager, or doctor).[13] It needs to be emphasised that the distinction between slave and freed status was not so much a gulf as a process of continuation at a personal level. As it is pointed out, an average freedman would have been a slave almost half of his life, and above all, the relationship of master and slave was expected to continue as freedman and patron in the forms of social respect (*obsequium*) or work obligation (*operae*).[14]

The way in which a slave receives manumission might also affect their notion of freedom, especially when slaves had a good chance of receiving freedom on their deathbed.[15] Such a last-minute freedom might have had spiritual importance for the individual's mind, but what real effect did it bring otherwise (doubtlessly most of the manumissions at deathbed were unplanned occurrences and therefore informal)? Despite Augustan legislation on the age of formal manumission (above thirty years old), the ages of freedmen known from epitaphs varied greatly; early manumission was not unusual, and others of advanced age over thirty, though comparatively few, still died as slaves.[16] The same situation is clearly observable in our *columbaria* evidence. Some slaves had already attained freed status even by their early teens,[17] whilst some others had to remain slaves after their thirties.[18] If, then, even a five-year-old boy could call himself '*libertus*', why would anyone need to be so anxious to record the title for themselves? Unlike those freedmen who managed to establish their own funeral monuments, having been freed or not did not matter as much for the people buried within the *columbarium* together alongside their families and friends. For some, in that context, to boast of their freed status might even be perceived as something of a vulgar thing to do.

In fact, as is well observed by scholars, the status indication of freedmen, except those of emperors, tends to be increasingly omitted from the mid-first century AD. As one contributing factor to this 'decline of traditional nomenclature', it was claimed, the Familia Caesaris with the designation of 'Aug. lib.', which came to establish its position as courtiers and abiding civil servants, consequently led to a trivialisation of the status of non-imperial freedmen,[19] thus increasing the omission of status indication of 'ordinary' freedmen. This observation has a point, but is not entirely convincing. Emulating the same terms as already existing government offices was a norm for slaves and freedmen as seen in their *collegia* or job-titles. Unless the designations were banned or perceived as too pompous, which is clearly not the case here, if the significant 'others' (i.e., Familia Caesaris) came to use the status designation, they would probably use it even more. If freedmen in the *columbaria* came to drop the designation, this probably owed more to a change in the conception of freed/slave status among 'themselves', rather than a feeling of being 'trivialised' in comparison to the 'others' above them. Indeed, most of the imperial slaves were manumitted with citizenship and there were very few imperial freedmen of Latin status, as emperors were not constrained by the regulations of formal manumission, which left less ambiguity about their status for this already highly institutionalised group.

In sum, I think that lack of attention to the recording of precise legal status in the *columbaria* is to be explained first of all by a degree of ambivalence in conceptions and conditions of freedom in this period, and also by the pretext of the familiar environment of the *columbaria*. A freed status certainly opened up enormous possibilities in social and political life, and some freedmen were probably powerful and independent enough to arrange their own burial place outside the *columbaria*. However, there were many freedmen in the *columbaria* keeping

---

quadraginta servivi; nemo tamen sciit, utrum servus essem an liber' (Petr. 57).

[13] Roman law leaves freedmen living in the patron's household under that patron's discipline: *Dig.* 48, 19, 11, 1 (Marcian).

[14] Restrictions on a freedman to bring legal action against a patron: *Dig.* 37, 14-15 (Ulpian); the debates in the Senate to annul the emancipation of ungrateful freedmen: Tac. *Ann.* 13. 26; cf. Suet. *Claud.* 25; a freedman might have to provide a certain fixed amount of labour for a patron as a deal to gain freedom: *Dig.* 38, 1 (Ulpian); a freedman was required to support his patron and his children in need: *Dig.* 25, 3, 5, 18-26 (Ulpian); cf. *Dig.* 48.19.11.1 (Marcianus); Hopkins, 1978, 129-131; Gardner, 1993, 20-25; Duff, 1928, 197-198.

[15] Masters might initiate the manumission of dying slaves for sentimental reasons: Plin. *Ep.* 8, 16: *unum facilitas manumittendi (videor enim non omnino immaturos perdidisse, quos iam liberos perdidi)*; Mart. 1, 101 (describing his dying slave Styx), *Munere dignus erat convaluisse meo. Sensit deficiens sua praemia meque patronum dixit ad infernas liber iturus aquas*; cf. Plin. *HN.* 7, 39, 129; Weaver, 1972, 97-104, raises this motive as the cause of many under-age freedmen on epitaphs.

[16] Early manumission under thirty years old is discussed by Wiedemann, 1985, 162-163; according to Weaver (1972, 97-104) about 24% (N=173) of the slaves of the emperors were manumitted before 30 years old.

[17] e.g. (A137) Condicio, Posidippi liberti, vixit annos V; (A256) T. Statilius T. l(ibertus) Mena Aucti frater dispens(ator) an(nis) XIIX; (A135) Chryseros Dorcadis libert. hic insitus est annorum VIIII; (A406) Statiliae Messallinae l(iberta) Primillae haec vixit ann. X; (A230) ...Statilia Capsulae et ((duarum mulierum)) l(iberta) Sabina, vix(it) a(nnis) XIIII; (A208) T. Statilius T. l(ibertus) Optatus, a manu, v(ixit) a(nnis) XXVI... ; (B017) Statilia Tauri l(iberta) Albana, pia in suos hic requiscit v(ixit) a(nnis) III; (A333) Statilia Quadrati liberti l(iberta) Venusta, vix(it) an(nis) XVII.

[18] e.g. (A397) Invento Tauri Statili servo Prima conservo suo merenti fecit v. a. XXXV; (A394) Sperato, tabulario, Messallinae Neronis servo, vixit annis XXX; (A383) Epapho, Corvini a manu, ann(orum) XXXV. Diodorus, conser(vus), cubicularius, fecit; (7371) Pancarpo exact. v(ixit) an(nis) XXXIIII, Aucta vicaria fecit; cf. a vicarius still at the age of twenty-five years old, (A313) Euenus Chresti Auctiani vicar(ius) de amphiteatro v. a. XXV; (A320) Apollinaris Chresti Auctiani vicarius, v(ixit) a(nnis) XXV.

[19] Taylor, 1961, 120-121; Weaver, 1972, 42ff.

their ties with fellow dependants of the *gens*, and many did not care to specify their apparent freed status. Freedmen used to be slaves, and as we will see below, difference of legal status as designated in epitaphs could not be seen as the factor that structured hierarchy and working units in the *domus*.

Familia or *domus*?

Before we look at individual cases of ownership, let us ask a question concerning the application of terms to describe servile dependants in the *columbaria*. Can we call *columbaria* dependants by any existing Latin term? The two most important Latin words that designate a group of domestic slaves are '*familia*' and '*domus*'. Both words could simply mean 'family' (esp. agnatic family) excluding slaves, which R. Saller closely examined in search of the Roman conception of 'family'. According to his study, the range of people centred on the *paterfamilias* that each term designates as 'family' varies in different contexts of different authors, and all we can observe with certainty is that both words did not point to a nuclear family, a couple and their children, to the exclusion of other extended members of kin or dependants in a household.[20]

When the words include servile dependants of the family, which is our concern here, they are equally ambivalent. The '*domus*' was occasionally used in the sense of '*familia*', referring only to the slave / freedman staff of a master, and one can say that the two words were virtually synonyms in ancient sources. But there were certain points of emphasis for each term. The '*domus*' generally designates a master (*paterfamilias*), his family, and their slaves, where emphasis is put on those who share the living space of the 'house' (*domus*). With this notion of shared physical space absent, the term *familia* refers to the group of slaves under the ownership of a single *dominus*. In this sense, a mistress in *sine manu* marriage might have a *familia* of her own, separate from that of her husband.[21] Technically, '*domus*' is a broader term in the sense that it might contain several *familiae* in a household,[22] whereas '*familia*' becomes broader when it includes slaves who were working for the master outside the *domus*, for example, the *institores* (business agents) as shopkeepers etc. Both words seem to have no problem in including freedmen, particularly those who continued to live in the master's household as servants.

Let us return to the question, what would be the most appropriate term (if any) for those buried in a *columbarium*? As for Livia's *columbarium*, their mistress was primarily Livia, but a handful of others were owned by her husband Augustus, or her sons Tiberius and Drusus etc. If they were all personal servants working in the household of Livia where her husband and other relatives cohabited from time to time, they should probably be called the servants in the *domus Liviae*. However, their range of occupations is so diverse that it is unlikely that all the servile staff lived in the same household, and in that sense the *familia Liviae* seems a more suitable term for them. As for the Statilii and Volusii, it is clear that the *columbarium* contained more than one *familia* of a single *dominus*; however, to categorise them as a *domus* becomes difficult because, even though individual masters or mistresses were under the *potestas* of a *paterfamilias* for a large part of their lives, they eventually become independent and at some point live in separate houses.

In fact, some servants established personal ties (by marital union or kinship) beyond the category of *familia* or *domus*. For instance, Phyllis, a slave *sarcinatrix* of Statilia, was united with Sophro, a slave *tabularius* of Statilia's brother Sisenna (A330, A337). If the brother Sisenna and sister Statilia lived in different houses while the couple were united,[23] did they also live apart from each other, or were they allowed to live together in the household of either master? One would imagine that slaves' kinship and *contuberium* was vulnerable to disruption by change of ownership, but at least there were moral and legal obstacles to this kind of cruelty: not only ancient moralistic writers, but also legal experts recommended masters to avoid inconsiderate action causing the separation of a slave family.[24] What seems to be the case here, in my view, is continuation rather than disruption or distress in slave marital life, with the couple only separated by death. Another such example we find is T. Statilius Diodotus, the freedman of Taurus, and his *coniunx* Vedusia Auge, who is recorded as the freedwoman of Taurus' sister (A047).[25] Auge might actually be the *liberta* of (a Statilia's) husband, a Vedusius, though the nomen Vedusius is not listed among the known senatorial families. The epitaph at least informs us that, as far as their nomenclature go, the couple once belonged to different masters though of the same *gens*. The undivided *gens Statilia* prepared the common context for the dependants associated to it, which eventually united these couples.[26]

---

[20] Saller, 1994, 74-101.
[21] *Dig.* 24, 1, 31, 10 (Pomponius).
[22] Not only a wife's *familia*, but also the *familiae* of bilateral family members might share a household. According to Plutarch (*Vit. Aem. Paull.* 5, 4-5), one of Aemilius Paullus' daughters married Aelius Tubero in extreme poverty: they lived in a household with fifteen other members of the Aelii with their own wives and children.

[23] Sisenna had a *domus* (house) on the Palatine, which had previously belonged to Cicero. The house was originally built by M. Livius Drusus, the tribune in 91 BC, incidentally the adoptive grandfather of Livia (her father was adopted by him), and after a period of time passed to Cicero and a certain Censorinus; then, by the time of Velleius Paterculus' writing (presumably in AD 30), it had been occupied by Statilius Sisenna; Vell. 2, 14, *aedificaret domum in Palatio in eo loco, ubi est quae quondam Ciceronis, mox Censorini fuit, nunc Statilii Sisennae est.*
[24] Ulpian thinks it reasonable for a testator not to separate slave families: *Dig.* 33, 7, 12, 7: *uxores quoque et infantes eorum, qui supra enumerati sunt, credendum est in eadem uilla agentes uoluisse testatorem legato contineri: neque enim duram separationem iniunxisse credendus est.*
[25] *PIR* V 215; cf. Mommsen's comments in *CIL* VI, p.995, 8.
[26] Others married freedwomen from other families; e.g., (A239) T. Statilius Pharnaces with Claudia Caenis; (A042) T. Statilius Tauri lib.

In sum, the range of servile dependants who were buried in a *columbarium* was so extensive that straightforward application of either term *domus* or *familia* is problematic. It might be better said in reverse; the *columbaria* certainly 'included' the *familia* or servile members of the *domus*, but those who were in other ways associated with the aristocratic family were also admitted. After all, as we will see in what follows, not all slaves and freedmen in the *columbaria* were directly subordinate to members of the aristocratic family.

II. Ownership

As is already clear, all the servants in a *columbarium* were not owned by a single mater. Table 4.2 shows the distribution, in terms of whom these slaves and freedmen recorded in epitaphs as their master or patron.[27]

Table 4.2 Proportions of those under aristocratic masters and under sub-owners in the *columbaria*

	STATILII	VOLUSII	LIVIA
aristocratic masters	80 (12%)	57 (19%)	145 (24%)
sub-owners	121 (19%)	20 (7%)	70 (11%)
unknown / others*	456 (69%)	224 (74%)	393 (65%)

* Instances of the uncertain relationship expressed on epitaphs as person 'A' of person 'B' (in Latin genitive), which could be either ties of ownership, or filial or marital relationship, are included in this category.

Unfortunately, only 26-35% of total individuals recorded their masters/patrons, and the contexts of the remaining individuals are untraceable because of the absence of information on epitaphs. Around 12-24 % of the individuals in the *columbaria* articulated their connection to their aristocratic masters, and 7-19% to non-aristocratic slave-owners (and also *vicarius*-owners), which I call 'sub-owners' or 'intermediate' owners. Alongside the masters of high birth, those who were originally slaves of the aristocratic families formed their own ownership units. Hermann-Otto, in her study of *vernae* (home-born slaves), has noted this feature as "substructural ownership relationships" (substrukturalen Besitzverhältnisse), which, aside from the ownership of aristocratic masters, is the one mainly represented in servants' epitaphs.[28] Within the limits of speculation, it can be said from the figures that the Statilian *domus* formed a pyramid shaped hierarchical structure, while those of Volusii and Livia formed an inverted pyramid (or trapezoid) structure, by which more servants were directly connected to aristocratic masters.

Direct ownership by aristocratic masters

One of the characteristics visible in the pyramid shaped Statilian ownership structure is the extended connection of ownership, from the aristocratic masters to the 'inferior' via the 'superior' members of staff. There appears to be a tendency for the privilege of serving aristocratic masters to go to the children of (or slaves under) slaves or freedmen who were already engaged in service, as if nepotism were at work. In other words, parents or sub-owners connected to the aristocratic masters seem to be able to prepare favourable career paths for their children or for their slaves. The following examples provide a detailed picture regarding the conditions of their employment.

First of all, we can reconstruct the family of Euticus, a Statilian staff, in which the father Euticus was the '*veteranus*' ('a long-serving servant'?) of the mistress Cornelia, and his daughter Logas was a *pedisequa* (attendant) of Cornelia's daughter-in-law Messallina. Though the master of the rest of the family members is not recorded, their job-titles suggest that they all worked close to the aristocratic *domini*. Zena, who commemorates Euticus, is recorded as a *velarius* (responsible for taking care of some kinds of *velum*, perhaps his mistress' clothing, hence bed-chamber servant?), and the same job title is held by one of Eucticus' sons Aphrodisius (Fig. 4.1).[29]

It seems natural that a slave born of a servant in a privileged post could begin his service with an advantage compared to servants who arrived as unknowns. In the case of an Atticus, his mother's job as *nutrix* of the young master Sisenna gave him the status of *conlacteus* (foster-brother) to her nurseling (A345). If Atticus lived longer, he would have inherited from his mother an indisputable and solid connection with his young master.[30] And this was the very strength and advantage of the so-called *vernae* (home-born slaves). Primus, a twenty-one-year-old slave *opsonator* (caterer), was a *verna* of Messalina (wife) of Nero (Fig. 4.2), which means that his parents (or at least the mother) were also slaves of Messallina. A certain Hesychus commemorates him as his paternal uncle (*patruus*) (A405), and Hesychus was in fact the father of ten year old Primilla, the freedwoman of Messallina (A406). These two brothers' families show their clear connection to the mistress Messallina.[31]

Eros Parra with Hetereia P. l. Chreste; (6208) T. Statilius Chrestus with *coniunx* Gella Aetheatice.
[27] The number and proportion of servants who belonged to the aristocratic masters were already shown in Table 2.1-3.
[28] Hermann-Otto, 1994, 50.
[29] The pattern of commemoration between the same family members is shown in Fig. 5.2 in Chap. 5.
[30] (A345); cf. (5939) *Arruntia L. l. Cleopatra nutrix, L. Arruntius L. l. Dicaeus conlacteus*; Suet. *Nero*, 35: Nero exiled his nurse's son Tuscus because he had bathed in the baths in Egypt which were built for Nero.
[31] The pattern of commemoration of the same family members are shown in Fig. 5.3 in Chap. 5.

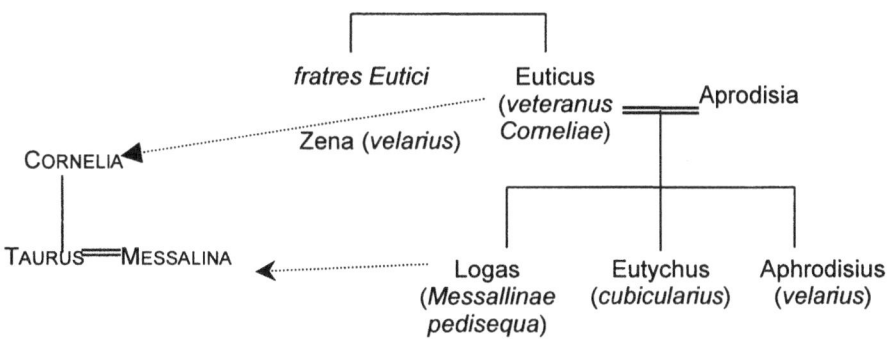

Fig. 4.1 Euticus family

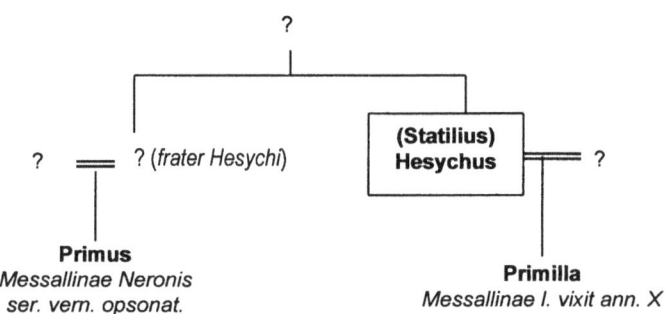

Fig. 4.2 Hesychus family

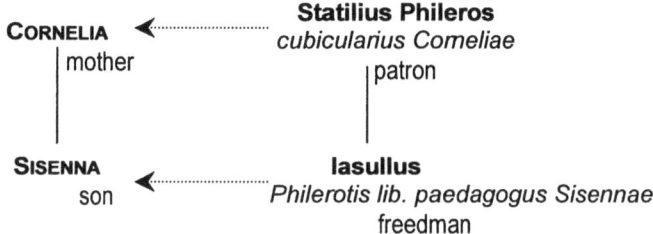

Fig. 4.3 Phileros ownership

The same kind of patronage system was exercised by Cornelia's *cubicularius*, Phileros (A344), who is known to be the patron of a freedman Iasullus who became a *paedagogus* of Sisenna (A242) (Fig. 4.3). As the protege of Phileros, who was a close servant of Cornelia, Iasullus was entrusted with the job of tutoring Cornelia's son Sisenna.

It is to be noted that even a 'freedman of a Statilian freedman', who was legally outside the ownership of the aristocratic Statilii, was still working for them as a servant. Such a complex allocation of servants to the *domini* might be caused by the transfer of slaves by inheritance, a topic of frequent discussion in legal texts.

Intermediate ownership

Serving the aristocratic masters face-to-face was not everything required in a large household. The chains of ownership could go deeper than the point of contact with aristocratic masters. As we have seen in Table 4.2, admission to the *columbarium* was extensive, comprising freedmen's slaves, slaves' slaves, and aristocratic master's direct servants all together. Sub-ownership vis-à-vis direct ownership is frequently found here, most notably as the *vicarious* (under-slave).[32] Roman literature

---

[32] The *vicarii* of the Statilii: A203; A091; A030; A031; A118; A054; A120; A121; A123; A125; A126; A045; A046; A124; A122; A269, A006, A236, A001, A320, A119, A313, A253, A407, A319; the Volusii: 7283; 7286, 7295; 7298; 7371; 9425; 11851 (dedication from a *vicarius* to a *vicaria*); 7307; 9757; on *vicarii*, see Merola, 1990, 133-187.

often describes a *vicarius* as in a state of 'double' slavery, in a lineal hierarchy of master, slave, and *vicarius*.[33] Apart from an ideological significance that it connotes as 'double' or even 'triple' slavery,[34] sub-ownership was enormously functional, constituting the basis of workforce upon which a large *domus* stood.

P.R.C. Weaver, in his study of the *familia Caesaris*, considers the function of a *vicarius* in the imperial court to be that of an 'occupational replacement' rather than a personal servant of the *ordinarius*.[35] In the *columbaria*, it is usually not possible to say whether a *vicarius* performed personal service or worked as an occupational assistant, though I suppose they often did both. We are reminded that in Apuleius' *Metamorphoses* (8, 26), the band of the eunuch priest purchases a slave from a common fund; while this shared-slave plays pipe along with his masters as a co-worker, he also serves them in the same way as a domestic slave, and his role is described as '*partiarius concubinus*' (shared male concubine). A similar example might be found in the Statilian *columbarium*; a *vicaria* Caliste, together with certain Philologus and Felix, commemorates Agatho *lecticarius* (litter-carrier) (A091). The same Caliste and Philologus reappear as commemorators in the epitaph of another *lecticarius* Iucundus (A093). From these two epitaphs, it appears that Caliste and Philologus were 'communal' *vicaria* and *vicarius* shared by several *lecticarii* and worked in a more general context – as it is difficult to imagine Caliste being trained as a '*lecticaria*'. In this sense, the *vicarii* here (especially Caliste) are closer to personal servants or assistants than apprentices.

At the same time, we also find occupational continuity passed on from a slave to a *vicarius*. The Statilian *horrearii* (storehouse managers), Felix and Protogenes, were recorded in two separate epitaphs as the *vicarii* of a Hipparchus (A319, A045). They worked at the *horrea* (storehouses) as professional *horrearii*, but at the same time they were also *vicarii*, under the supervision of Hipparchus, who, therefore, must be himself a senior *horrearius*. Incidentally, this same Hipparchus apparently possessed a *vicaria* Felicla who is attested to elsewhere (A046). Altogether, it may be supposed that Hipparchus possessed his two male *vicarii* for his occupation work (*horrearius*), and let the *vicaria* Felicla who did not have a job-title serve him in other more personal service. The *vicarii* as *horrearii* here is understood as a subordinate, assistant colleague of Hipparchus in the same occupation. The presence of a *vicarius*, in this respect, attests to the hierarchy of slaves within the profession. One might recall here the slaves in Plautus' comedy: a *promus* (butler) kept a *subpromus* for managing the wine storage room (*cella vinaria*) (*Miles*, 857).

Intermediate ownership on one of the most extensive scales known from the *columbaria* is that of a certain Chrestus Auctianus, the master of Euenus *de amphiteatro* (*sic*) (manager of the amphitheatre) and two other *vicarii*. His agnomen 'Auctianus' indicates that he was previously a slave or *vicarius* of an 'Auctus'.[36] This Auctus might probably be the *dispensator* Auctus, the only individual of that name in the *columbarium*; he was so much the central figure of the family unit that his name was referred to in the epitaphs of his two brothers, the mother, and two females related to him (vd. Fig. 4.4).

What makes this case potentially more intriguing is that, apart from 'Chrestus Auctianus', the *columbarium* knew two other 'Chresti', one without *agnomen*, that is 'Chrestus Tauri', and one with the *tria nomina* 'T. Statilius Chrestus'. I suspect that this second and third Chresti are both identical with the first 'Chrestus Auctianus', as the names appear similarly in the possessive to identify certain *vicarii* or slaves. Besides, if Chrestus Auctianus was 'previously' in apprenticeship as a *vicarius* under Auctus *dispensator*, and if he was then transferred and promoted to a slave of the aristocratic master Taurus, as going through the sub-ownership of an influential *dispensator* before serving an aristocratic master seems a resonable career path, it is fitting that he was referred to either as 'Chrestus Auctianus' or as 'Chrestus Tauri'.

Finally, we find the third figure 'T. Statilius Chrestus', from an epitaph recovered outside the *columbarium* but in a close proximity to it (near the Porta Maggiore) (B001). This Chrestus was commemorated by his spouse of alien nomen, Cellia Aetheatice. The 'Chrestus' buried outside the *columbarium* is likely to be identical to the 'Chrestus' found in the *columbarium* who was only mentioned by name by his slaves. Supposedly, he did not choose to be buried in the *columbarium* because of his marriage with a non-Statilian woman and the independence he achieved.[37]

---

[33] *Vicarius* in literature; Petr. 30; Mart. 2, 18, 7, *esse sat est servum, iam nolo vicarius esse*; id. 2, 32, 7-8, *non bene, crede mihi, servo servitur amico: sit liber, dominus qui volet esse meus*; Hor. *Sat.* 2, 7, 78-80, *nam sive vicarius est, qui servo paret, uti mos vester ait, seu conservus, tibi quid sum ego?*; cf. Fitzgerald, 2000, 72.

[34] Double (or triple if we taken into account aristocratic masters) slavery of the Statilii: (A123) *Rufa, Menandri Saeni vicaria ani* (Saenus - Menander - Rufa *vicaria*); the Volusii: (7295) *Zosimus Hymni medicus, Ampelioni cognatae et vicariae suae, coniugi Tyranni Daphni, vix. ann. XIIX* (Hymnus - Zosimus - Ampelio); Livia: (3976) *Auctus lanip(endius) Augustae l(ibertus), M. Livius Aucti l. Lydus a sede Augustae*, (4166) *Livia Lydi l(iberta) Chloe* (Auctus - Lydus - Chloe).

[35] On *vicarius* and *ordinarius* in the institutionalised body of the *Familia Caesaris*, Weaver, 1972, 200-206.

[36] The *agnomen* was derived from either the *cognomen* or *nomen* of a previous master, as a result of a change of ownership, either by inheritance, gift, or by purchase. A range of unusual *agnomina* held by slaves might have been caused by the transfer from the Statilian freedmen left to the Statilii by will. The *agnomen* might also originate from a Junian Latin or a slave, by the death of which their slave or *vicarius* was automatically absorbed into the Statilii; cf. Petr. 47-48: when Trimalchio asks his cook whether he was purchased or born on the estate, the cook's answer is neither, but instead that he was left to Trimalchio under Pansa's will ("*empticius an*" inquit "*domi natus?*" "*neutrum*" inquit cocus "*sed testamento Pansae tibi relictus sum.*"); on the use of an *agnomen* by members of the *familia Caesaris* see in Weaver, 1972, 90-92.

[37] The fourth T. Statilius Chrestus 'Barbianus' (A365) is problematic, though doubtlessly distinguishing himself from Chrestus 'Auctianus'; cf. 'Chrestus' the instigator of Jews in the city during Claudius' reign (Suet. *Claud.* 25, 3).

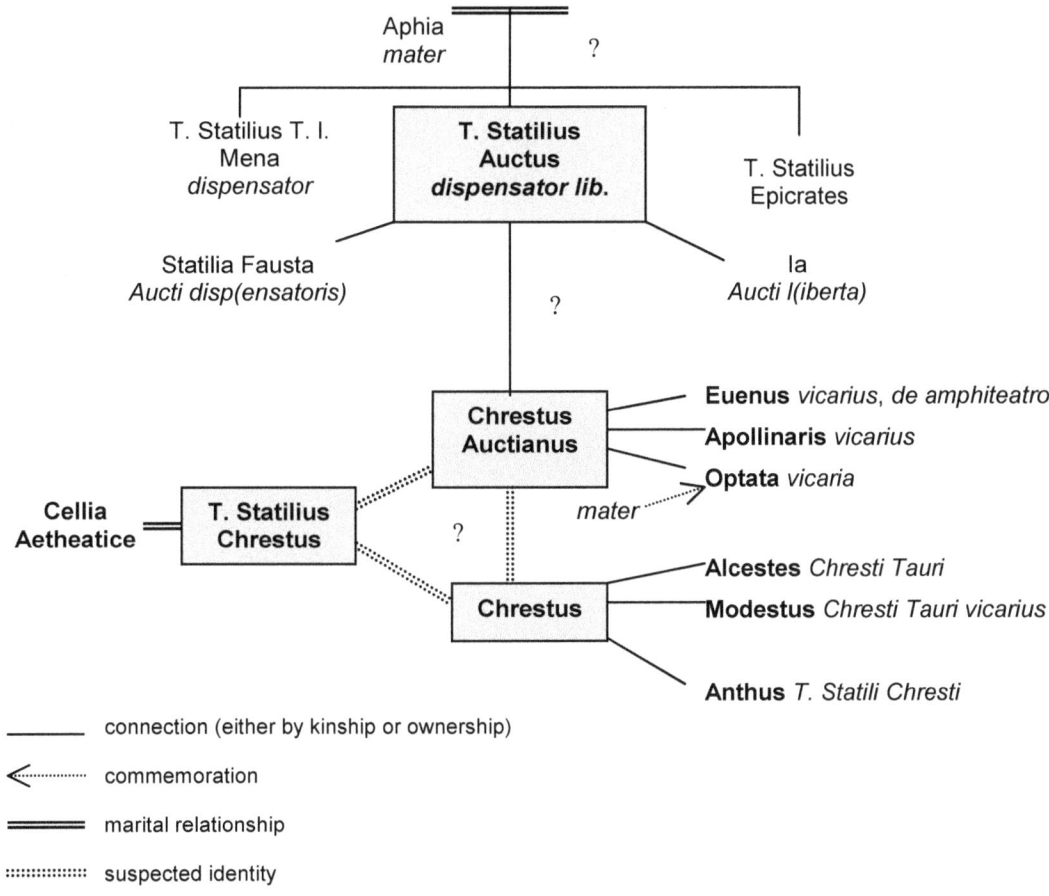

Fig. 4.4 Familial-ownership unit of Auctus the *dispensator*
(A278, A256, A335, A328, A240, B001, *CIL* VI 6270)

If 'Chrestus Auctianus' and 'Chrestus Tauri' and 'T. Statilius Chrestus' were all the same person, with a total of six *vicarii* under him, which included three- and four-year-old children. If this identification as shown in Fig. 4.4 is correct, Chrestus Auctianus' career path would have been as follows: he first served apprenticeship under Auctus for the respectable profession of *dispensator*, and then was transferred into the direct ownership of T. Statilius Taurus, and was eventually manumitted as T. Statilius Chrestus. It seems fitting that Chrestus who went through such an 'elite' career among the Statilian servants had six *vicarii* and that one of them was a manager of the amphitheatre. This amphitheatre, of course, would be the one constructed by the founder T. Statilius Taurus, and the family's continuous charge of it would have been the pride of the whole *gens Statilia*. It was perhaps the *ordinarius* Chrestus to whom the commission was directly given from Taurus (as he was called 'Chrestus Tauri'), and Chrestus himself involved in the amphitheatre management with his *vicarius* Euenus. Furthermore, I suppose that Chrestus' previous master Auctus, as the *dispensator*, had been heavily involved in the finance of the amphitheatre business. It is noteworthy that in this instance, a string of connections is arguably visible from the aristocratic master, through sub-owners, to a *vicarius* at the very bottom of hierarchy, who was still part of the workforce for the Statilian *domus*.

Another, but less obvious, connection to the aristocratic masters is the sub-ownership unit of the Statilian freedman called Posidippus. He owned no less than nineteen slaves and freedmen,[38] which is incidentally the largest single ownership known from the *columbaria*. Nothing about Posidippus himself is known - except that he was a freedman of the Statilii (vd. A137; A058) -, since his own epitaph has not been found in the *columbarium*. Despite his absence, the presence of

---

[38] (A021) *Philemo Posidippi dispensator, vixit an(nis) XX*; (A052) *Hilarionis, Posidippi, cub(icularii), ossa hic sita sunt; vixit ann(is) XX*; (A254) *Appollonius Posidippi ser.*; (A053) *Gratus, Posidippi, disp(ensator)*; (A057) *Eros, cocus, Posidippi ser. hic situs est*; (A058) *Eros, T. Statili Posidippi ser., disp(ensator)*; (A133) *Beata, Posidip(pi)*; (A137) *Condicio, Posidippi liberti, vixit annos V*; (A163) *Iazemus, Posidippi lib.*; (A183) *T. Statilius Posidippi l. Eros*; (A201) *Urbana, Posid(ippi) vixit annos XXVII*; (A267) *Iucundus, Posidippi ser. cubucularius, verna, annor(um) XXI.*; (A268) *Stablio, Posidipi l. disp(ensator)*; (A270) *Isidorus Posidipp(i) lib.*; (A271) *T. Statilius Posidippi l. Apella*; (A277) *Ianuarius Posidippi l. v(ixit) a(nnis) IXV (!)*; (A310) *Peregrinus Posidippi ser. vix(it) ann(is) XX*; (A355) *Onesimus, Posidippi T. Statili ser., vixit an(nis) VII*; (A369) *Statilia Posidippi l. Phoebe, v(ixit) a(nnis) XII.*

Posidippus' slaves and freedmen in the *columbarium* attests to his unbroken connection to the Statilii. The fact that he owned four *dispensatores* (financial managers) might indicate that Posidippus was himself the *dispensator* who trained young slaves into the profession. Intermediate owners of similar or lesser scale are also known from Livia's *columbarium*: a certain Tertius is named as the master and patron of at least ten slaves and freedmen,[39] while a man called Attalus owned no less than five slaves and freedmen, some of whom were in skilled professions such as *ab argento* or *a manu* (Fig. 4.5). In addition, even though these slave-owners of a substantial scale were generally male, there were also *dominae* of smaller-scale, of which Livia Musa, freedwoman of Livia, and a certain Antonia Lyde, are noted in Fig. 4.6-7.

In sum, these freedmen and freedwomen owning slaves or slaves owning under-slaves appear to be an essential part of the ownership structure of a *domus*. It was probably these compact-sized units that constituted a workforce and stock pool of extra personnel for the *domus*. After nurtured and given training by senior freedmen or slaves, the young servants could be passed on to the aristocratic master, who would be by now familiar with their faces through their intermediate owners. Such a situation accords with the practice of the Elder Cato's selection of his servants. Plutarch recounts one of his domestic schemes: he lent money to his slaves to buy slave boys, and allowed them to keep these new slaves under their command for a year, and then receive them back. Instead of "playing the role of slave-dealer himself", Cato cleverly made his slaves recruit

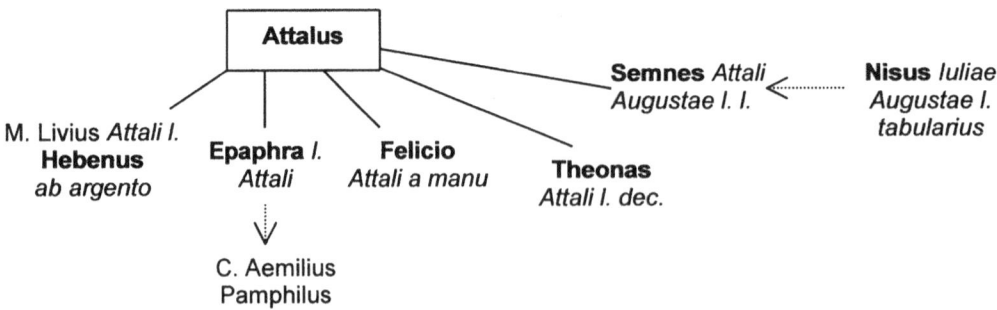

Fig. 4.5 Attalus (4121, 4232, 4243, 4250, 4256)

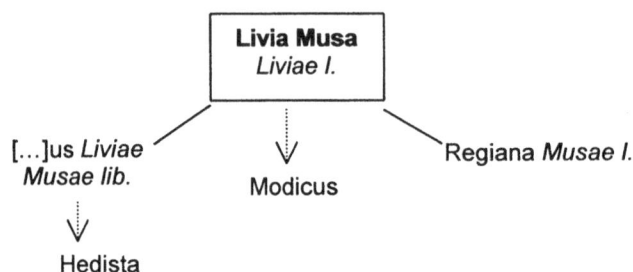

Fig. 4.6 Livia Musa (4175, 4131, 4176)

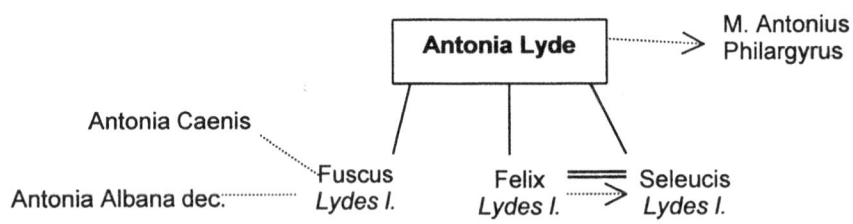

Fig. 4.7 Antonia Lyde (4275, 4268, 4276)

---

[39] Tertius' slaves and freedmen/-women (3926-3934): *Euphro Terti aedituus, Rufa Terti l., Philomusus Terti l. inaur(ator), Philomusus Terti l. vilicus, M. Livius Terti l. Nicephor dec., Olympia Terti l. (coniunx Nicephoris), Agatho (et) Phosice Terti l., Atimetus Terti, Haline Terti lib.*; cf. Solin, 1996, 152-3.

prospective servants and obtained them at a higher quality since some discipline and training had been given.[40] Such a system would also have relieved the aristocratic masters from fears about security; through the period of intermediate ownership and familial units, hierarchical order and sense of community must have been established, placing every slave under tight supervision and control. It was beneficial in these regards for masters to protect and encourage intermediate ownership units.

Conclusion

We have seen that a straightforward application of terms such as *domus* or *familia* to the group of people buried in the *columbarium* is not strictly accurate; nor are most of their legal statuses unambiguous. The members admitted to a *columbarium* belonged to different *familiae* of masters living under different roofs (*domus*), and slave and freed status ought to be viewed as transitional rather than hierarchical. At this point, one might perhaps feel that the individuals in the *columbaria* were rather self-serving, disparate groups of people. However, our close observation of intermediate ownership units yielded some constructive evidence, in which we can see continuous delegation of service for the *domus* at the very bottom of the hierarchy or sequence of ownership. These sub-ownership structures would have been useful especially for aristocratic families in need of a number of personnel but unable to engage in full supervision over them. Moreover, in the first place, to be accepted in the *columbarium* essentially required a certain degree of duty and respect towards the aristocratic masters, and also loyalty and co-operation towards their fellow slaves and freedmen, since, although they were free to make their own burial arrangement separately, 'to be excluded' from the family tombs imputed a disgrace and connoted their disloyalty and illegitimacy.[41] In this sense, being admitted to the *columbarium* acknowledges your readiness to assist the *domus* to prosper. The labour of the individuals in the *columbarium*, I suppose, was thus in one way or another directed collectively towards the *domus* in which they themselves were a part, and was available for the aristocratic masters.

---

[40] Plut. *Cat. Mai.* 21, 7; Schneider, *RE,* viii, a2, 1958, 2046.
[41] In Roman family tombstones, the formula '*libertis libertabusque meis posterisque eorum*' occurs commonly, by which patrons intended their freedmen and their descendants to be buried with them. The burial places of families accepted their freedmen as extended family members who would share the same name (*nomen* and *praenomen*) (Rawson, 1986, 42-43). Moreover, some patrons refer in more detail to the prohibition or acceptance of certain freedmen in their family tomb. *ILS* 8365, 8283 et al, *GARS* no. 38, 39; exclusion of certain freedmen from a patron's tomb, *ILS* 1984, "...*ceteris libertis libertabusque meis omnibus posterisque eorum, praeter quos testamento meo praeteriero*", about this epitaph from Ostia, Gardner, 1993, 32-33, note 53; (11027=*ILS* 8285) "...with the exception of his freedman Hermes whom he forbids, because of his ungrateful and offensive behaviour, to approach, walk around or draw near to this tomb." (tr. from Shelton, 1998, 200, n.246).

Chapter 5

The women, children, and servile families

'Free-born' women and children in Roman society, as in most pre-modern societies, were second-class citizens. Women could neither vote, hold public office nor serve in the army as a Roman citizen, though they could make valid contracts and wills or manumit slaves, usually under guardianship. Children were under the *potestas* of their father (or grandfather etc.) who had an absolute control over life and death (at least in principle), and above all, rearing of children, not infrequently abandoned in Roman society (child exposure), depended upon paternal acknowledgement. Women and children were legally and socially inferior to adult male citizens, and are rarely visible outside the context of household and family. In this sense, it is hardly surprising that modern scholarship of the ancient family is ultimately the study of women and children, in contrast to political and military history centred upon adult male citizens.[1]

Aristocratic women and children are in certain respects similar to slaves, as all are subordinate to the adult male *paterfamilias* in *domus* (though there are certainly distinctions).[2] When it comes to those within servile status, unlike their free equivalents, adult male slaves did not have the same privileges over their fellow women and children, since they were altogether deprived of legal rights. In the first place, slaves possessed no kin: slaves were disqualified from having claim to 'legitimate' family, and in this sense, freedmen did not have ancestors. Only free Roman citizens (*ingenui*) were entitled to publicly enumerate their fathers and ancestors.[3] As a matter of fact, however, slaves could maintain kinship and newly establish their own family, outside of recognition by Roman law. The ties of family were real for many slaves, and they might retain their ties intact until after they obtained freedom. Augustus' measures to encourage people to have families were directed towards freedmen as well as free-born citizens, and ultimately having children in slavery was advantageous in attaining a better life after manumission.[4] In that quasi-family unit, it is obvious that men generally dominated women and children both in work place and family life, but a crucial difference from the leisured class is that our subjects had work to perform. Neither servile family nor occupational group could accommodate parasitical members: their life (even as children) was constrained by a workload in order to survive. In this sense, the dominance of men over women and children in families and at the workplace might be less symbolic than in the context of the more wealthy aristocratic household.

It was not a problem for the wealthy Roman matrons who could easily delegate their domestic tasks to slaves. But how did slaves and ex-slaves conduct their family life, despite the workload inherent in their status? A freedwoman was relieved from the *operae* after marriage, with her patron's consent (*Dig.* 38, 1, 48, pr.; Duff. 1928, 47), but still need to make a living. In general, servile women must have had to make much effort to juggle between the family (husband and children) and work.

There is also the problem of "broken" families. The epitaphs often do not provide the picture of a complete (i.e. parents and children) family, but plenty of cases of children and single parents (usually mothers) as we will

---

[1] On scholarship of ancient family, Dixon, 2001c, 1-17; Dixon, 1992, 1-35.
[2] Similarities and distinctions: Saller, 1991; in terms of corporal punishment, Saller, 1998, 85-91; cf. in terms of loyalty in literature, Holt Parker, 1998, 152-173.
[3] Liv. 10, 8, 10, *qui patrem ciere possent, id est nihil ultra quam ingenuos*; *Dig.* 38, 8, 1, 2 (Ulpian), *pertinet autem haec lex ad cognationes non seruiles: nec enim facile ulla seruilis uidetur esse cognatio*; on servile kinship in Roman law, Buckland, 1908, 76-79; *Dig.* 38, 8, 1-2 (Ulpian); 38, 10, 10, 5 (Paul), *non parcimus his nominibus, id est cognatorum, etiam in seruis: itaque parentes et filios fratresque etiam seruorum dicimus: sed ad leges seruiles cognationes non pertinent*; Duff, 1928, 68, cites Martial, 11, 12, and 10, 27.

[4] Firstly, if a freedman was only manumitted into Latin status but had a child, they could later apply for Roman citizenship. Secondly, a freedman with two children was relieved from the obligation of the *operae*. Thirdly, a rich freedman (property of more than 100,000 sesterces) with three children could exclude the patron from inheritance. In the case of freedwomen, though the patron became the guardian of his freedwoman and could claim all her property (since she could not make a will without the patron's approval), a freedwoman was released from a patron's control if she gave birth to four children (*lex Papia Poppaea*); Gai. *Inst.* 3, 41-44; Gardner, 1993, 21; Watson, 1978, 35-39; vd. Chap. 4. n. 9.

CHAPTER 5: THE WOMEN, CHILDREN, AND SERVILE FAMILIES

see below. Does this actually indicate incomplete family units, caused by death or separation from the partners? If unions were frequently dissolved, were fathers at least supporting children financially? The limitation of the evidence does not always provide satisfactory answer to these questions, but data from the epitaphs shows some unsettling aspects of family life and the conditions of women and children. This chapter explores in what way and to what extent the *columbaria* epitaphs represent aspects of family life, and what we can construe from the result.

Evidence of familial ties

Measuring the relationship of individuals from a set of inscriptions is a difficult task. To quantify personal ties in a certain given population, modern scholars usually consult epitaphs of commemoration. Saller and Shaw (1984) counted the relationships in commemorative epitaphs from the various regions of the Roman Empire, and appeared to present a solid picture of the situation from large-scale epigraphic data. They demonstrated, rather unsurprisingly, that most people relied on their immediate family members for commemoration at death. The commemoration was most often made between *coniuges* (or *contubernales*), and secondly between parent and child(ren). The commemorations in the *columbaria*, the pattern of which largely coincides with the one drawn out by Saller and Shaw, were certainly centred on the family, or more specifically, immediate family members; 63% of all commemorations in the Volusian, 48% in the Statilian, and 45% in Livia's *columbarium*, was either between couples, parent(s) and child(ren), occasionally brothers and sisters, or other extended family members (i-iv, Table 5.1).

But then, what can be inferred from this result? The commemorations between close family members are proved most frequent, but the conclusion made by Saller and Shaw, that the nuclear family was the basic form of ancient family structure, has been questioned and invalidated, though not disproved. D. B. Martin, in a 1996 article, cast a fair criticism on their methodology and concept of the nuclear family. Martin is rightly sceptical about the dichotomy of nuclear family and extended family prevalent in Saller and Shaw and other scholars. The frequent commemorations within the nuclear family, Martin points out, only attests to 'degrees of social intimacy and the importance of immediate family relations' in funerary custom, but this cannot be equated with 'the boundary of the family.' In other words, it is rather natural that the deceased were commemorated by their immediate family members, but this trend concerning epitaphs does not become the proof of the exclusive cohesion of the nuclear family unit detached from other extended members of family. Our belief in the nuclear family all the more weakens, when we recall that the Romans did not have a term for the 'nuclear family' in differentiation from the usual terms *familia* or *domus*, both of which included more than the members of a nuclear family.[5]

Quite apart from the argument of Saller and Shaw, nevertheless, the prevalence of small living units based on nuclear families can hardly be denied. There are much fewer evidences speaking of the living units of extended family members, and their absence is not difficult to imagine especially for urban domestic slaves and freed persons. Notably, in epitaphic evidence, it appears that even the standard family structure of children with parents was frequently not maintained. In other words, only a very small proportion of the epitaphs (whether in the *columbaria* or elsewhere) actually attest to a 'complete' nuclear family, with wife and husband and child(ren) together (less than 5% in the *columbaria*). Though about half or more of all commemoration is unmistakably from those related by kin (i-iv, Table 5.1), they are more often only a single parent and child(ren), couples with no mention of a child, or siblings with no mention of their parent or spouse.[6] As if a substitute for familial ties, another bulk of commemoration is conducted between those bound by ties of ownership, i.e., from a freedman to a patron, from a slave to a master (non-aristocratic), or from a *vicarius/-ia* to a slave, or in each case vice versa (v, Table 5.1). The other substantial proportion of commemorators is indeed 'relationship uncertain', they do not define their relationship at all or merely address themselves as *conservus*, *conlibertus*, or *amicus* (vi, Table 5.1).[7]

As is shown in the Table, the three *columbaria* present a more or less similar pattern of commemoration. To be more precise, however, the 'commemorative' epitaphs are merely a fraction of all epitaphs, and their proportion varies significantly between the *columbaria* (vii, Table 5.1).[8] There are many epitaphs composed which lack commemorations altogether. Some of these 'non-commemorative' epitaphs still have recorded the relations of the deceased, though not as commemorator. For instance, in an epitaph (A229) "*Statilia Fortunata, Heraclaes uxor, vixit annis XXIIII*," we know Statilia Fortunata as wife of Heracla, but Heracla is not explicitly recorded as commemorating her. In such cases, we know the existence of the kinship or familial tie of a person, though we do not know the actual involvement or

---

[5] Saller and Shaw, 1984; Martin, 1996.
[6] On the prevalence of 'broken' families in the epitaphs of the lower-class, Rawson, 1966.
[7] A number of epitaphs attest to the commemoration between male and female '*conservi*' or '*colliberti*' in the same *familia*. Though they do not specify any further relationship, they are likely to have been in marital relationships: cf. Flory, 1978, 83, considers that the couple preferred commemorating each other "as fellow members of the same household," instead of referring to their ties of illegitimate marriage.
[8] Of all 429 Statilian epitaphs, only 67 (16%) epitaphs make clear the dedication from person(s) to the deceased. The majority of Statilian epitaphs simply give the name of the deceased in an ambiguous combination of nominative and possessive genitive. The proportion in Livia's *columbarium* is a little higher than the Statilii (33%), but the Volusian *columbarium* is outstanding in the proportion of commemorative epitaphs (64%, i.e., 101 of total 158 epitaphs).

Table 5.1 Patterns of commemoration (Statilii, Volusii, and Livia)

COMMEMORATION PATTERN (% in total commemorative epitaphs in each *columbarium*)	NUMBER OF EPITAPHS (% of all commemorative epitaphs in each *columbarium*)		
	Statilii (N=429)	Volusii (N=158)	Livia (N=322)
(i) btw. nuclear family or more extended family members	3 (5%)	4 (4%)	3 (3%)
(ii) btw. *coniunx/contubernalis*	14 (21%)	36 (36%)	20 (19%)
(iii) btw. *parens* & *filius/-ia*	10 (15%)	16 (16%)	17 (16%)
(iv) btw. *frater /soror*	5 (7%)	7 (7%)	7 (7%)
(v) btw. master & slave, freedman & patron, *vicarius* & slave	10 (15%)	14 (14%)	5 (5%)
(vi) others and relationship uncertain, incl. dedication by *conservus / conlibertus / amicus / collegia / familia*	22 (32%)	24 (24%)	54 (51%)
(vii) total (% of commemorative epitaphs in total epitaphs)	67 (16%)	101 (64%)	106 (33%)

presence of that person at their death. Another problem is caused by the presence of 'multiple' commemorations in an epitaph. In a handful of instances in the *columbaria*, there are more than one person commemorating the deceased or included as the deceased in an epitaph.[9] In such cases, for the purpose of sorting in number, those who attest to both kinship and ownership are arbitrarily included in the kinship group (e.g., *coniunx* rather than *libertus*); if both were related to the deceased by kin, blood relation is chosen over marital relation (e.g., *frater* over *coniunx*); finally, the relation to the commemorator is chosen over those merely named together in an epitaph unless the relation of the commemorator to the deceased is 'unspecified' or unknown. Thus, the revised Table 5.2 is drawn from the information of both commemorative and non-commemorative epitaphs.[10]

Table 5.2 The types of relationship in the *columbaria*

	Statilii	Volusii	Livia
In kinship	127 (19%)	161 (53%)	142 (24%)
In ownership	154 (23%)	21 (7%)	63 (10%)
In unspecified relationship or in *amicitia*	141 (22%)	54 (18%)	310 (51%)
No relationship recorded	235 (36%)	65 (22%)	93 (15%)

From the Table, we find more Statilian individuals bound in ownership than in kinship, whereas those in kinship far outnumber those in ownership in the Volusian *columbarium*. This seems to have some correlation with the ownership structure of each *domus* as we have seen in the previous chapter (Table 4.2): the Statilii of a pyramid shaped ownership structure (predominately intermediate ownership) tended to substitute and reduce individual familial ties, while the Volusii and Livia of inverted pyramid structure (predominately direct ownership, i.e., more individuals were connected directly to the aristocratic masters) tended to preserve ties of family, which did not facilitate as much necessity for intermediate ownership.[11]

In all three *columbaria*, ties of family were certainly prevalent, but at the same time, there were also a substantial proportion of individuals without ties of family – or to be precise, those whose familial ties were not mentioned. It is not possible to say from the record of epitaphs whether family ties for slaves and freedmen were common or not. Slaves in general might have understandably had more difficulty in establishing families than those in other social groups because of their status. As the agronomists such as Cato or Varro relentlessly stated, systematic provision of females for males controlled their sexual activity, and that might have resulted in successful procreation even without a stable family life.[12] Alternatively, they might have shared the reluctance towards marriage felt by those in the upper reaches of society.[13] To be emphasised here is that ties of

---

[9] e.g. (A330) *Sophro, Sisennae Statili ser., tabul(arius); Psyche soror et Optata coniunx fecer(unt)*: I categorised the relationship of this epitaph as between brother and sister in Table 5.1.

[10] Clearly, (a) the ownership by aristocratic masters is not considered here, and (b) two (or more) individuals that appear together in one epitaph without mention of their relationship are considered as in an unspecified relationship.

[11] The epigraphic data indicate that the Volusian *columbarium* was generally more 'compassionate' than other *columbaria*, at least in outlook. For instance, the use of epithets ('*carissimus*' etc.) was exceedingly higher in the Volusii than in Statilii and Livia; cf. on epithets, Nielsen, 1997.

[12] Varro, *Rust.* 2, 10, 6, talks about 'breeding' of herdsmen with fellow female slaves. When herdsmen were away to tend herds at a distance, he suggests sending women to accompany them for breeding as well as for other supporting work such as cooking; Columella, *Rust.* 1, 8; Plut. *Cat. Mai.* 21.

[13] Brunt, 1971, 136-140, argued that celibacy was common among the upper class, and also that, even though we do not have enough evidence, the marriage rate was equally very low (or lower) among the lower class (especially the Roman *proletarii*, in Brunt's words), because of their lack of financial resources to support a family.

family and of ownership coexisted - sometimes they were even identical - among the people in the *columbaria*.

Gender imbalance in the *columbaria*

In Rome during the early Empire, there were allegedly far more males than females among the free-born, according to Cassius Dio. He claims that it was because of this lack of females that Augustus formally acknowledged the right of Roman citizens except senators to marry freedwomen and recognised their offspring as legitimate: such marriages, though not illegal, had previously incurred disgrace.[14] It is tempting to interpret this lack of females in society in Dio's account as the background to the statistical estimation made by modern scholars regarding the groups of inscriptions, which generally yield a preponderance of males over females.[15] Our *columbaria* inscriptions likewise yield nearly twice as many male slaves and freedmen as female counterparts (Table 5.3).[16]

Table 5.3 Proportion of male and female in the *columbaria*

columbaria	male (%)	female (%)	uncertain (%)
Statilii (N=657)	65	32	3
Volusii (N=301)	62	35	3
Livia (N=608)	62	33	5
Arruntii (N=61)	57	43	0
Iunius Silanus (N=58)	69	31	0
Abuccii (N=99)	59	41	0
Annius Pollio (N=26)	65	35	0
overall (N=1799)	63	36	1

As far as our evidence is concerned, the figures indicate that the *familiae urbanae* of the aristocracy were, perhaps not surprisingly, male dominated. Admittedly, the figures may not reflect the real composition of the servant body in a large elite household; one may claim that females were not absent, but merely tended to be 'not commemorated'. But even if this was the case, it is significant that females were generally considered 'unworthy' to receive the recognition of commemoration in an epitaph.

If we look more closely, the ages of death recorded in epitaphs show that the female population at certain ages appears to be significantly reduced or 'unrecognised' in comparison to the male equivalent (Fig. 5.1.1-3). Certainly, we are aware of the restrictions of the data. Firstly, these are the number of deaths, not the number of people alive at any one time, though we might be able to assume that the more death records of males in comparison to those of females means more males or more males who received commemoration, rather than that males of a certain age group were more likely to die. Secondly, those who recorded the age of death are a small minority of the whole. For instance, the Statilian *columbarium* has 103 individuals (including 7 of uncertain sex) with age at death recorded; of 428 individuals who are recorded as deceased (excluding commemorators and others only named to identify the deceased), 24%, i.e., less than a third, of all the deceased, notes the age at death. Other *columbaria* are worse still; we find only 79 individuals altogether (in seven *columbaria*) with records of ages of death. Moreover, it is clear that deaths of children, especially of infants of less than one year old, are severely underrepresented in epigraphic evidence in general, in comparison to the probable death rate of infants for a typical Roman population. It has been generally accepted by scholars that the average life expectancy of the ancient Romans was about 25 years from birth. This means that approximately one third of newborn babies died within twelve months, or half died before the age of ten.[17] In contrast to this theoretical proportion of infant death, the surviving epigraphic evidence, for instance as revealed in K. Hopkins' study, with a sample of 16,000 tombstones from Rome and elsewhere in Italy, only 1.3% were infants under twelve months old.[18] Indeed, in the Statilian *columbarium* amongst others, we find no epitaphs that record a child's age as under one year old.

A number of factors make intelligible the thought that the epigraphic evidence might generally under-represent infants, particularly under 12 months old. As modern scholars have argued, children, particularly infants, received different treatment at burial from adults,

---

[14] Dio, 54, 16, 2; Rich, 1990, 193.
[15] According to Weaver, 1972, 170-173, the inscriptions of the *familia Caesaris* in Rome and Italy give the proportion of approximately 60% male and 40% female. If we look more closely, females are only 6% of those who carry status indication as Imperial freedmen/slaves (against 94% male *familia Caesaris*); in any other given samples of data, males generally dominate females in number: Treggiari, 1975, 395; Bradley, 1987b, 73-74.
[16] The gender of a person in inscriptions can be determined by looking at the gender used in descriptive nouns or adjectives in the Latin, though they are not always available in generally concise *columbaria* epitaphs. The secondary clue then is the name itself; certain names are customary for either male or female, though the problem is that certain other names are common to both sexes. For example, the name 'Daphnis' or 'Felix' could be given to both male and female. In this sense, a certain degree of presumption on our side is inevitable, as it is impossible to tell whether '*cubicul. Felix*' is really a male though we think most certainly that there was no '*cubicularia*'. The category of "gender unknown" is for those persons whose name is reversible in both gender and for whom no other clues as to gender are available; the catalogue of slave names is in Solin, 1996, vol. I-III, especially 86 and 92, on 'Felix', and 515, on 'Daphnis', both held by male and female.

[17] Saller, 1987a, 68; id. 1994, 15-16; Frier, 1982, 213-51; Garnsey, 1991, 51-52; Hopkins, 1983, 225.
[18] Hopkins, 1983, 225; Shaw, 1991, 74-77, argued that dedications to children varied in proportion in different regions of the Empire and in different periods, that is to say, more children were commemorated in the urban centre (Rome) and in the Christian era (*c*. AD 250-500); McWilliam, 2001, 79.

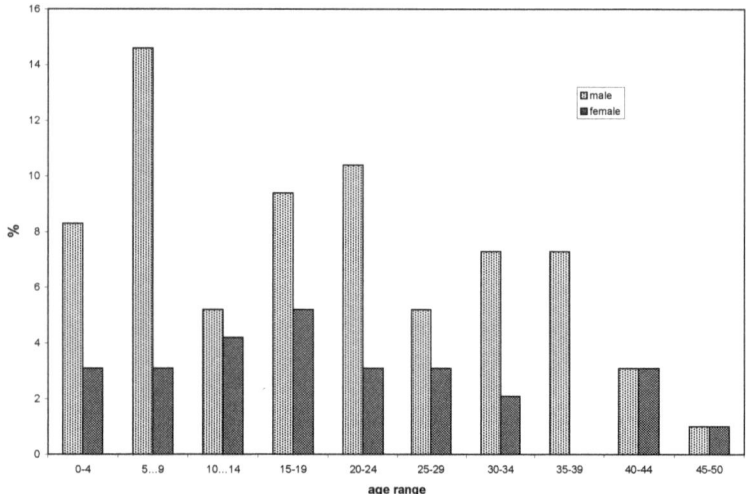

Fig. 5.1.1 Recorded age of death: Statilii (N=96)

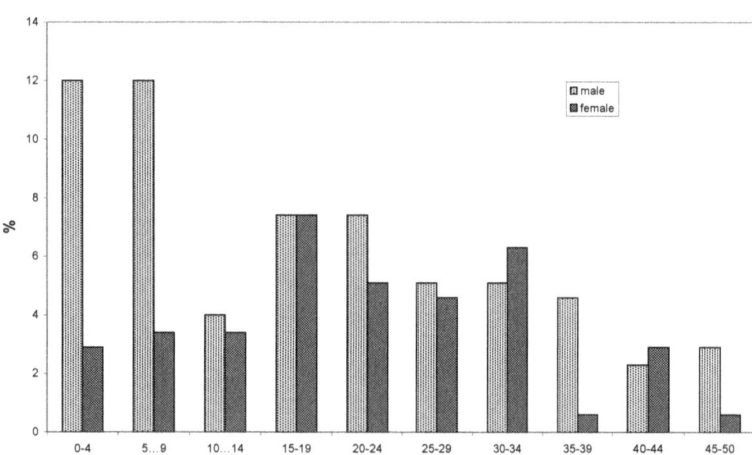

Fig. 5.1.2 Recorded age of death: Volusii, Iunius Silanus, Abuccii, Arruntii, C. Annius Polio, Caecilii, Livia (N=79)

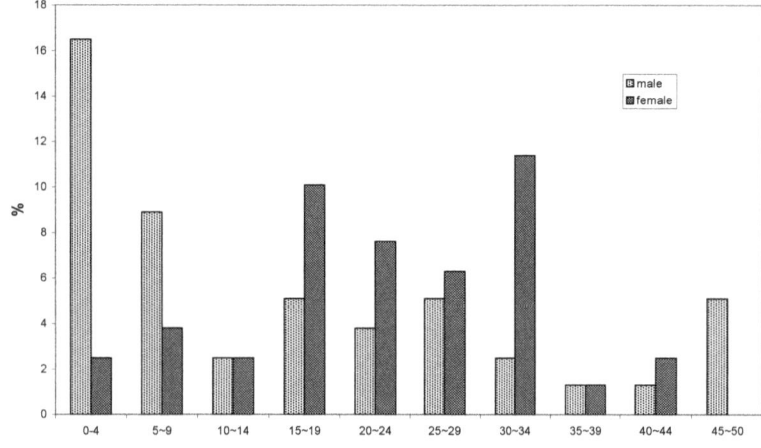

Fig. 5.1.3 Recorded age of death: all (N=175)

as religiously 'marginal' figures. For instance, it was the custom attested by Pliny and Juvenal not to cremate babies who died before cutting their teeth;[19] their funeral took place at night and they were buried within the confines of the house, even inside the city.[20] The rituals of the *dies lustricus* were to take place on the ninth day for boys and the eighth day for girls, when children received names and marked their formal acceptance into society. The period before the *dies lustricus* was when yet unnamed children were most often exposed,[21] and babies who died of natural causes before names were given were obviously not to be commemorated in epitaphs. Even though slave children might not necessarily go through the same rituals of purification and of admission into the household as free-born children, the same timing of naming a child or special treatment at funerals for new-born babies are likely to have been applied to them.[22]

Despite elements of distortion, however, ages of death in epitaphs are still enormously valuable as one of few available sources of data on the age composition of a certain group of people in ancient society.[23] As we can see in Fig. 5.1.1-3, although certain variations occur between the Statilian and other *columbaria* data in advanced ages, both sets of data attest equally to a lack of females against males in ages under 10-14 years old. A strikingly similar result is found in B. Shaw's surveys, which consulted a larger scale of epigraphic samples. B. Rawson's study on inscriptions of *alumni* (foster-children) and *vernae* (home-born slaves) also presents a similar situation, where the male/female ratio of recorded age at death shows the greatest disparity for those under five years old, while the disparity declines from ages 5-9 on.[24]

---

[19] Plin. *HN*. 7, 72, *hominem prius quam genito dente cremari mos gentium non est*; Juv. 15, 139-140, *naturae imperio gemimus... terra clauditur infans et minor igne rogi*.
[20] Wiedemann, 1989, 5-25, 176-182; McWilliam, 2001, 75-77; cf. Sen. *brev. vit.*, 20, 5.
[21] Corbier, 2001, 57-58; Garnsey, 1991, 52-53; name-giving on the *dies lustricus*, Suet. *Nero*, 6, 2; cf. Suet. *Calig.* 5.
[22] Shaw, 1991, 69; Garnsey, 1991, 51.
[23] Saller (1987b) and Shaw (1987) argued the standard age of the first marriage of the men and women respectively, by looking at the ages of death when commemorators of the deceased shift from parent(s) to husband / wife.
[24] Rawson, 1986b, 170-200, her sample is 415 *alumni* and 564 *vernae* from *CIL* VI; it also shows the visible under-representation in epitaphs of infant *alumni* and *vernae* under the age of one.

Why then, as shown in Fig. 5.1.1-3, did the *columbaria* lack females in particular in the first ten years after birth? One might be duly obliged to consider as one possibility the often-discussed social custom of infant exposure.[25] Infant exposure was commonly practised in ancient society even at the very top of the social hierarchy, though, in such cases, it was not so much out of poverty as a strategy to control the division of inheritance among children and protect family property. At other occasions, the adulterous lifestyle of imperial women prompted the emperors to order exposure of their children to eliminate disgrace.[26] Roman society had few qualms about leaving infants to die, and doing so, or if not, selling or sending them away,[27] were practical decisions not infrequently made by either master or slave parents.[28] An often cited papyrus letter from Egypt contained the instruction from a husband to his pregnant wife, "if it is a male, let it live; if it is a female, expose it".[29] It was not that boys were immune to exposure, but chances were less when compared to girls and they were probably more likely to be rescued. We know from Suetonius of the cases of two boys who were free by birth but exposed as infants; they were both given training by foster parents (*nutritor* or *educator*), manumitted later, and became famous grammarians of the time.[30] In the widespread practice of child exposure, daughters were more likely to slip out of parents' protection than sons and lose contact with them.[31]

If not necessarily child exposure, it has been suggested that girls born in large households were sent to be brought up in a rural household (though it is obscure why rural household particularly needed girls); more often, I suppose, they might be sold or sent away to smaller (or poorer) households to serve as a servant - like Photis, the only slave maid in Milo's poor household in Apuleius' *Metamorphoses*. Whereas slave children meant an increase of property in the long term, the negative side of rearing a slave baby was that it cost a master (or parents) subsistence with no profits at least for the first 3-5 years. In a society that heavily valued men over women, females in servile status were supposedly most vulnerable to exposure and other means of dismissal. According to Dionysius of Halicarnassus, the legendary Romulus obliged people to raise 'all male children' and 'the first-born daughter'.[32] Such a view towards daughters seems to be clearly demonstrated in the following data from the *columbaria*; we know a total of 75 brothers and sisters from the *columbaria* (Statilii, Livia, Volusii, Arruntii), which is 35 blood-related groups (with or without parents). Among them, females (sisters) constitute only 14 out of 75 (19%). Moreover, only two groups consisted of more than two sisters, while 23 groups consisted of more than two brothers (Table 5.4). In other words, except in two cases (one in Livia's *columbarium* and one Statilian but both epitaphs were recovered from outside the *columbarium*, and both groups consisting of one brother and two sisters), we do not find a family with more than one daughter. From the figures, servile families in the *columbaria* do not seem to have been willing to accommodate more than one daughter.

Table 5.4 Brothers and Sisters in the *columbaria*

TYPES	THE NUMBER OF GROUPS	INSCRIPTIONS
M+M+M (three brothers)	2	3950 / A278+A256+A335+A328
M+M (two brothers)	19	5954 / A141+A429 / 3945-3948 / 7379 / 4237 / 7426 / 7370 / A109 / 4050 / A159 / 3956 / 4302 / 4049 / 4124 / 7283a / 7286 / 4061 / 4080 / 3937
F+M+M (one sister and two brothers)	2	A296+A038+A080+A114 / 4053
F+M (one sister and one brother)	10	7304 / 7386 / 5953 / A330 / A185/ 7373 / 4022 / 4151 / 4251 / 7341
F+F+M (two sisters and one brother)	2	B019 / 4193
Total	35	

This supposition is further strengthened by the fact that daughters were less likely to receive epitaphic commemoration by parents. In the Statilian *columbarium*, only two out of 18 commemorations from parent(s) to child were to a daughter, and similarly in the Volusian *columbarium*, only one out of ten commemorations was to a daughter. In Huttunen's sample, which is every fifth epitaph in *CIL* VI, the gap is reduced but certainly male-favoured; about 60% (N=581) of the commemoration from parent(s) to child (N=964) was to sons, while 40% was to daughters (N=383).[33]

---

[25] Infant exposure as a major source of slaves, Harris, 1994; the Roman attitudes towards, and rules about exposure, Corbier, 2001.
[26] Augustus did not allow the rearing of a newborn child of his granddaughter Julia in exile (Suet. *Aug.* 65, 4); Claudius ordered his newborn daughter to be exposed, laying her naked outside the doorstep of her mother Urgulanilla, because he found out that her real father was one of his freedmen: id. *Claud.* 27; Corbier, 2001, 54; Saller, 1987a, 69.
[27] Slave children might be sent off to the country estate and brought up there; *Dig.* 50, 16, 210 (Marcian), *is qui natus est ex mancipiis urbanis et missus est in villam nutriendus, in urbanis servis constituetur*; id. 32, 99, 3 (Paul), *eum, qui natus est ex ancilla urbana et missus in uillam nutriendus, interim in neutris esse quidam putant*.
[28] In comparison to infant exposure, exposing or killing the 'grown-ups' was probably to incur more moral guilt. In AD 47, Claudius ordered to set free those slaves who were exposed by their master for illness without giving treatment, and for masters who killed sick slaves for the same reason to be charged with murder: Suet. *Claud.* 25; Dio, 60, 29; *Dig*, 40, 8, 2 (Modestinus), *seruo, quem pro derelicto dominus ob grauem infirmitatem habuit, ex edicto diui Claudii competit libertas*.
[29] *P. Oxy.* 744 (1 BC): Frank, 1936, ii, 281.
[30] Suet. *Gram.* 7; 21.
[31] *vd. supra*, n. 27; Treggiari, 1975b, 400-1; 1979b, 189.

[32] Dion. Hal. *Antiq.* 2, 15, 2; Brunt, 1971, 148-154, holds the view that girls were more likely to be exposed or killed at birth, and that this led to lack of women in society and as a result a tendency for women to marry at a much earlier age than men; cf. Ulpian (*Dig.* 34, 5, 10, 1) assesses the case in which a master promises freedom for a female slave on the condition that the first child she bears is male.
[33] Huttunen, 1974, 62-63.

After the ubiquitous absence of females in childhood, the ages 10-14 were the turning point: the number of females dying at these ages comes closest to that of males or even exceeds it (Fig. 5.1). B. Shaw's survey gives a similar result where females of the slave population in Rome dramatically increase their appearance on epitaphs in their teens onwards after a comparative rarity of appearance under ten years old.[34] These ages mark the legally marriageable age for the free(d) females, and many females could and supposedly did give birth to children. Since children born of female slaves meant an increase to the master's property,[35] the legal experts, as well as agricultural writers, saw the benefit of female slaves in terms of their procreative capacity. They were well aware of the fertility of female slaves on sale when assessing their value.[36] The pregnancy of a female slave might be regarded as a burden or disturbance to their work, but at the same time, pregnant slaves were put on sale apparently for a good price, specifically intended for buyers who were looking for a *nutrix* (nurse) to suckle other babies, or wanting a slave baby as a domesticated *verna* and to give him training from an early age. Certainly, legal experts do not assume that fertility was all that was needed for female slaves; physical and intellectual ability for work mattered most on the platform of slave-dealers, as they did for male slaves. Nonetheless, the increased appearance of females at the age 10-14 after being visibly underrepresented during childhood in our *columbaria* data, along with a similar result from other studies seems to indicate that there was in fact an overt change in the value of females accorded to age. If a substantial increase of females at these ages was taking place, many were those brought in for 'marriage', and consequently more females died partly because of childbirth.[37] On another interpretation, it is possible that the change in the proportion of female deaths is in record only, namely, that there were actually more women but they were not mentioned by name. Even in that case, it is important to note that female children were not regarded as meriting an epitaph, whereas at least from these more advanced ages onward, females come to receive proper 'recognition' in terms of being commemorated by an epitaph.

In either case, it is clear that the underlying expectation of society towards female slaves/freedwomen concerned, for better or worse, their role in the family. More data will follow to confirm this point. Despite the overall lack of females in the *columbaria*, there were more women commemorated in epitaphs as *mater* or *coniunx* (or *contubernalis* etc.) than men as *pater* or *coniunx* (or *contubernalis* etc.). Table 5.5 gives the numbers of females and males in familial context, namely the deceased addressed as *coniunx*, *contubernalis*, *mater*, *pater* etc., commemorated by their spouses or children.

Table 5.5 The number of epitaphs recording the death of male and female with family relationship

	a. death of mother / wife	b. death of father / husband	ratio (a : b)
Statilii	13	8	1.6 : 1
Volusii	29	18	1.6 : 1
Livia	19	7	2.7 : 1
Every fifth inscriptions in *CIL* VI (Huttunen, 1974, 61)	933	707	1.2 : 1

This shows that both the Statilian and Volusian *columbaria* contained 50% more epitaphs of female as *coniunx* or *mater* than male as *coniunx* or *pater*. In other words, under the premise that death occurred equally to male and female spouses/parents alike, the death of a mother/wife was much more likely to be commemorated in a familial context than the death of a father/husband was. Moreover, though the sample is very small, we find more mothers acting as the commemorators of children than fathers (11 mothers and 6 fathers in the Statilian and Volusian *columbaria*). In sum, we find more mothers/wives than fathers/husbands, in reverse proportion to the number of females (only one third of the overall population as we have seen in Table 5.3).

In Roman law, the children of a slave woman, whether the husband was slave or free, became slaves of the mother's master. This might have resulted in many children living closer to mothers than to fathers, and consequently closer ties of children and mother and the higher rate of familial commemoration between them. Besides, the fact that job titles attested in epitaphs are overwhelmingly for men (Table 3.1, Chap. 3) indicates that fathers tended to receive commemoration by (or commemorate) work colleagues more often than mothers, and this presumably reduced their appearance as *pater* or *coniunx* in epitaphs.

This aspect of funerary commemoration is glimpsed in the following examples. The epitaphs of the family of the

---

[34] Shaw, 1991, 80-83; 1987, 30-31; however, as a rather odd exception, his data of those of 'freed' status in Rome presents female predominance over male throughout from age zero to the late twenties.
[35] *Dig.* 5, 3, 27, pr. (Ulpian): "The children of slave-girls and also the children of their children, though not thought of as fruits because slave-girls are not acquired solely as breeding stock, are still additions to an inheritance."
[36] *Dig.* 21, 1, 15 (Paul): "One who menstruates twice within a month is not healthy any more than one who never menstruates, unless this latter be by reason of her age."; *Dig.* 21, 1, 14, 1-3 (Ulpian): "All are agreed that a pregnant woman, the object of a sale, is healthy; for it is the highest and particular lot of woman to conceive and conserve what she conceives. A woman in labour is also healthy, unless some extrinsic factor affects her body with some form of ill-health. Where a barren woman is concerned, Caelius says that Trebatius took a distinction: If she be naturally barren, she is healthy, but not if her infertility be due to some bodily defect."
[37] Cf. Bradley, 1984, 54-55, examined the ages of female slaves at sale, as recorded in the papyrus transactions from Roman Egypt. His sample is too small (only thirty), but the distribution of ages at which females were sold largely concentrates on above 10 years old while females under ten years old are relatively few.

CHAPTER 5: THE WOMEN, CHILDREN, AND SERVILE FAMILIES

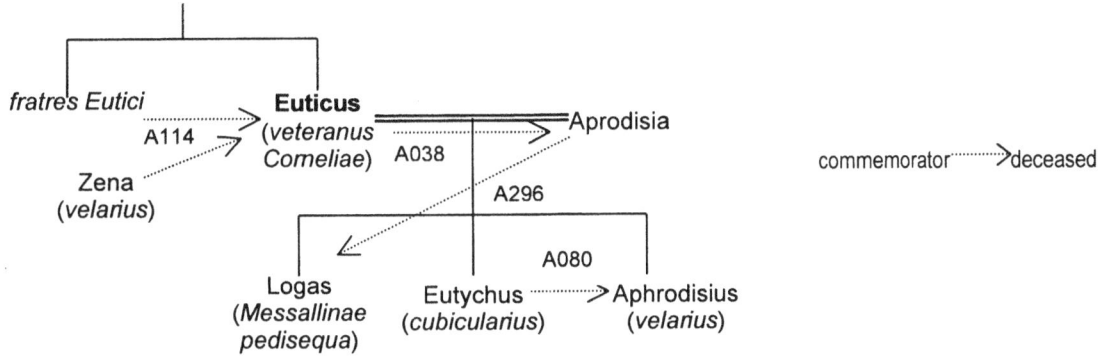

Fig. 5.2 The commemorative pattern of Euticus' family

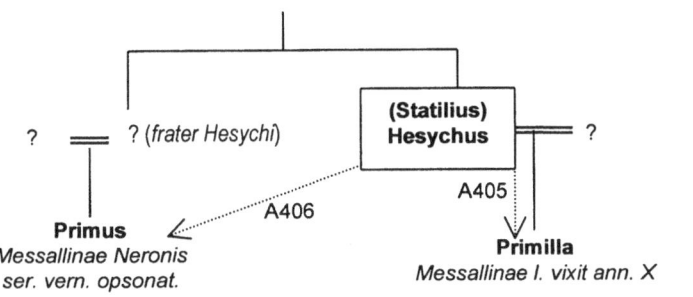

Fig. 5.3 The commemorative pattern of Hesychus' family

Statilian servant Euticus (Fig. 5.2) were already discussed in the previous chapter (Fig. 4.1). This family could easily have escaped our notice since the members of the family were all commemorated separately, without reference to the other family members.

In the first epitaph, we find an 'Aprodisia' the *mater*, commemorating her sixteen-year-old daughter 'Logas', who was a *pedisequa* of Messallina (A296). Then, 'Aprodisia' the *coniunx* is commemorated in another epitaph by 'Euticus' (A038). This Euticus appears in another epitaph as the *veteranus Corneliae* ('a long-serving servant of Cornelia'), commemorated by his anonymous brothers (*fratres*) and a certain Zena the *velarius* whose relationship to Euticus is unknown but presumably one of his colleagues (A114). Finally, there is the fourth epitaph, where a slave called Eutychus is commemorating his brother Aphrodisius. From their nomenclature, they are most likely the sons of Euticus and Aprodisia (A080). If these members were thus related to each other, the question remains why only mother Aprodisia but not father Euticus took pains to commemorate the daughter Logas on her death.

For men in the Euticus family, commemorative activities seem to be centred on brotherly ties, and this is also observed in the case of Hesychus' family (Fig. 5.3; cf. Fig. 4.2). Hesychus, unlike Euticus, did not have a problem commemorating his daughter Primilla (A406), but as *patruus* (paternal uncle), he also took responsibility of his nephew Primus (A405).

Fraternal ties are again evident in the *dispensator* Auticus family (vd. Fig. 4.4), where Auticus is named, though not as commemorator, in epitaphs of his two brothers. In contrast, such consistently close ties between brothers are not found between sisters. In both Statilian and Volusian *columbaria*, no commemoration between sisters is known. As I have discussed above, we rarely find more than one daughter in a family in the *columbaria*, while many brotherly ties were preserved until death. Family planning at the outset (i.e., exposure etc) could be an important contributing factor to the daughter-less situation. But from another viewpoint, it may be explained that at a later stage sisters tended to lose contact with their original family by marriage, which is the opposite side of the coin from the situation that we have seen, that women were more likely to be commemorated as mother or spouse.

The work and family life

So far we have seen an overall situation of familial ties and peculiar appearance of women in the *columbaria* epitaphs. Our evidence attested to both servile women's role in the family (as wife and mother) and their participation in labour. In what way, then, was their family life achieved (or compromised) in relation to work obligations to their master or mistress? Let us look at several examples of servile families on this issue.

The three spouses of Spendo, apparently separated by death, had their own professions as well as their relationships to their husband.[38] In the first epitaph, Spendo commemorates his two spouses (*contubernales*) together, Panope *ornatrix* (hairdresser) and Phoebe *a speculum* (*sic*) (mirror-holder? caretaker of mirrors?). Both of them probably worked for Torquata, the wife or daughter of Q. Volusius Saturninus (*cos.* AD 56).[39] The second epitaph indicates that Spendo himself was also a member of Torquata's *familia*: here the same name 'Spendo', this time with the agnomen 'Torquatianus' appears with his third spouse Primigenia, commemorating their daughter Spendusa who lived only five months.[40] Similarly, we find the case of a Sophro, a slave *tabularius* of Statilius Sisenna, who first commemorates his *coniunx* Phyllis, a *sarcinatrix* of Statilia (A337). When Sophro died, he was commemorated by his sister (*soror*) Psyche and *coniunx* Optata (A330). It is assumed that Optata became Sophro's second spouse after Phyllis' death. To be noted here is that the first spouse Phyllis, a slave of Statilia, was married to Sophro, a slave of her mistress' brother Sisenna. If they cohabited as a couple, they might have to commute to different households for work (or different office and workshop) every day.

In the view of agricultural writers, a female companion and children served to bind male slaves more strongly to the estate.[41] Cato bluntly instructed the slave *vilicus*: "if the master has given her to you as wife, keep yourself only to her. Make her stand in awe of you. Restrain her from extravagance." [42] Female slaves in entering *contubernium* might be allowed to engage in the care of their spouses; the legal expert Scaevola refers to this practice in a hypothetical case, where a *pedisequa* (female attendant) was relieved from the duty to her master when she was united with an *actor* (bailiff) in the *contubernium*, though she remained a slave of the same master.[43] Women's retirement from their own profession at the point of marital union supposedly depended on the husband's profession. Women might be required to perform tasks in support of him, such as a *vilica*. But other female professionals might retain a full-time job of their own. Such was probably Scaeva the *tabellarius Tauri* (courier of Taurus) and his *coniunx* Italia the *quasillaria* (spinning-woman) (A100), or that of Diadumenus *Liviae mensor* and Lochias *Liviae sarcinatrix* (3988), who continued to identify themselves by their job-titles alongside their marital ties. As we have already seen (Table 3.1), however, most of the professionals were males, and a much smaller number of females recorded job-titles. Without a specialist job of her own, a woman would have had a much lower prospect of accumulating *peculium*, and therefore, much less control of their own lives, since *peculium* would have enabled them to buy their own freedom, and even their spouse's or children's freedom.

Typically for those in servile status, family and work were not to be separated, but intermixed without boundary. Slaves, who by nature were not their own master (but wore price tags in themselves by someone else's value estimate), were inevitably disposed to bringing ownership further into family relations. Masters might have relationships with their slave women, which might lead to granting her freedom, and marrying her as his freedwoman. Marrying a slave woman after freeing her under the civil law was one of the much predicted scenarios, as the Augustus law entitled even a master under twenty years old to initiate a formal manumission, if this was the intention.[44] If not her own master, it was also a usual custom for a man to buy his prospective female companion from slavery and secure her for himself. 'Buying' the freedom of one's spouse or children technically made the buyer their patron, and inevitably placed him in a position of superiority. One may recall one memorable scene in Petronius, where Trimalchio silences his jealous wife Fortunata by throwing a cup at her face, and then goes on to assert his superiority by reminding her that it is him who saved her from the wretchedness of slavery. The fact that Trimalchio paid for Fortunata's manumission enabled him to assert his superiority over her years later. One of Trimalchio's fellow freedman Hermeros likewise boasted that he bought his *contubernalis*' freedom (Petr. 57).[45]

---

[38] In the *columbaria* we only know of examples of men achieving the *de facto* remarriage: L. Volusius Comicus first commemorates his '*coniunx karissima*' Volusia Eo, then sometime later, his '*uxor optima*' Valeria Celsilla (7389) (*Volusiae Eo, coniugi karissimae bene merenti. L. Volusius Comicus et sibi. permissu Luci n. et Valeriae Celsillae, uxori optimae b. m.*). The first Volusia Eo was allegedly the consort united in slavery according to her nomen Volusia and the term '*coniunx*' (not '*uxor*' for the free or freed) he used for her, and after her death and his manumission, Comicus married Valeria Celsilla of alien nomen, probably his first legally valid marriage; cf. presumably two *coniuges* of Epaphroditus the *dispensator*, himself commemorated by his homonymous son: (9326) *Volusiae Primae coniugi karissimae; Epaphroditus Q(uinti) n(ostri) disp(enator) et Volusiae Olympiadi coniugi sanctissimae et Epaphroditus filius Epaphrodito Q(uinti) n(ostri) dis(pensator); locus d(atus) a Quinto n(ostro)*.

[39] (7297) *d. m. s. Panope ornatrix Torquate Q. Volusi, vixit annis XXII et Phoebe a speculum vixit annis XXXVII, Spendo contubernalibus suis bene merentibus fecit et sibi loc. d. dec. decu*.

[40] (7303) *d. m. s. Spendusae, vixit m(ensibus) V, d(iebus) XXVI, Spendo Torquatian(us) et Primigenia filiae dulcissimae fecer(unt)...*

[41] Varro, *Rust*. 1, 17, 5, *praefectos alacriores faciendum praemiis dandaque opera ut habeant peculium et coniunctas conservas, e quibus habeant filios. eo enim fiunt firmiores ac coniunctiores fundo. Itaque propter haec cognationes Epiroticae familiae sunt illustriores ac cariores*; Herrmann-Otto, 1997, 254; Westermann, 1955, 76-77.

[42] Cato, *Rust*. 143, *si eam tibi dederit dominus uxorem, esto contentus; ea te metuat facito; ne nimium luxuriosa siet*.

[43] Scaevola discusses whether such a former *pedisequa* should also be manumitted if she was a *pedisequa* when the master's testament explicitly ordered those with such job-titles to be free: *Dig*. 40, 4, 59 pr., *inueniatur actori in contubernio tradita...quod pedisequa esse desiit*.

[44] Manumission by under-aged masters normally granted a freedman the status of Junian Latin: Gai. *Inst*. 1, 12-17.

[45] Petr. 74, "*ambubaia non meminit, sed de machina illam sustuli, hominem inter homines feci. At inflat se tanquam rana, et in sinum suum non spuit, codex, non mulier.*"; id. 57, "*contubernalem meam redemi, ne quis in sinu illius manus tergeret.*"; cf. id. 71, a master might bequeath a slave woman to her slave husband by will: (Trimalchio speaking) "*ad summam, omnes illos in testamento meo manu mitto. Philargyro etiam fundum lego et contubernalem suam.*"

The epitaph of a Volusian slave Pancarpus is an example of servile families originally connected by ownership (*Pancarpo exact. v. an. XXXIIII, Aucta vicaria fecit. Sabina Pancar. f. v. a. XIII. Volusia Aucta v. a. XXXI*) (7371); after Pancarpus the *exactor* (probably the supervisor of slaves) was commemorated by his *vicaria* Aucta, the commemoration of Pancarpus' daughter Sabina was added on, and finally, when Aucta, previously a *vicaria*, died, she was now a freedwoman Volusia Aucta. Whatever the relationship between the three (the *vicaria* Aucta appears to be a spouse of Pancarpus and the mother of Sabina), to be commemorated in the same epitaph indicates their virtual identity as a familial unit.[46] Even without any real ties of kin, a living unit bound by ownership was an important substitute for family for those in servile status. For slaves, ties of ownership were the basis from which any extensive familial ties might be nurtured.

This could start from the day when they were born. Children born from female slaves (*ancillae*) belonged to the mother's *dominus*. In the same way, children born from a *vicaria* belonged to the slave *ordinarius* who owned the mother in his *peculium*. Such children were specifically called *vernae* (home-born) for the *dominus* or for the slave *ordinarius*. For instance, Irene, a *vicaria* of a Statilian slave Deucalio (A269), had a five year old son (*filius*) Faustio. Wherever the biological father was, it was solely the mother's master who could exercise paternal authority towards the child born in slavery. Thus Faustio was a *verna* of her master Deucalio (A266).[47]

'*Verna*', the popular designation in literary sources of slaves born in a household, was a term of affection from the *dominus* and the proud designation of slaves themselves. One might expect that the title *verna* would be plentiful in the *columbaria* epitaphs, since frequent references to familial ties means that many slaves were born in household. However, as is shown in the Table 5.6 below, the use of the word *verna* is extremely rare in the *columbaria* epitaphs and not at all common as a status indication.

Table 5.6 The number of vernae in the columbaria

columbaria	Number of vernae	% of total individuals
Statilii (N=657)	6	0.9%
Volusii (N=224)	8	2.7%
Livia (N=608)	1	0.2%
Abuccii (N=99)	1	1.0%
Marcellae*	4	0.5%
Nero Drusus*	1	0.8%

*The figures from Hermann-Otto, 1997, 50, n.62.

Apart from the Volusii's 2.7%, the persons recorded as *verna* are less than 1% of total individuals in the five *columbaria*. According to Weaver, the designation of '*verna*' was also very rare in the Familia Caesaris before Hadrian.[48] Herrmann-Otto, in her study of children born from *ancillae* (i.e., home-born slaves), suggests that use of the term *verna*, which is found more often in epitaphs of a later period, especially during the second century AD, was not yet common at the time of the *columbaria*, in the early Empire. Although the word *verna* had already appeared in Plautus' plays, the epigraphic evidence does not show sign of its spread as a personal title until much later. This delayed spread of the term for home-born slaves might perhaps indicate that the first century AD was still a period of transformation in the consciousness of slave-owners and the *familia* alike; that slaves tend now to be born into the household rather than being introduced from abroad, given significant reduction in the supply of war prisoners.[49]

As Hermann-Otto recognised the problem of the title '*verna*', her analysis of home-born slaves naturally extended the subject to the so-called 'verkappte *verna*' ('hidden *verna*'), namely those assumed virtually as home-born even though they were not called so in epitaphs.[50] In our *columbaria* inscriptions, the aforementioned daughter Logas, and her brothers Euticus and Aphrodisius (Fig. 5.2), would be categorised as such "verkappte *vernae*" of a master (possibly Logas' mistress Messalina's husband Taurus), to whom the mother Aprodisia belonged as an *ancilla*.[51] The evidence of such 'virtual' *vernae* in the *columbaria* is plentiful.

Slave children, whether born as *vernae* or acquired at an early stage, could not constitute an immediate workforce. Yet they were placed in ownership or under the apprenticeship of a third party in early age. A three-year-old Optata, while she was commemorated by her anonymous mother, belonged to Chrestus Auctianus as a *vicaria* (A123). Rufa, who died at the age of one, was already the *vicaria* of the Statilian slave Menander (A124). A master and nurturer, who employed an infant slave, might have done so because of a blood relation: a Volusian slave physician Zosimus had his *cognata* (a relative) Ampelio as a *vicaria* (7295).

Thus, in servile families, ownership tends to be disguised as familial ties. After being unemployable for a certain period of time, children are swiftly placed in the hierarchy of the adult as workforce.

---

[46] cf. (7286) *Logo, L. Volusi citharoedo, vixit ann. XX. Cerialis frater, Agathopus vicarius.*
[47] *CIL* VI, p.1004 (Mommsen); Herrmann-Otto, 1994, 49.
[48] Weaver, 1972, 51f.
[49] Five out of six *vernae* in the Statilian *columbarium* were not slaves of the aristocratic masters, but those of freedmen of the Statilii or other masters of alien nomina: A020, A267, A266, A237 (alien nomen), A364 (alien nomen), A405 (a *verna* of Statilia Messalina, Nero's wife); cf. Volusii: 7316, 7318.
[50] Herrmann-Otto, 1994, 50.
[51] Also, Atticus, the son of Stacte, the *nutrix* of Sisenna Taurus' son, was possibly *verna* of Sisenna (A345).

Conclusion

The servile world of the *columbaria* centred on males, as the epitaphs found from there record nearly twice as many male slaves/freedmen as female counterparts. If we look at the ages of the deceased in epitaphs, females under ten years old keep a low profile in comparison to males but the number of appearances improves thereafter. Infant exposure was probably one reason to blame for the disparity, as our evidence clearly shows that very few sisters, especially not more than one daughter in a family, are found in the *columbaria*, while we know of more brothers. Besides, more sons than daughters received epitaph dedications by parents. In fact, females were more likely to identify themselves as mothers of children and companions of males than as daughters. Women are more often commemorated in the epitaphs as spouse or mother than are men as spouse or father, and mothers, rather than fathers, tend to commemorate their children. These seem to indicate that they were more valued for their role as spouse and mother in the family. Some women might continue their professional work even after united with partners, but not many could have pursued independent occupations, but probably engaged mainly in both household and assisting tasks for male partners. Servile families were often closely connected to ownership, and in such families both ties of kin and those of subordination intertwined. From ownership-based living unit, some might go to find their own genuine familial tie elsewhere: or others might continue to be trapped in ownership-familial ties even long after manumission.

Chapter 6

Slave names

In the previous chapter we considered the family relationship prevalent among the servile dependants, and it is observed that a number of slaves were certainly born in the *domus* virtually as *vernae* (home-born). At the same time, however, there must have been other groups of slaves who did not originate from the master's household, or not even from Rome. In the early Empire, the city of Rome was a cosmopolitan society, which embraced people from all over the provinces or even beyond. Many such foreigners were presumably brought into the city to be the domestic slaves of wealthy families. Tacitus reports C. Cassius Longinus' speech to the senate, to the effect that a large household of the elite had become highly international, comprising slaves of a variety of nationalities; such a household would be mixed with slaves of different skin-colour, and some of their Latin might not be good enough for communication; others might have their own religious beliefs or customs, or none at all, and a person so different in background would not behave in an entirely predictable way (Cassius Longinus advanced this as an argument for ruling them by terror, i.e., the execution of all four hundred slaves in the murdered master Secundus' household).[1] Earlier, the agricultural writer Varro advised his readers not to have too many slaves of the same *natio*, in order to avoid domestic conflict.[2] What Cassius Longinus and Varro concede in their alarmist statements is that basic characters or customs deriving from locality or race could not be completely obliterated, even though the institution of slavery formally deprived slaves of their identity, either that of national or individual altogether.[3]

In modern scholarship, the problem of slave 'foreigners' in a household raises two related topics of debate as to its cause and consequence; the sources of slaves at the outset, and the proportion of the foreign or servile people in the city as an outcome. The former questions to what extent home-born slaves dominated the slave population (sources of slaves), and the latter the issue of foreigners (many arguably servile by origin) and their descendents vis-à-vis the 'pure-blood' citizen population.[4] The proportion of home-born slaves certainly seems to have increased a great deal after the Augustan peace, though the import of slaves of non-Italian birth did not cease altogether either. We also hear voices among the contemporary elite authors alarmed at the situation and lamenting that Rome was full of foreigners, particularly of servile origin, as a result of large-scale and long-term assimilation of the servile population into the citizen body.[5]

In considering the question of mixed nationalities in a household, the records on epitaphs I will examine in this chapter are personal names of servile dependants. Although it is to an extent a speculative business, their servile names are often the only available indications of their roots, and a close analysis of their servile onomastic practice provides us, I believe, with a clue to the question of what it meant to have been slave 'outsiders'.

Names in the *columbaria*

While aristocratic Romans usually designated themselves by three names inherited through generations (*tria nomina*), their slaves were not entitled to such a privilege, but were bearers of a single name. Servile names, with a great range of vocabulary, could be comical, or reminiscent of their ethnic origins, or totally out of context. The names borne by slaves were generally signifiers of their servile status. It was only some 'outlaw' masters that allowed slaves to bear names that might invoke the status of *ingenui*.[6] At the point of being

---

[1] Tac. *Ann.* 14, 44.
[2] Varro, *Rust.* 1, 17, 5: *neque eiusdem nationis plures parandos esse; ex eo enim potissimum solere offensiones domesticas fieri.*
[3] The awareness of racial difference in slaves: Petr.102, *servi Aethiopes*; Juv. 2, 23; 6, 600; Tac. *Dial.* 29, *at nunc natus infans delegatur Graeculae alicui ancillae*; Greek women as *nutrices*, Evans, 1991, 195-199; on slavery contributing to the diffusion of nations in the Empire, Barrow, 1928, 208-229.
[4] On sources of slaves: Scheidel, 1997; Harris, 1999; on freedmen and their descendants in the city population: Frank, 1916; Taylor, 1961.
[5] The argument was advanced in the senate in AD 56 that the majority of those in equestrian and senatorial rank were in fact descendants of former slaves: Tac. *Ann.* 13, 27; Appian, *B Civ.* 2, 17, 120, "For the plebeians are now much mixed with foreign blood, freedmen have equal rights of citizenship with them, and slaves are dressed in the same fashion as their masters."; Suet. *Aug.* 40, 3-4 (as the motive of the *lex Aelia Sentia* in 4 AD) "Considering it also of great importance to keep the people pure and unsullied by any taint of foreign or servile blood, he was most chary of conferring Roman citizenship and set a limit to manumission."
[6] Cic. *Tusc.* 5, 22, 58, a certain Dionysius collected slaves and foreigners from the wealthy households and made them into his entourage and bodyguards, removing their servile names (*ex familiis locupletium servos delegerat, quibus nomen servitutis ipse detraxerat, et quibusdam convenis et feris barbaris corporis custodiam committebat*).

Table 6.1 Proportion of Greek, Latin, and other names

	STATILII (N=657)	LIVIA (N=608)	VOLUSII (N=301)	TOTAL (N=1566)
Greek names	381 (58%)	412 (68%)	205 (68%)	998 (64%)
Latin names	235 (36%)	145 (24%)	65 (22%)	445 (28%)
local / ethnic	20 (3%)	12 (2%)	0	32 (2%)
Unclear	21 (3%)	39 (6%)	31 (10%)	91 (6%)

Table 6.2.1 The most common servile names (male)

ranking	Name	Number of holders of the name							Total	% of the male population
		Statilii	Volusii	Livia	Iunii	Annii	Abuccii	Arruntii		
1	Felix	14 [4]	4	12 [4]	1	-	1	-	32 [8]	3.4%
2	Eros	17	1	6	3	2	2	1	32	3.4%
3	Hilario / -us	10	-	7	2	1	-	1	21	2.3%
3	Faustus / -io	10	2	4	2	-	1	2	21	2.3%
5	Phileros	8	-	3	-	-	1	-	12	1.3%
6	Antigonus	1	5	5	-	-	-	-	11	1.2%
6	Antiochus	6	1	2	-	-	-	2	11	1.2%
6	Iucundus	7	-	3	-	1	-	-	11	1.2%
9	Agatho	4	1	3	1	-	-	-	9	1.0%
9	Alexander	5	-	3	-	-	-	1	9	1.0%
11	Epaphra	4	1	2	-	-	1	-	8	0.9%
11	Amaranthus	4	-	4	-	-	-	-	8	0.9%
11	Onesimus	4	-	1	-	-	3	-	8	0.9%
11	Primus	4	1	1	-	1	1	-	8	0.9%

Note: [n] in cell is the number of holders whose gender is uncertain.

Table. 6.2.2 The most common servile names (female)

Ranking	Name	number of holders of the name							Total	% of the female population
		Statilii	Volusii	Livia	Iunii	Annii	Abuccii	Arruntii		
1	Secunda	6	-	6	-	-	-	1	13	2.6%
2	Erotis	5	1	5	-	1	-	-	11	2.2%
3	Helpis	2	2	3	-	-	2	1	10	2.0%
4	Hilara	6	1	1	-	-	1	-	9	1.8%
4	Prima	6	2	-	-	-	1	-	9	1.8%
4	Iucunda /-e	5	-	2	-	1	1	-	9	1.8%
7	Nice	4	1	2	-	-	1	-	8	1.6%
7	Aucta	2	3	2	-	-	1	-	8	1.6%
7	Helena / -e	4	-	2	-	-	-	2	8	1.6%
10	Hedone	2	2	1	-	-	2	-	7	1.4%
10	Felicula / -icla	5	-	1	-	-	1	-	7	1.4%
10	Fausta	5	-	1	1	-	-	-	7	1.4%

Table 6.2.3 Total readable names in seven *columbaria*
(N=1429) (excluding those whose gender is uncertain)

	female	male
(a) Total number of individuals (=number of names)	498	931
(b) Number of 'kinds' of names (i.e. without duplication)	296	512
Ratio of shares per a name (a)/(b)	1.68	1.82

manumitted into a Roman citizen (we do not know what the nomenclature of a Junian Latin was like), a slave encounters the onomastic practice of the free. A freedman, his single name in slavery now turning into *cognomen*, preceded by the *praenomen* and *nomen* taken from the former master, awkwardly adopts both elements of two separate naming practices, servile and the free.

In examining the *columbaria* inscriptions, the slave's single name and freedmen's *cognomen* are not distinguished for the reason that their exact legal status is often not stated (vd. Chapter 4, Table 4.1.), and here it is assumed that the two are ultimately the same thing. One of the characteristics of the servile names is the predominance of Greek names over Latin names.

While Greek names occupy a large majority (average 64%), Latin names were held by about one third of servile dependants in the *columbaria*. Aside from the sheer number of the holders, a wider range of names were available in Greek than in Latin. If we look at the names most frequently found in the *columbaria* (Table 6.2.1-2), apart from Greek name 'Eros', three out of the four most common male names in the *columbaria* were all Latin names, 'Felix', 'Faustus', 'Hilario', and for female, the Latin name 'Secunda' is at the top of the list.[7] This, together with the fact that the number of those holding Latin names was less than half of those who held Greek names (Table 6.1), means that much less variety of Latin names was available for slaves. In particular, some Latin names could be dangerously confused with the *cognomina* taken by aristocrats. For instance, taking the same name as the aristocratic master Lucius and Quintus Volusius 'Saturninus' would have been carefully avoided by their servants – and there were none called as such –, whereas the *columbaria* of the Statilii, Livia, and others, certainly had slaves or freedmen called 'Saturninus'. I suppose that even though there were typically 'servile' names (such as 'Eros'), it was in the end a very grey area especially when it came to the distinction of 'servile' Latin names and 'elite' cognomen.

The diverse variety of slave names seems to imply a degree of mixture of people from different areas of the Empire and beyond. In a rough estimate, three out of five people had their own distinct names that were not shared with anybody else in the seven *columbaria* (Table 6.2.3). The situation is sharply contrasting to the image envisaged by Pliny that there used to be only slaves called Marcipor or Lucipor belonging to the master Marcus or Lucius. Pliny goes on to say that nowadays so many outsiders had come into the household (he talks of a 'crowd of outsiders in a house', *in domo turba externa*) and consequently their names had become so diverse that owners needed some help to be reminded of their names.[8]

While popular servile names or a diversity of names in the *columbaria* do not themselves provide any clearer a picture of the members' places of origin, there are some distinct names that connote the 'foreignness' of their bearers and are likely to suggest their native locality, that is the names given in the local languages (Table 6.3). In the laborious compilation of slave names known from inscriptions and literary sources, Solin (1996) classified all slave names by derivation in three volumes; for the most part they are either Latin or Greek names, but also included are ten additional small categories of names derived from other languages, so-called 'barbarischen Namen.'[9] The famous example of a 'barbarian' name is Spartacus, a Thracian shepherd and then a captive at war, sold into slavery to become a gladiator at Capua. His name is said to have been one of those peculiar to Thracians.[10]

As is shown in Table 6.3, the Statilian *columbarium* contained about twelve kinds of such 'barbarian' names, held by the servants. An equivalent set is also found in Livia's *columbarium*. In particular, a Semitic name might indicate a bearer's background as Jewish; it is reported that Livia actually received legacies that include slaves from Herod and his sister Salome.[11] We find the Statilian *paedagogi* with Semitic names in both *columbaria* (Zabda and Malchio), and of two *ad vestem* (in charge of clothes), one had a Semitic name (Malchio; the other with Illyrican name, Dasius). But these might not necessarily practice Judaism, since, if so, they would be likely to have joined a Jewish community for burials if they could, which were numerous in Rome, instead of sharing the *columbarium* with those who were perhaps of a variety of different religious beliefs.[12] Three *lecticarii* (litter-carriers) and a *strator* (groom) of the Statilii, both

---

[7] Solin, 1996, 680, gives the top ten slave names among more than 28,000 attestations found in inscriptions from Rome; from the top, Felix (m.) (461 attestations), Eros (346), Hermes (328), Hilarus (248), Prima (213), Antiochus (189), Alexander (186), Onesimus (185), Faustus (184), Primus (184); cf. the review of Solin's works by Bodel, 2003.

[8] Plin. *HN*. 33, 6, 26.
[9] As Solin (1996, xxii) admits, the distinction between each language group is to a degree subjective.
[10] Plut. *Vit. Crass.* 8; Solin, 1996, 610.
[11] Barret, 2002, 176.
[12] Although there were sporadic expulsions of Jews from Rome by Tiberius and Claudius, the Roman government generally acknowledged and protected the right of Jews living in their closed community: Sherwin-White, 1967, 96-100; Tac. *Ann.* 2, 85; Dio, 57, 18, 5a; Dio 60, 6, 6; cf. Suetonius' account that Claudius expelled Jews from Rome because they were causing constant disturbances at the instigation of 'Chrestus' (*Iudaeos impulsore Chresto assidue tumultuantis Roma expulit*) (*Claud.* 25, 3); cf. Tac. *Ann.* 15, 44; Mottershead, 1986, 149-157; on slavery and various religious cults, Barrow, 1928, 223-229.

Table 6.3 'Barbarian' names

Language group	Statilian servants with 'barbarian' names	Livia's servants With 'barbarian' names
Semitic	(A284) T. Statilius Malchio ad vestem (A166) Marta (A311) Statilia Martha Alexandri l. (A105) Barnaeus Sisennae strator paternus (B004) Masa Tauri l. (male) (A048) Zabda faber (A212) T. Statilius Zabda paedag. Statiliae	(4289) M. Livius Alconis l. Barnaeus (3999) Malchio Drusi paedagogus decurio
Anatorian	(A163) **Iazemus** Posidippi lib. (A022) **Aba** lecticarius	(4095) **Anna** Liviae Maecenatiana (4178) **Ninna** Lamachi l.
Thracian	(A308) **Teres** cubicularius (A232) **Bithus** Tauri lecticarius (A096) **Trucunda** lecticarius	-
Iranian	(A276) **Sasa** ex hortis topiarius	(4100) **Arsames** Antoniae (mater Cissi) (4183) **Sasa** Liviae
Egyptian	-	(4169) Livia Aug. l. **Thermutario**
Illyrian	(A237) T. Statilius Tauri l. **Dasius** ad vestem avi (A187) (A325) T. Statilius **Dasius**	-
African	-	(4171) Lullu Liviae l. (coniunx Antigoni Liviae l.)
Celtic	-	(4072) **Litto** Liviae l. decurio (male)

'masculine' jobs, held Thracian names 'Bithus', 'Trucunda', an Anatorian name 'Aba', and a Semitic name 'Barnaeus'. It is tempting, though misleading, to draw 'racial stereotypes' from their names and occupations, as the ancient elite authors often did.

Although more ambivalent a category, the other group of names refers to certain geographical areas or foreign tribes, which might suggest the holders' association to them. 'Falernus' the *dispensator* of Statilia seems to point to the Falernus ager in Campania. An unusual name 'Bithynicus' implies that this slave of Statilius Corvinus might come from Bithynia (A244). Likewise, 'Suebus' *Germanus* coincides with the name of a Germanic tribe (A064), and 'Milensia' (A297) with Miletus, or T. Statilius Tauri l. 'Cnidus' (B014) with Cnidus, both towns in Caria, and 'Medus' *lecticarius* may be Persian by birth (A061), and so on.[13] Many of these names are unusual enough to carry specific ethnic connotations, and they or possibly their parents might have originated from such places.

Though certainly not always the case, there are some examples of coherence of name and origin. According to Macrobius, Publilius Syrus, the author of mimes and protégé of Caesar, was a Syrian by birth, and brought into Rome as a slave, although eventually his master gave him his freedom in reward for his intelligence.[14] Though Macrobius does not give any reason for describing him as a Syrian, the cognomen 'Syrus', which was probably also his name in slavery, coincides with his alleged racial origin. A similar connection of *natio* and name is found in Terence, i.e., Publius Terentius Afer. This most celebrated writer of plays in the second century BC was born in Carthage, and started off as a slave of the senator Terentius Lucanus, and was later manumitted by him.[15] Strabo refers to an Athenian custom, which gives slaves the names of the peoples from whom they were imported, such as 'Lydos' or 'Syros', or the names which were common among these people, like 'Manes' or 'Midas' for a Phrygian, or 'Tibios' for a Paphlagonian (7, 3, 12). Varro also mentions the practice that a slave might be named after a slave-dealer or place, from whom and where the master made a purchase.[16] As Ulpian states that slave-dealers should always declare slaves' nationality (*natio*) at auction, slaves' national origin was one of the first options from which their names might be derived.[17]

---

[13] (A373) 'Zmyrna' Postumiana and (A343) 'Ismyrne' veterana, both from Smyrna, the town in Ionia? (A236) 'Hellas' Epinici vicaria; (A351) 'Hellas'; (A252) 'Lesbia'; (A425) 'Corinthias' Statili Faustionis et Statiliae Hedones delicium; (A255) 'Chius' l. Sisennae silentiarius, from Chios?; (6221) 'Helico', the mountain in Boeotia? ; (A240) 'Ia' Aucti l., an Ionian?; Statilia Tauri l. 'Albana' (B017); In other *columbaria*; the Arruntii (5944) L. Arruntius L. l. 'Halus'; the Volusii (7307) 'Delphicus' L. Volusi Saturnini ser.; (7307) 'Donysa' vicaria; Livia (4620) 'Donusa', etc.; the *columbarium* of Iunius Silanus records a slave called 'Celtus', and the *columbarium* of Annius Pollio, 'Dacus *insularius*; (7612) *Celtus M. Silani a munera*; (7407) *Dacus insularius*; Solin, 1996, 39, 372, 377 et al. Note a slave 'Romanus' of Livia (3970).

[14] Macrobius, *Saturnalia*, 2, 7, 6-8.

[15] Suet. *vita Terentii*, 1, *Publius Terentius Afer, Karthagine natus, serviit Romae Terentio Lucano senatori, a quo ob ingenium et formam non institutus modo liberaliter sed et mature manumissus est. Quidam captum esse existimant, quod fieri nullo modo potuisse Fenestella docet, cum inter finem secundi Punici belli et initium tertii natus sit et mortuus; nec si a Numidis et Gaetulis captus sit, ad ducem Romanum pervenire potuisse, nullo commercio inter Italicos et Afros nisi post deletam Karthaginem coepto.*

[16] Varro, *Ling.* 8. 21.

[17] If the nationality of a slave had not been rightly given at this point, the unsatisfied purchaser could take back the slave to the seller for reimbursement: *Dig.* 21, 1, 31; 50, 15, 4, 5 (Ulpian); cf. Suet. *Aug.*

M. L. Gordon has examined the names of slaves that indicated specific geographical area or race, as a possible indication of the bearer's birth. Kajanto, in his study of Latin *cognomina*, also refers to such names as an evidence of one's origin, pointing out a "considerable amount of correlation between geographical *cognomina* and the findspots of the inscriptions". He could list 162 such *cognomina* that corresponded to their actual localities.[18] Certainly it is wrong to suppose that these names always corresponded to the bearers' origins, and a slave might be given the name of a particular *natio* without any relevance. As Kajanto (1965, 45) cautions, names such as 'Atticus' or 'Graecus' were "so common as adjectives in Latin that they were unlikely felt to be foreign at all".[19] Indeed, it is obscure to what extent the names of the Statilian *ancillae* such as 'Acte' *quasillaria* (A050), 'Italia' *textrix* (A033), or 'Italia' *quasillaria* (A100), actually reflect their descents. Nevertheless, it is worth taking notice of other less ambiguous references to geographical areas in personal names, which indicate a certain degree of mixture of people from different localities in a household.

If these are the names 'possibly' linked with the bearers' places of origin, other slaves gave more straightforward sign of their origins, as a second name or as an adjective appended to the name (but not as an agnomen or as the name itself).[20] This type of record of *natio* is almost exclusive to the Statilian *columbarium*.

Table 6.4 Individuals with clear indication of *natio*

Syria	(A099) Auge Sura quasillaria (A028) Prima Sura Alexandri l. pist. (A035) Dapnis Sura
Asia Minor	(A301) Prima Erotis, Cappadoca (A165) Laudica Cilicissa (A095) Phileros Paplago lecticarius
Balkan	(A312) Secunda Thraecida (A101) Messia Dardana quasillaria; fecit Iacinthus unctor Dardanus
Africa	(A005) Preima Afra
Sicily	(A178) Rufio Siculus

There was a woman called 'Statilia Sura' (A059) (Sura as cognomen), but here, this indication of Syrian birth was attached to Auge *quasillaria*, Prima, and Dapnis, as if a second name. Others are Prima a Cappadocian, Laudica a Cilician, Phileros *lecticarius* a Paphlagonian, and Secunda a Thracian. Messia *quasiallaria* was distinctively a Dardanian, commemorated by a certain Iacinthus *unctor*, who also identifies himself as a Dardanian. Messia and Iacinthus might be kinsmen, enslaved together and sold into the Statilian household from the same slave-dealer's platform. The Dardanians were an Illyrian tribe, and Strabo describes them as utterly wild and as living in caves, but as having a taste for music, constantly playing flutes and string instruments.[21] Slaves from the areas of Cappadocia, Thrace, Dacia, or Moesia evoked in the minds of the ancients 'masculine' and untamed nature and were often found performing 'masculine' work, as litter-carriers (porters) or as shepherds.[22] There was also one African woman called Preima, probably correctly 'Prima', and lastly, Rufio 'Siculus' from Sicily.[23] One may notice that eight out of eleven with *nationes* are females,[24] and they held extremely 'ordinary' Latin names despite their specific ethnic mark. Three of them were similarly called 'Prima' and one 'Secunda' (vd. Table 6.2.2, common names for females). Other names (Auge, Dapnis, Laudice, Phileros, and Rufio) are also the sorts commonly held by slaves.[25] It appears that the names of 'ethnic minorities' were chosen, without much thought, from the most typical Latin slave names. I suggest that this is indicative of the consequence of enslavement, their supposedly original 'barbarian' names struck off from them and replaced with the most banal slave names. It is often mentioned in literary sources that slaves of certain nationalities cost a fortune and were highly valued as luxuries.[26] Wealthy masters liked to keep foreign slaves as waiters at banquets or for other kinds of services. The

---

7: Augustus originally had the name 'Thurinus' (from the place name Thurii), which Mark Antony used to ridicule.

[18] Gordon, 1960; Kajanto, 1965, 43-53.

[19] Some such names clearly conflict with the implications of the mother's name, though the father's nationality might have influenced the children's name; (A345) '*Atticus*' *f(ilius), Stactes nutricis*; (A261) *Statilia Athenais, mater 'Campani'*; (A348) *Statiliae Hilarae, 'Attice' posuit matri suae bene merenti*.

[20] On the records of *natio* in the Statilian epitaphs, *CIL* VI, p.1002.

[21] Strabo, 7, 5, 7; cf. Varro, who finds that women involved in agriculture or pastoralism in Illyricum are not inferior to men at work but continue a proper workforce side by side with men (*Rust.* 2, 10, 6-7).

[22] Petr. 63, *habebamus tunc hominem Cappadocem, longum, valde audaculum et qui valebat: poterat bovem iratum tollere*; Mart. 6, 77, 4, *quid te Cappadocum sex onus esse iuvat?*; Cic. *red. sen.* 6, 14, *Cappadocem modo abreptum de grege venalium diceres*; Juv. 9, 142-144, *et duo fortes de grege Moesorum, qui me ceruice locata securum iubeant clamoso insistere circo*; Mart. 7, 80, 11-12, *tibi captiuo famulus mittetur ab Histro qui Tiburtinas pascere possit oues*; Mart. 10, 76, *de Cappadocis eques catastis*; Noy, 2000, 214-218.

[23] From the *columbarium* of the Abucciii, we find 'Eros Graecus': (8142) L. Abuccius Eros Graecus; in Livia's *columbarium*, a mother and a son related to a person originated from Maronia, a town in Thrace; (4173) *Mima l. Maronia dat...Timotheo Aug. l. Maron. filio suo*; cf. the Iunii (7614) *Eutacto pictori 'Eudaemoni'*.

[24] cf. D. Noy's study on foreign immigrants in Rome shows the majority of foreign civilians in pagan inscriptions (76.7%) are male: Noy, 2000, 60-61.

[25] vd. the catalogue of Solin, 1996; 'Rufio' as a common name of slaves, Cic. *Mil.* 22, 60; cf. a royal member of the German tribe Cherusci, kept in Rome, bore the name 'Italicus' (Tac. *Ann.* XI 16).

[26] Juv. 11, 147-8, dinners served by Phrygian and Lycian slave waiters as well as by *vernae*; Hor. *Sat.* 2, 8, 14, a dark-coloured slave called 'Hydaspes', which was also the name of a river of India, works as a waiter at the dinner of a rich Nasidienus; Petr. 31; 34-35, slave boys from Alexandria, Egypt, and Ethiopia at Trimalchio's dinner: *tandem ergo discubuimus pueris Alexandrinis aquam in manus nivatam infundentibus...ubinde intraverunt duo Aethiopes capillati cum pusillis utribus, quales solent esse qui harenam in amphitheatro spargunt, vinumque dedere in manus; aquam enim nemo porrexit...circumferebat Aegyptius puer clibano argenteo panem*; Quintilian (1, 2, 7) noted, among others, corrupted manner of speech of *deliciae Alexandriniae*; cf. a general taste of the elite Romans for things Alexandrian, Suet. *Nero*, 20; Caes. *B Civ.* 3, 110, 2.

Statilii's preference of 'female' foreign slaves (over 'male') might perhaps be a clever strategy to produce children from such ethnic slaves; above all, it would have been cheaper to buy female than male, and their children would be home-born *and* have distinctive precious 'foreign' blood.

Among many apparently plain neutral names, those who retained their 'foreignness' look particularly distinct. If we compare occupational groups of the Statilii, that of the litter-carriers (*lecticarii*) stands out for the uniqueness of its members' names. The fourteen *lecticarii* recorded in this *columbarium* included an unusual number of persons who retained names suggestive of non-Latin origin: Phileros 'Laplago' (A095), and Aba (A022), Bithus (A232),[27] Trucunda (A096) of 'barbarian' names, and Medus (A061) and Potamo (A294) are names indicating Persia, and finally, Astragalo 'Afrianus' (A023), the agnomen, which perhaps indicates that he was previously a slave of a certain 'Afer', possibly an African by birth. In contrast, ten *Germani* of the Statilii generally held 'ordinary' Latin names (except the aforementioned 'Suebus' *Germanus*). Likewise, among twelve bedchamber servants (*cubicularii*), only one had a 'barbarian' name (A308), and among ten financial-managers (*dispensatores*), none indicates any connection with alien *natio*. This 'foreignness' of the Statilian *lecticarii* in comparison with other groups seems to suggest something unique about the recruitment of this professional group.

The question of slaves' origins might be perceived as closely connected to the question of the sources of slaves. It is generally assumed that the Augustan peace brought a significant reduction in slave supply by way of wartime captivity, and that what followed in consequence was a relative shift from the purchase of slaves to self-reproduction. Scheidel (1997) and Harris (1994) disagreed as to the degree of importance of slave breeding as major source of slaves.[28] K. Bradley makes a good point regarding the limitations of the ancient sources that we rely on for our understanding of Roman society: while the historical reports by Polybius or Livy naturally emphasise the numbers of war captives, it does not follow that slave-breeding was unimportant during the Republic. Although references in legal sources to home-born slaves are more abundant in the Imperial period, our knowledge of the laws that derive from the Republican period is generally very little in comparison to those of the Imperial period, and the same is true for the epigraphic evidence. Occasional mentions of female captives and female slaves on the farm may suggest that breeding was not necessarily neglected even during the period of great warfare.[29] Moreover, it must be noted that brutal means of adult enslavement did not totally lapse even after Augustus; there was in fact plenty of warfare on the Northern frontier down to AD 16 and it continued to bring in war captives,[30] and it is reported that groups of kidnappers operated under the name of the *collegia*, and caught travellers and confined them in the *ergastula*, a situation which forced Augustus and Tiberius to set up a police force to keep a constant watch.[31] Such criminal activities could not be a substantial source of slaves, but as the slave trade remained profitable during the first century AD,[32] it appears that neither means of enslavement of the people from outside Rome ran out.

The total number of individuals with positive indications of foreign origin is admittedly a small minority. Those who recorded the *natio* constitute only 1.7%, and those of 'barbarian' names are 3.1% of the whole population of the Statilian *columbarium*. However, it is reminded here that 'barbarian' names tended to be Graecised or Latinised so as to make them sound familiar, or simply struck off and replaced with another. In this way, there is always the possibility of 'hidden' ethnic identities under ordinary Latin or Greek names.[33] Besides, an inconceivable degree of grey area surrounds the issues in regard to the sources and origins of slaves. Even though we can say some slaves in the *columbaria* were foreign, we do not know how they were originally enslaved, or more importantly, I think, how they ended up there. Entrance to slavery might be either through war-captivity, child exposure, self-enslavement, or birth. But the process a slave went through after their initial enslavement would have been greatly varied and some probably transferred through more than one master in the vicissitudes of a life, and even more so depending on what kind of slaves we are talking about: the Familia Caesaris, for instance, might have been consisted of more self-enslaved people, if compared to ordinary domestic servants of private individuals. It was probably unusual that 'foreign' slaves could immediately serve the elite family without training. Even if elite households were full of foreigners as claimed by literary authors such as Tacitus' Cassius Longinus or Pliny, it seems doubtful that many such domestic foreign slaves were ones purchased

---

[27] 'Bithus' was a common Thracian name. According to Noy, 2000, 220-221, among the bearers of the name Bithus (or Bitus or Vitus), 34% were of servile origin, while 36% were soldiers.

[28] Harris, 1994 and 1999; Scheidel, 1997.

[29] Bradley, 1987b, 49-50.

[30] e.g., in 12-9 BC, Tiberius defeated the Pannonians and after he disarmed them, deported and sold the majority of the adult male inhabitants into slavery (Dio, 54, 31, 2-3); Harris, 1980, 122; Bradley, 1987b, 48-49; Tac. *Hist*. 1, 68, the Helvetii defeated in AD 70 were sold into slavery (*multa sub corona venundata*); cf. some of the Frisii in Germany, handed over as slaves to a Roman governor as part of tribute in AD 28: Tac. *Ann*. 4, 72.

[31] Suet. *Aug*. 32; id. *Tib*. 8, *repurgandorum tota Italia ergastulorum, quorum domini in inuidiam uenerant quasi exceptos supprimerent non solum uiatores sed et quos sacramenti metus ad eius modi latebras compulisset;* Apul. *Met*. 7, 9.

[32] Bosworth, 2002, argued that Vespasion, around AD 62 returning from Africa as proconsul before he becomes emperor, impoverished, started to invest in the slave trade and eventually made profits, which helped to enhance his position in politics; Suet. *Vesp*. 4, 3.

[33] Gordon, 1924, 98-109, suggests that slaves captured or purchased by Romans have often held the name of their original nationalities in "a Graecised or Latinised form" of either translation or of similar sounds. For instance, 'Vitalis' from the Celtic name 'Venobius', or 'Acme' from the Syrian 'Hacma'. Some familiar slave names might be the result of this transformation; cf. Joshel, 1992, 41.

Table 6.5 Naming practice from father to son

	T. FRANK'S SAMPLE (N=1347)				COLUMBARIA (N=40)			
Father	Greek name 859 (64%)		Latin name 488 (36%)		Greek name 30		Latin name 10	
Son	G 460 (34%)	L 399 (30%)	G 53 (4%)	L 435 (32%)	G 20	L 10	G 2	L 8

*G=Greek name, L=Latin name

from the slave-dealers. More often, I suppose, the newly-acquired slaves had to go through constant small-scale exchanges between intermediate owners or acquaintances before they could even see the face of their aristocratic master.[34] The possible routes by which slaves were circulated were probably far too complicated and dynamic a process to be neatly classified under a few headlines.

The second generation of slaves

If the question of the sources of slaves is a very obscure territory, likewise that of freedmen and their descendants in the city population. Tenney Frank's article 'Race mixture in the Roman Empire' (1916) examined epigraphic evidence and asked a bold question, to what extent people of 'foreign' extract dominated over 'native' inhabitants in Rome. On the assumption that a Greek cognomen indicates the foreign birth of its bearer or his ancestor, and a Latin cognomen native Italian birth, his reading of a bulk of urban inscriptions made him remark that nearly 90% of the people in Rome had foreign ancestry originating in a recent generation and that most of them arrived as slaves. Furthermore, he suggested that slaves of Greek names mostly came from Greece and the Hellenised East, whereas Latin names were given more to the Western 'barbarians'. Not surprisingly, his thesis has received much criticism from subsequent scholars; Greek names were held even by those with a clear record of their non-Greek *natio*, such as the emperor's Germanic bodyguards (apparently one third of them held Greek names).[35] M. L. Gordon's alternative view was that Greek was the language of slave-dealers rather than that of the slaves themselves, and that Greek names became customary as servile names since the slave trade was once largely in the hands of Greek merchants.[36]

I cite Frank's observation of epigraphic evidence here because, despite the criticisms, I think that his method is relevant and useful in asking the question as to the assimilation of servile population in terms of transmission of slave names. He found 1347 sets of names of father and son from his original sample of total 13,900 inscriptions in the section 'Sepulcrales' in *CIL* volume VI, and examined the correlation of Greek and Latin names between father and son:

The figures show that while two thirds of fathers in samples held Greek names, when we turn to their son's generation, the proportion is almost reversed. What made the most difference is that fathers with Latin cognomen rarely gave sons Greek names. Accordingly, Greek names were to diminish from 64% to 38% in a single generation of fathers and sons. When this is compared with the small sample of the *columbaria* inscriptions, from which I could find only 40 pairs of fathers and sons (and daughters included), the trend observed in Frank's data is noticeable here as well; in the *columbaria* - a population which presumably consisted of more slaves than Frank's sample (which was taken from the section 'Sepulcrales') - Greek names are naturally higher in proportion to Latin names, but the proportion of Greek name likewise drops from 75% to 55% in a generation.

This seems to lead to the fairly reasonable conclusion that Greek names were considered as, in Frank's word "a sign of dubious origin", and hence, it might follow, "the presence of a Greek name in immediate family is good evidence that the subject of the inscription is of servile or foreign stock."[37] Duff agreed in a more moderate tone that "the first thing that a Greek name suggested was servile origin or extraction".[38] One may recall Suetonius' account of the prominent grammarian Lucius Crassicius, a former slave of Tarentine birth, who changed his servile Greek cognomen 'Pasicles' into the Latin name 'Pansa' some time after manumission. Similarly, Icelus the trusted freedman of emperor Galba was honoured (for reporting the life-saving news of the death of Nero to his patron) and was given the Latin name 'Marcianus', thus called 'Ser. Sulpicius Marcianus'.[39] The change of the Greek cognomen into Latin was perceived as one

---

[34] Petr. 47, "*ex quota decuria es?*" *Cum ille se ex quadragesima respondisset,* "*Empticius an*" *inquit* "*domi natus?*" "*Neutrum*" *inquit cocus* "*sed testamento Pansae tibi relictus sum.*"

[35] A total of eleven *Germani* of the Statilii also included two with Greek names.

[36] Frank, 1916; Gordon, 1924, 101-103; Duff, 1928, 5-8; Westermann, 1955, 96; Taylor, 1961; Treggiari, 1969, 5.

[37] Frank, 1916, 693; Taylor, 1961, 125-127; cf. Salway, 1994, 131; Noy, 2000, 179-183, suggests that some foreigners might have both a local name and a 'Roman' name.

[38] Duff, 1928, 56; cf. Taylor, 1961, argued that Greek *cognomina* were predominant in inscriptions from the city, and that most of Greek *cognomina* were originally slave names, and therefore that freedmen dominated the free population.

[39] On Cassicius, Suet. *Gram.* 18; *L. Crassicius, genere Tarentinus, ordinis libertini, cognomine Pasicles, mox Pansam se transnominavit*; cf. Mart. 6, 17, *Cinnam, Cinname, te iubes uocari: non est hic, rogo, Cinna, barbarismus? tu si Furius ante dictus esses, Fur ista ratione dicereris*; cf., Wiseman, 1985c, 189; Kaster, 1995, 196-198; on Icelus, Tac. *Hist.* 1, 13; Suet. *Galba*, 14, 22; Plut. *Galba*, 7; Sandys, 1969, 221.

effective way of lessening the disadvantages and stigma carried by former slaves.

Of course, attitudes towards servile names differ according to individual perception. Some freedmen in the *columbaria* regard the *cognomen* as hereditary, where father and son are homonymous: the freedman father 'T. Statilius Tauri l. Mystes', gave the same *cognomen* (but Latinised?) to one son 'T. Statilius Mystus' and a different one to the other son 'T. Statilius Thallus' (A419). Likewise, we find the *pater* 'Q. Volusius December' and the *filii* 'Q. Volusius Merops' and 'Q. Volusius December' (1868); the *pater* 'L. Volusius Hamillus' and *filius* 'Hamillus' (7379); and finally 'Q. Volusius Antigonus' in three generations (7376). In these families, the conventional praenomina (Titus, Quintus, Lucius) apparently stop functioning, but instead their servile cognomina are treated as personal names. On the other hand, the following two examples seem to lack the notion of cognomen as hereditary but reminiscent of servile single names: the *pater* L. Volusius Hermes and *filius* L. Volusius Primanus (Latinising) (7374); the *pater* L. Volusius Diodorus and the *filius* L. Volusius Zenon (7380).

Despite the differences in the treatment of their own *cognomina* (formerly servile names), the way freedmen in the *columbaria* adopted the nomenclature of the aristocratic masters is strictly conventional. The novel mode of *tria nomina* adopted by the masters of the *gens Statilia* (vd. Chapter 2) did not affect their freedmen: at the event of manumission, freedmen unanimously received the conventional *praenomen* 'Titus' of the Statilii; the special *praenomina* ('Taurus', 'Sisenna') never became part of their nomenclature. As for the Volusii with conventional nomenclature, slaves received each master's *praenomen* (either Quintus or Lucius) upon manumission. But for those who possess *tria nomina* in the *columbaria*, whether the Statilii or the Volusii that remained conventional, the original function of the *praenomina* is largely ceased though they still continue to record one.[40] It would have been hardly necessary to employ differentiating *praenomina* over already distinctive servile cognomen. It was the *cognomen* that distinguished the status of aristocratic masters and their freedmen, and amongst the descendants of servile origin it was again the *cognomen* that might be changed through generations or between brothers, while the *praenomen* and *nomen* of the aristocratic masters were equally shared by their freedmen and thus could expand indefinitely.

Conclusion

In the *columbaria* the people who possess proofs of their *nationes* are overall a minority, though we find a variety of names that indicate certain particular areas or tribes, which seem to suggest the presence of people from outside Rome. However, one's status as a foreigner does not immediately tells us the manner of their enslavement. No matter how much (or how little) we find slaves coming from outside Rome, it was perhaps exceptional for slaves fresh from the slave-dealers' platform to serve the Statilian or any other aristocratic families. To an extent, a common perception was that all slaves, even those born in household, were outsiders and therefore foreign. Naturally, the state of mind of servile families would have been a mixed one. On one hand, there was an urge to obliterate any trace suggestive of servile origins or 'outsider' status, whether born in Rome or outside. Some traces of their origins were no doubt forcibly struck off in the process of enslavement or in that of integration into the master's society. On the other, they were equally inclined to preserve their roots and retain the mark of their own local origins. The few people who retained the mark of their foreign birth would be all the more visible, even though it might be otherwise felt as a stigma. The fulfilment of either desire – especially the acts of giving names – is essentially checked by the masters' disposition. The slaves are generally more likely to possess Greek names than Latin ones, and the Greek vocabulary could offer a wider variety of names befitting to those in servile status and distinctive future *cognomina*. Understandably, some wished not to pass them on to their sons, or they themselves adopted more familiar Latin names when they were freed. We like to think that the *columbaria* at least allowed them freedom in dictating their own epitaphs, giving vent to their desire, whether that was desire for integration or for the preservation of roots.

---

[40] Even though the conventional *praenomen* had been losing its function, particularly for the Statilii, freedmen generally did not regard it as unimportant: the percentage of abbreviated praenomina (the cases of nomen and cognomen only) are 11% for the Statilii (9 out of 74), 10% for the Volusii (6 out of 52), and 8% for Livia (6 out of 83).

Chapter 7

The burial clubs for slaves and freedmen

Despite their marginal and hampered legal status in general, it is known that slaves could join various kinds of social clubs. One witnesses slaves and freedmen being associated with the *collegia* as early as the late second century BC. The epigraphic evidence from Campania and Minturnae shows that slaves, even female slaves, were an important part of various local religious organisations.[1] We also come across slave members in the often cited *collegium* of Diana and Antinous at Lanuvium; a regulation of this *collegium*, known in the inscription dated from AD 136, specifies that if a slave member gained his freedom, he should contribute an amphora of good wine (*quisquis seruus ex hoc collegio liber factus fuerit, is dare debebit uini [boni] amphoram*).[2] Clearly, slaves were not prevented from joining a club as long as they could fulfil the club's obligations, including the payment of entry fees and other regular dues. By doing so, slaves might have hoped to gain social connections and enter the community of the free, anticipating the day when they would finally achieve freedom and walk out of the master's household. At the same time, however, such freedom of social activity open to slaves had to be under supervision. The legal expert Marcianus emphasises that slaves could join a *collegium* only with the consent of their masters; if they neglected to secure the permission, the *curatores*, the officials of the *collegium*, were fined one hundred gold pieces (*centum aurei*, that is 2500 denarii or HS 10,000) for each illegal slave (cf. Table 7.2).[3]

In parallel to such funeral clubs in society, there appear to have been other sorts of formal or informal funeral organisations, the so-called *collegia domestica*, domestic funeral clubs, whose membership and governing body centred on the slaves and freedmen associated with a certain wealthy aristocratic household or *gens*. To take a clear example of a *collegium domesticum*, we have a series of epitaphs of the dependants of a mistress called Sergia Paullina, the daughter of L. Sergius Paullus (the consul around 150 AD). It is remarkable that her slaves and freedmen talk of their burial club located in the household, the '*collegium quod est in domu Sergiae Paullinae.*' We find seven such epitaphs, which uniformly refer to the *collegium domesticum*, along with individual commemorators who were in personal ties with the deceased – a common twofold structure of *collegium* and commemorator operating at a person's death.[4]

Setting aside the *collegium domesticum* of Sergia Paullina, can we find the operation of a similar organisation in the inscriptions of the *columbaria*? In other words, how did a household conduct the burials of a large number of servile staff members? Unfortunately, the degree of articulation found in the household of Sergia Paullina is quite exceptional, and it is rare to find clear records of *collegium* operations elsewhere. The *collegia domestica*, nonetheless, were certainly included as one category of the *collegia* by scholars of this subject in the late 19th century, J. P. Waltzing and T. Schiess, amongst others.[5] In what follows, I shall first investigate the indications of *collegia* operations from the *columbaria* inscriptions. The fragments of evidence thus gathered will further lead us to consider how the burials of slaves and freedmen of notable elite Roman families were taken care of and epitaphs set up for them. Such burial establishment, along with provision of food, clothes, and shelter, indicates a degree of welfare available for the servile members of privileged families in

---

[1] Westermann, 1955, 78; Waltzing, 1900, iv. 252, observes that there were many funeral clubs composed mainly of slaves, either as *collegia domestica* or *collegia* of public slaves; cf. slaves and freedmen as *magistri* or *magistrae* of the *collegium* in Minturnae, ILLRP 724-746.
[2] *ILS*, III, 7212; Hopkins, 1983, 213-215.
[3] *Dig.* 47, 22, 3, 2 (Marcianus): *seruos quoque licet in collegio tenuiorum recipi uolentibus dominis, ut curatores horum corporum sciant, ne inuito aut ignorante domino in collegium tenuiorum reciperent, et in futurum poena teneantur in singulos homines aureorum centum.*

[4] (9148) *Hermeroti arcario u(ixit) a(nnis) XXXIV, collegium quod est in domu Sergiae Paullinae, fecerunt Agathemer et Chreste Arescon fratri piissimo b. m.*; (10262) *Sergio Pio, Sergia Hesperis coniugi benemerenti fecit, ex collegio quod est in domo Sergiae Paullinae; uixit annis LXX*; (9149) *Hilaro aurifici collegium quod est in domo Sergiae L. [f.] Paullinae item...*; (10261) *d. m. Pardo quae et Hiarine, collegium quod est in domo Serg(iae) L(uci) f(iliae) Paullinae, item Pyrrus coniugi b. m. fec*; (10263) *d. m. L. Sergio Trophimo, patri piissimo Sergia Eutychia fil(ia), ex collegio familiae Serg(iae) Paulinae fecit*; (10264) *d. m. Eutychia[e, col]legium m[ajorum] et mino[rum?...qui] sunt in [domo] Sergiae L. f(iliae) Paull[i]na[e]*; (10260) *colleg[i]um [familiae] Serg(iae) [L(uci) f(iliae)] Paulli[nae] Cerdoni conseru[o] m(emoriae) c(ausa).*
[5] Waltzing, vol. IV, 1900, 167-176; Schiess, 1888.

Table 7.1 Signs of operations of the *collegia* in each *columbarium*

columbaria	The words used in inscriptions				v. Signpost / collective actions
	i. *collegium*	ii. *decurio*	iii. *curator* (*curo*)	iv. *quaestor* / *magister*	
Statilii	√	√	√	√	√
Volusii	√	√	√		
Livia		√	√		
Arruntii			√		√
Marcellae	√	√	√	√	
C. Annius Pollio		√			√
L. Caninius Gallus		√			
Abuccii					√
Nero Drusus		√			

Roman society. In this sense, the question here is related to the role of *domus* for slaves; the *domus*, as the *res publica* for slaves (and to a large extent for freedmen, too), provided them with a basic necessity of life and at the same time prospered by their labour.[6]

The signs of the *collegia domestica*

There are several indications or titles recorded in epitaphs that mark the operation of the *collegium*. Some simply refer to a *collegium* with nothing but the mention of occupational groups they belonged to.[7] A more elaborate one, the burial of a certain Statilia Ammia, was undertaken through the funeral club (*conlegium commorientium*), and five individual caretakers are listed:

(A066) Statilia Ammia hic sepulta est, quoius sepult(urae) curam egerunt conleg(ium) commorient(ium): Cerdo, ins(ularius), uir eius, Bathyllus, atriens(is), Musaeus, ost(iarius), Eros, ins(ularius), Philocal[us], unctor.

Some of the names appear again as caretakers for the burial of the freedman called Chius (A255, vd. *infra*). Apart from a small number of these cases clearly referring to the *collegium*, we may also take certain particular titles as indicating the officials of a *collegium*.[8] First of all, the *decuriones* functioned as a governing committee authorising the admission of certain individuals (ii, Table 7.1). Such *decuriones* are often, if not always, clearly of freed status.[9] The formula '*ex decreto decurionum*', '(the deceased was allowed to be buried in here) according to the decision of the *decuriones*', was recorded in two Statilian epitaphs, both addressed to individuals of non-Statilian *nomen*.[10] In the Volusian *columbarium*, at least five epitaphs were set up by permission of the *decuriones* (with phrases such as *ex permissu decurionum locus datus* etc.).[11] It is noted that the slave/freedman staff of some large households seem to have had their own *consilium* of *decuriones* as their representatives, at least for matters relating to burials.[12]

The references to another *collegium* official, *curator* (funeral caretaker), are found mostly in more elaborate epitaphs recording grander funerals (iii, Table 7.1). For instance, the funeral of a Statilian freedman Chius was undertaken by three caretakers, the *ostiarius* (door-keeper) Musaeus, the *insularius* (rent-collector) Eros, and the *colorator* (dyer) Amaranthus:

(A255) Chius l(ibertus), Sisennae silentiarius ex conlegio hic situs est. Curatores Musaeus, ostiar(ius), dec(urio),

---

[6] The household (*domus*) as a miniature state: vd. Chap.1.
[7] (A306) *T. Statilius Anoptes, pistor de conleg(io)*; (A305) *Antiochus lecticarius de conlegio*; (A067) *Philologus cellarius ex conlegio commorientes*; (7282) *Volusia L(ucii) l(iberta) Athenais de collegio*.
[8] The rank and order of officers within a *collegium*, from *magistri* or *quinquennales* to *curatores* and *quaestores* etc., are in Kornemann, *RE* IV, 1901, 417-8; Waltzing, 380-383; Royden, 1988, 12-17.
[9] Freedman *decuriones*: (10358) *M(arcus) Aemilius M(arci) libertus Anteros, decurio, primus ollas habet continentes VI. M(arcus) Aemilius M(arci) l(ibertus) Aescinus, Aemilia M(arci) l(iberta) Simene, M(arcus) Aemilius M(arcorum) duorum l(ibertus) Gihllo (sic); from the columbarium of C. Annius Pollio (7395-7429) in vinea Amendola: (7397) C(aius) Annius C(ai) l(ibertus) Familiaris, dec(urio); u(ixit) a(nnis) XXX.*
[10] (A015) *Familia T. Statili Tauri patris, ex d(ecreto) d(ecurionum), Antoniae M. l. Chryse, in bonore (sic) Statili Storacis, ollam dederunt*; (A202) *M. Iunius Ueiento, ex d(ecreto) d(ecurionum); u(ixit) a(nnis) XIII, infelix parentibus.*
[11] (7304); (7297) *loc(us) d(atus) dec(reto) decu(rionum)*; (7373) *p(oni) c(urauere?) d(ecreto) d(ecurionum)*; (7379) *loc(us) dat(us) d(ecreto) d(ecurionum)*; (7387) *l(ocus) d(atus) d(ecreto) d(ecurionum)*.
[12] An inscription of Anchialus, the *cubicularius* of an unknown household in Rome during the Augustan period, attests that he entered the status of *decurio* by agreement of the *decuriones* and of the *familia*: (9288) *Anchialus cub(icularius), aed(ilis), q(uaestor) ter(tium), in aedilitate decurio adlectus ex consensu decurionum et familiae uoluntate.*

Amaranthus, colorat(or), l(ibertus), Eros, insular(ius), dec(urio), de suo dant.

The first two *curatores*, Musaeus and Eros, were marked as *decuriones*, and apparently the same Musaeus and Eros also acted as caretakers at the funeral of Statilia Ammia mentioned above (A066). Furthermore, in this epitaph, the phrase '*de suo dant*' indicates that the *curatores* undertook the funeral for the deceased with money they contributed.

The important function of funeral clubs in general was to provide members with financial or material support for a part of or for a whole *funeraticium*, the sum expended on a funeral.[13] We do not know exactly how the *collegia domestica* were financially involved with members' burials. We ocasionally find, however, a *quæstor* elected as the treasurer of the *collegium* (iv, Table 7.1). T. Statilius Diodotus, a freedman of T. Statilius Taurus, was the *magister* (the 'president' of a *collegium*) and previously the *quaestor in familia* (A047). Also, a certain Zena Sutorianus was the *magister*, previously the *quaestor*, and *ad locationes* (in charge of leasing of the property?) (A026). The *columbarium* of the Marcellae knew as many as ten *quaestores* including a female.[14] These posts in *collegia* (*magister, quaestor*) must be distinguished from regular occupations and sources of livelihood; the officials of the *collegium* belonged to their own occupational groups at the same time.[15]

Apart from references to the *collegium* officials, certain collective actions of the *familia* and/or freedmen might also be considered as indications of virtual organisation as a *collegium*. Firstly, there are the inscriptions that claim group ownership of sepulchral buildings as, for instance, '*libertorum et familiae*' of certain masters. These inscriptions were usually erected as a signpost at a conspicuous place inside or outside the building. The *columbarium* of the Arruntii on the Esquiline was equipped with inscriptions of this type, one for the '*liberti et familia*' of 'L. Arruntius L. f. Ter(etina tribus)', and another for the '*liberti*' of Arruntia Camilla, daughter of Camillus.[16] Likewise, the *columbarium* of C. Annius Pollio on the via Appia gives the signpost inscription '*libertorum et liberarum et familiae C. Anni C. f.* Cor(nelia tribu) Pollionis' (7395).[17] Not confined to the *columbaria* structures, the signpost of ownership is often put up to specify and protect the territory of sepulchral space (*religiosus locus*).[18] In other cases, the '*liberti et familia*' or '*decuriones et familia*' etc. make dedications to a certain individual in honour either of his patronage or of meritorious service.[19] Even without formal recognition as a *collegium*, this is evidence of equal importance, since the *liberti* (or *decuriones*) and *familia* were acting together for burials and other related matters. Both Waltzing and Schiess loosely applied the term *collegium* to such collective bodies that appear in inscriptions even without specific evidence of formal organisation. In other words, collective actions, namely the dedication by a whole body of *familia* and/or *liberti* or the signposting of the burial space as such, are also recognised as *collegia domestica* at work, which is reasonable enough, since these individuals worked cooperatively for burial purposes beyond the obligation or ties of the *familia*. In this respect, the word *collegium domesticum* is taken in such a way as to indicate the group unity of slaves and freedmen, which excluded their aristocratic masters.[20]

As we see in Table 7.1, each *columbarium* presents its own characteristic evidence of the *collegia domestica*. We witness fairly complete indications of the *collegia* establishment in the *columbaria* of the Statilii and Marcellae. The Volusian *columbarium* contained two isolated cases of the operation of the '*collegium castrense*', with the *sumptuarius* (casher) and *a manu* (secretary) acting as caretakers (*curatores*). These two odd references to *collegium castrense* give the impression of a group somewhat seperate from the committee of the *decuriones* attested to in other epitaphs (*vd. infra*).[21] In Livia's *columbarium*, we witness persons with the status mark of '*decurio*' most frequently, though their specific function or authority is not mentioned at all. The other minor *columbaria* seem to lack presiding *collegia* officials as a regular feature, presumably because they were considered unnecessary.

The information on an issue of this kind that did not involve aristocratic masters is naturally only fragmentary, and no literary sources seem to refer to this manner of collective activity of slaves and freedmen. Admittedly,

---

[13] *Dig.* 11, 7, 37 (Macer).
[14] *CIL* VI, 4451, 4467, 4470, 4474, 4480, 4481, 4692, 4693, 4709, 4711.
[15] This seems an important distinction; cf. an epitaph from the *via Latina* (9409) recorded the career of sixty year old M. Allius Apollonius, as the *faber tignuarius* (carpenter), the *magister in familia* (the president of the *familia*), and *praefectus decuriae* (or *praefectus, [et] decurio*) (the head of a *decuria*); in the absence of formal *collegium*-officials, the *dispensator* (the financial manager of the household) might instead take over the responsibility of *quaestor* and *curator* and preside over the burials of the *familia*: (9322) *Libertorum et familiae M(arci) Corneli Maturi, curatore Timone disp(ensatore)*: (9320) *Familiae L. Coccei et liberteis et eorum, Dasius disp. de suo fac. coer.*
[16] *CIL* VI, 5931 and 5932: the latter was set up (*curante*) by a certain Arruntius Firmus; Waltzing, vol. III, 1900, 234.

[17] The same *columbarium* knew a *decurio*, a freedman of the Annii (7397).
[18] e.g., (11998) *monumentum circumdatum maceria cum protecto et area pertinet ad libertos et familiam Antoni Isochrysi*; (12361) *libertorum C. Arreni Marciani et posteris eorum, et qui in hoc monumentum tuendum contulerunt.*
[19] (A015); (10352) *Asinia M(arci) l(iberta) Prima, dec(uriones) et fam(ilia) h(onoris) c(ausa); uixit a(nnis) XXX*; (10357) *C(aio) n(ostro), decurion(es) et familia*; (10045) *decurionibus et familiae panni russei C(ai) Ceioni Maxim(i), quaestore Yperego. In fr(onte) p(edes) XXII, in agr(o) p(edes) XX.*; (9323) *Liberti et familia, Hilaro Camilli dispens(atori), honoris causa.*
[20] On group unity of the *familia* (including freedmen) in arrangement of funerals, Flory, 1978, 78-95; Parri, 1998, 58-59.
[21] (7281a) *Philomuso fulloni colleg. castresem, curatoribus Daphno sumptuario et Hedylalo a manu*; (7281) *[Ca]llistioni cellar(io) conleg(ium) castriense, Daphno sump(tuario), Hedylalo a manu, curatorib(us).*

the epitaphs with indications of the *collegia* are as a whole extremely small in proportion to the total number of epitaphs. For instance, from a total of 427 inscriptions in the Statilian *columbarium*, indications of the *collegium domesticum* are found in fewer than twenty epitaphs. Nonetheless, as is shown in Table 7.1, every *columbarium* contains indications of *collegia* operations in one way or another. The evidence overall seems to point to a *collegium*-like arrangement as customary for the running of the *columbarium*. In sum, despite scattered references to the *collegia*, we certainly see the shadow of the *collegia domestica*, either in the form of regular governing committees with leading officials, taking control of running the *columbaria*, or merely the *familia* acting together with freedmen without clear recognition as a *collegium*.

Functions of the *collegia domestica* for individual funerals

Having thus looked at the range of evidence available, we may reasonably suppose that the *collegia* or some sort of corporate activity of the *familiae* was taking place in the *columbaria*. Let us now consider in more detail the functions of the *collegia domestica* and the manner of the funerals as they appear in the *columbaria* epitaphs.

The first question is how the money and personnel were (or were not) assembled in order to conduct a burial and set up an epitaph for the deceased. The evidence on this point is very sparse, but we have some information from the following two Statilian epitaphs which record the actual cost of funerals. One is the epitaph of the freedman Antiochus, which recorded that his friends (*amici*) contributed money for his burial and provided for the *novendialia*, the feast held on the ninth day after the funeral. The reading of the costs spent for these is problematic, recorded in *CIL* as ✶ CCCCLXXXX (490 denarii), but Caldelli and Ricci transcribe it as MCCCCLXXXX ('1490'), in which case the amount was probably given by sesterces (Table 7.2, a).[22] For this special event, ten freedmen and slaves are named as the *curatores* (caretakers). The other epitaph with a record of funeral expenditure is that of Donatus, the *Germanus* (Germanic bodyguard) of Taurus, which was attended by the *sodales*, the group of fellow members (presumably of the *Germani*) (*sodales ei funus fecerunt*). Three individual caretakers (*curatores*) were named, and the funeral was attended by 130 people and cost 225 denarii (Table 7.2, b).[23]

Table 7.2 Comparison of the prices relating to slaves and freedmen

Instances	denarii	sesterces (HS)
a. The cost of funeral and/or banquet of Statilian freedman11 Antiochus (A258)	372.5 or **490**	**1490** or 1960
b. Funeral cost of Donatus, Germanus of Taurus (A428)	225	**900**
c. Funeral grant of the *collegium* at Lanuvium per each member (*ILS* 7212)	63	**250**
d. Nerva's burial dole	63	**250**
e. The entry fee and monthly payment of the burial club at Lanuvium.	(entry fee) 25	**100**
	(monthly) 0.3	**5 asses** (1.25HS)
f. Augustus' distribution of money to the people in 29BC from the booty at his triumph (Dio, 53, 28, 1)	100	**400**
g. The fine imposed on *curatores* when a slave member neglected to obtain the master's consent (Dig. 47, 22, 3, 2)	2500	10,000
h. The funeral cost to be spent in the will of the rich freedman Gaius Caecilius Isidorus, who died in 8BC (Plin. *HN* 33, 134-135)	277,778	**1,100,000**

Note: numbers in bold are the prices originally stated in the texts

As far as the *columbaria* epitaphs are concerned, the funeral costs appear to have been raised not by the *collegium* but by individual contributions, probably voluntary, either by the deceased himself *ante mortem* or by colleagues, friends, or relatives. The act of recording funeral expenses was first of all one of ostentation, and the sum involved was undoubtedly far beyond the allowance from the treasury of the *collegium*. For comparison, if we ignore the fluctuation of prices through the period, we may estimate an average funeral budget from the following two pieces of evidence. The funeral club of Diana and Antinous at Lanuvium (*ILS*, III, 7212), in the early second century AD, granted each member 250 sesterces as a burial fund (Table 7.2, c). The same price was offered by the emperor Nerva for the burials of the plebs in Rome (Table 7.2, d).[24] If this was the standard cost of burial for the middle/lower class plebs, the recorded *funeraticia* on these Statilian epitaphs are well above the standard of the ordinary plebs. Provided that a sestertius is one fourth of a denarius, 225 denarii spent on the funeral of Donatus the *Germanus* are equal to 900 sesterces. There are some uncertainties for the freedman Antiochus' funeral cost, but it appears that a similar or greater sum was spent, certainly exceeding the standard allowance of the ordinary plebs. In this regard, these individuals, Antiochus and Donatus, are considered to be higher ranked or more influential men than the

---

[22] (A258) *Antiochi l(iberti) hic ossa sita sunt. Amici contulerunt curatoribus Pansa l(iberto), Cisso l(iberto), Heracleone l(iberto), Theophilo, Mithridate, Salvio, Nicarcho, Agathone, Philotimo, Musaeo. Consumptum est in funere et in ossibus e[t i]n nouendi{n}(alibus) MCCCCLXXXX*; cf. *CIL* VI ...*CCCCLXXXX*; However, according to Keppie (1991, 21), 'M' (mille) was not usually used with other numerals.

[23] (A428) *Donatus Tauri German. hic situs est sodales ei funus fecerunt hom. CXXX ✶ CCXXV curatoribus Maximo Helicone Dapno.*

[24] Duncan-Jones, 1982, 127, 131, 222-223; Hopkins, 1983, 210-215.

majority of ordinary individuals in the *columbarium*: their funeral gatherings were organised by caretakers and attended by a significant number of fellow slaves and freedmen.

Meanwhile, we know almost nothing about the funeral costs of the majority in the *columbaria*, but it is supposed that burials in the *columbaria* required something beyond the capacity of individual slaves. Apart from the cost of burning a corpse,[25] one needed to acquire an urn for ashes, place an order for an epitaph to a *lapidarius* (stone-cutter), give religious rites and possibly also funeral banquets. Even the minimum cost of a proper funeral would not have been financially insignificant, and therefore might remain unaffordable by some plebeians or slaves of modest means.[26] The *collegia domestica* or the *familia* were obliged, I suppose, to give a decent burial even to a colleague who died without savings or family. This was perhaps the most important difference between the *collegia domestica* and the 'ordinary' *collegia* in society. Existing burial clubs were never to function as charitable groups (at least until the time of Christian influence), and in principle, those who could not pay mandatory fees were expelled or not entitled to benefit as a member from the burial fund. On the contrary, the *collegia domestica* acted on behalf of the aristocratic masters who should have been responsible for the burial of their domestics. As the jurist Ulpian states, if a person buried another man's slave, he could reclaim the expense from that slave's master.[27] Without the *collegia domestica*, every *dominus* was expected to see to it as a moral obligation that dead slaves be buried and disposed of in a proper manner. Acknowledging their own responsibility, however, it was a natural consequence for a *dominus* with hundreds of slaves to leave the issue wholly in the hands of slaves and their seniors (i.e. freedmen). Above all, such *collegia domestica* might be regarded as 'internal funeral undertakers', as part of the autonomous system sought by large households,[28] since without them one would have had to rely on public undertakers.[29] In this way, the *collegia domestica* and the *columbaria* were to benefit both masters and slaves.[30]

In Schiess' view, not all the *liberti* or *serui* in a household belonged to the *collegium domesticum*, but were left rather with freedom of choice, either to make their own burial arrangements outside or to remain in unity with their fellows as members of a *familia*.[31] As Schiess suggests, there was no reason for the *dominus* to insist that all staff be buried under the supervision of the *collegium domesticum*. In fact, about 39 epitaphs that clearly belong to the Statilian slaves/freedmen in the same period were discovered outside the *columbarium*.[32] For some reason, they did not (or could not) join the *columbarium*. As alternative options, they might acquire their own family tombs or purchase niches in another *columbarium* owned by a separate funeral club (assuming they had enough money to pay the fees).

Choosing funeral clubs also depended upon individual preferences in terms of where they wished to belong and which circle of people to be associated with. We must not forget that the *collegia* were important in bringing people together on various occasions. In the *columbarium* of the Abuccii, an epitaph of L. Abuccius Nereus and Abuccia Pieris records that they gave '*porticus* (portico), *scamna* (benches, stools), *mensae* (tables)' for their fellow-freedmen from their pockets.[33] These items in the inventory are presumably to be used for gatherings and banquets of the *collegium domesticum* (though not articulated as such) of the couple's fellow freedmen, all of whom originally belonged to the same *domus*.

It has been pointed out that the burials of plebs belonging to a funeral club were often carried out by family members and the *collegium* together. For a cost, either an entry fee, or regular monthly or annual subscription, funeral clubs gave their members the assurance of a proper funeral. As J. R. Patterson suggests, "if a member died without leaving a family, he would be buried by the club and saved from the ignominy and anonymity of a pauper's burial. If on the other hand an heir did exist at the time of his death, the club would provide a sum of money for the heir to pay for the funeral or perhaps in some cases a niche in the club's *columbarium*."[34] It has been demonstrated from quantitative analysis of the inscriptions that the commemorators of the deceased were primarily drawn from family members, in particular the heirs of the deceased.[35] Likewise for slaves and freedmen, although not all of them had families, a significant number of the deceased in the *columbaria* are

---

[25] Even the simplest epitaphs refer to nothing but bones and ashes (*ossa* or *cineres*) of the deceased e.g., (A003) *ossa Italiae textric(is)*; (A129) *Antigonaes l(ibertae) ossa hic sita sunt*; (Volusian) (7315) *cineres Vestalis*, et al.; cf. one Statilian epitaph uses the word '*humatus*', which might indicate the practice of inhumation: (A188) *T. Statilius Tauri l. Princeps minor, hic humatus est*; the sarcophagus in the Livia's *columbarium* belonged to the final period of the *columbarium*; Morris, 1992, 42-47.

[26] When Cicero gave detailed instruction on the 'proper' manners of funeral rites and burials, he claimed that certain provisions and expenses at funerals should be common for the rich and poor alike (*de Leg*. 2, 55-60, *haec laudabilia et locupletibus fere cum plebe communia; quod quidem maxime e natura est, tolli fortunae discrimen in morte*.).

[27] *Dig*. 11, 7, 31, 1 (Ulpian), *qui seruum alienum uel ancillam sepeliuit, habet aduersus dominum funerariam actionem*.

[28] The idea of self-sufficiency: Veyne, 1979, 261-280; Finley, 1973, 109-110; D'Arms, 1981, 82-84, 99; Treggiari, 1973, 245-250.

[29] The inscription from Puteoli (*AE* 1971, 88), the so-called *lex libitinae puteolana*, records the regulations of a public funeral contractor, which at the same time, astonishingly, is said to have undertaken the punishment and execution of slaves for private owners.

[30] Otherwise, without a proper burial organisation and a *columbarium* or any other sepulchral structure, the reality might be the rather bleak picture described by Horace of a slave disposing of a fellow slave's body: Hor., *Sat*. 1, 8, 8-9.

[31] Schiess, 1888, 29-30.

[32] Caldelli and Ricci, 1999, 135-140.

[33] *CIL* VI 8117 ...*porticum, scamna, mensas collibertis suis sua pecunia donum dederunt.*

[34] Patterson, 1992, 22-23; Hopkins, 1983, 213-214.

[35] Saller and Shaw, 1984, 126.

commemorated by their family members in servile status, out of filial duty or family affection. In my statistics concerning the *columbaria* inscriptions, in general nearly half of the commemorations of the deceased were by family members (the Volusian *columbarium* 63%, the Statilii 48%, Livia 45%). Commemorations of dead slaves/freedmen were in the same way felt to be the responsibility of family members and relatives; and if such ties of family are not available, other personal connections, such as those connected in ownership (as *uicarii*, *serui*, or *liberti*), friends or colleagues (*amici*, *conserui*, *coliberti*) prompted the commemoration of the deceased. Otherwise, a large number of epitaphs with only the names of the deceased keep dedicators anonymous, many of which would be self-commemorations prepared by themselves *ante mortem*.[36] In parallel to these individual ties (or non-ties), the *collegium*-like corporate body of the *familia* and *liberti* stood in charge of the *columbaria* and burials as if a backup.[37] It is possible that some of the simple epitaphs in the *columbaria*, recording merely a name and without a commemorator, were routinely set up by a slave or freedman in charge of the burial of domestics.[38] The slave/freedman staff of a household was composed of those from various backgrounds and with diverse personal ties,[39] i.e. those with spouses, children, slaves, (non-aristocratic) masters/patrons, or loners, all of which the *collegia domestica* presumably embraced and took care of.

Unlike commemorators, the caretakers who actually carried out the burials are usually not mentioned at all in epitaphs. Irene, the *vicaria* (under-slave) of Deucalio of the Statilii, is commemorated by her son Faustio (A269). However, this Faustio actually died at the age of five as commemorated in another epitaph (A266: here Faustio is recorded as the *uerna* of Deucalio) where the commemorator is unknown.[40] This means that, when Faustio served as the commemorator at the death of his mother Irene, he was an infant under the age of five. Certainly, however, the procedure undoubtedly required adult caretakers to support an orphan Faustio, presumably the *ordinarius* Deucalio or other fellow slaves and freedmen, while the son Faustio, even though an infant and a slave, was deemed to be an appropriate commemorator of his mother. Ideally, this tripod of commemorator, caretaker, and *collegium* should properly function for a descent burial.

Permission for burial in the *columbaria*

In what respect then, or to what extent, did the aristocratic masters contribute to burials for their slaves and freedmen? Did the aristocratic masters donate money for the erection or acquisition of the *columbarium*? Though we lack evidence that directly answers these questions, the aristocratic masters of the *columbaria* were probably sponsors and benefactors rather than passive authorities merely lending their approval. It is considered that after their initial sponsorship of the construction of the *columbarium*, the *collegium* generally took care of the allocation of niches,[41] but some masters actually continued to exercise authority in subsequent business. It is recalled that prominent public *collegia* usually had patrons of high social standing, to whom they offered honourable titles in exchange for their financial and political support.[42] Such a patronage system, a norm in the *collegia*, would be even tighter in the relationship between the aristocratic masters and their own slaves and freedmen. In the Volusian *columbarium*, as we will see below, the aristocratic masters are found interfering in the management of the *collegia* and issue permission for burial in the *columbaria*, which seems to indicate their contribution to the erection of the sepulchral buildings.

As we saw above, giving individuals admission to the *columbaria* was first of all the duty of the *decuriones*, the governing committee of the *collegium*. Alongside the *decuriones* exercising this authority, we find five Volusian epitaphs where the aristocratic masters issued permission. Among them, the epitaphs of L. Volusius Paris, with the job title *a cubiculo et procurator L(ucii) n(ostri)* (*CIL* VI, 7368), and L. Volusius Heracla, the *capsarius idem a cubiculo L. n.* (7368), recorded the permission of the master Lucius Volusius Saturninus (*permissu L. n.*).[43] It is to be noted that Paris and Heracla both held double job titles of particularly privileged kinds, in a combination of *a cubiculo*, *procurator*, and *capsarius*. The post of *a cubiculo*, bedchamber manager, stood at the top of all the other *cubicularii*, and the *capsarius* and *procurator* were also in a highly trusted or intimate personal relationship with the master; the slaves of these professions could receive formal manumission even by masters under twenty years old, which the law ruled

---

[36] Only a (small) proportion of all the *columbaria* epitaphs are clearly 'commemorative', namely the dedicator and dedicatee specified (16% of the Statilian, 64% of the Volusian, and 26% of Livia's *columbarium*).
[37] Cf. Zmaragdus, the *cubicularius* of L. Domitius Apollinaris, is commemorated by Nicostratus, a *curator* of *collegium* and at the same time his friend (*amicus*); (9310) *D. M. Zmaragdi, L. Domiti Apollin(aris) cubicular(i) ex colleg(io), curan[t]e Nicostrato amico, b. m.* The master L. Domitius Apollinaris here is probably the consul in AD 97, the friend of the Pliny the younger (*Ep.* 2, 9; 5, 6) and cultured patron of Martial (6, 86; 7, 26; 89; 10, 30; 11, 15).
[38] Schiess, 1888, 30.
[39] Domestic slaves from various backgrounds: Tac., *Ann.* 14, 44; vd. Chap. 1 and 6.
[40] (A269) *Irene, uicar(ia) Deucalionis. Faustio filius posuit*; (A266) *Faustio, uern(a) Deucalionis, uixit an(nis) V. Ossa tibi bene quiescant et matri.*

[41] Caldelli and Ricci, 1999, 67.
[42] Patterson, 1992, 17-22.
[43] (7368) *L. Volusio Paridi a cubiculo et procuratori L. n., Claudia Helpis cum Volusia Hamilla et Volusio Paride filis suis coniugi suo, bene merenti, permissu L(uci) n(ostri)*; (7368) *L. Volusio Heraclae, capsario idem a cubiculo L. n., Volusia Prima patron(o) suo piissimo idem coniugi bene merent(i) fecit et sibi. p(ermissu) L(uci) n(ostri)*; cf. (7375) *Antiocho Q. Volusius Poebhus* (sic) *fecit* (sic) *filio suo pissimo, ben. mer. et suis permisum* (sic) *L(uci) et Q(uinti) nostri*; (7380) *L. Volusio Diodoro, L. Volusius Zenon filius fecit, permissu L. [n.], et Ma[...] Volus[...] siae b. m. f.*; (22811) *Diis manibus Mysti, L. Volusi Saturnini ser(ui), Volusia Irene et Dorio filio, uixit an(nis) XV, m(ensibus) VI. permissu Q(uinti) n(ostri).*

invalid under normal circumstances.⁴⁴ The job titles thus indicate the respected status of Paris and Heraclea, and the master's favouritism towards them is apparent. In general, the inclusion of the formula '*locus datus…*' connotes honour conferred either by the *decuriones* or by the *domini*, rather than their passive admission. In the case of Spendusa, who lived only for five months and was commemorated by her parents, both the masters and *decuriones* had jointly granted the niche in the *columbarium* (*locus datus a dominis et decurionibus*) (7303). This Spendusa's father Spendo was a slave of the master L. Volusius Saturninus' wife Torquata, and he, as a commemorator, had gained the permission of *decuriones* once already for a different epitaph.⁴⁵ Though such aristocratic masters' interference is only found in the Volusian *columbarium*, which seems to imply their patronage in the construction and maintenance of the sepulchral building, it does not mean that other *columbaria* did not receive their patronage; normally, the aristocratic masters of the *columbaria*, I suppose, would have simply waived their right to do so.

Otherwise, the aristocratic masters are generally absent from the context of their servants' death. In the *columbaria*, there are virtually no commemorations of slaves or freedmen by the elite *domini* (and *vice versa*). This is fully understandable when we consider the enormous social gulf between aristocratic masters and slaves. In this context, it is again worth mentioning the study of Saller and Shaw. As we saw above, commemoration of the deceased throughout the Empire was primarily carried out by their family members. When no family members were available, according to Saller and Shaw, people then come to rely on their slaves or freedmen for commemoration rather than on their friends (*amici*); commemorations by servile dependants are seven times higher than ones from *amicitia*, friendship. An exception to this pattern is the masters from the senatorial class, to which circle the patrons of our *columbaria*, the Statilii and Volusii etc., belong. In short, the aristocratic masters relied more on their *amici* than on their freedmen or slaves (ratio, 4 : 1) when they did not have family members or relatives. Masters from the senatorial class were reluctant to be commemorated even by their own freedmen. Saller and Shaw explain this phenomenon: "the social distance between a senator and his servile dependants was normally too great for the dependant to be chosen to succeed his master as head of the *domus*, and hence to appear as commemorator."⁴⁶

Because of the legal and conventional role attached to the commemorator, namely their claim to be legitimate heir of the deceased,⁴⁷ the aristocratic masters did not allow their social inferiors to act as commemorators, let alone themselves act as theirs. In the *columbaria*, this principle is most clearly demonstrated.

Nonetheless, those elite masters/mistresses who made the *columbaria* and the *collegia domestica* available to servile dependants did so out of goodwill. The underlying motive of such generosity would be primarily ostentation. But some factors might also be sought in contemporary politics, namely their timely response to the social atmosphere of the early Empire, as represented by Augustus' policy of encouraging stable family life and having children. ⁴⁸ Augustus' various measures to encourage people to have families were directed towards freedmen/women as well as free-born citizens, and ultimately having children in slavery helped them to gain freedom and a better life after manumission: above all, slaves were potential freed Roman citizens. ⁴⁹ We recognise the names of the masters of known *columbaria* as those who were closely linked to Augustus by ties of family (Livia, Nero Drusus and wife Antonia, and Marcellae) or else, those prominent senatorial figures during the Principate who would have been willing to toe the line in the Augustan social policy (T. Statilius Taurus, L. Volusius Saturninus, L. Arruntius, Iunius Silanus, and C. Annius Pollio). In this context, welfare to provide funerals and enable servile dependants to leave memorials with adequate funeral facilities may be considered as the aristocratic masters' (or Livia's) gesture of support towards the family in that context. Undertaking commemorative rituals for family members and frequenting the *columbaria* for such purposes would naturally strengthen the sense of *pietas* in slaves and freedmen, who were supposed to be 'kin-less' in another ideology in a different context.⁵⁰ We have seen that the commemoration of the deceased was most frequently made by spouses (*coniunx* or *contubernalis*) and secondly by parents or by children. At the same time, there were indeed many who did not mention any personal ties at all in epitaphs of *columbaria* (perhaps as some reflection of

---

⁴⁴ *Dig.* 40, 2, 11-13 (Ulpian), *si collactaneus, si educator, si paedagogus ipsius, si nutrix, uel filius filiaue cuius eorum, uel alumnus, uel capsarius (id est qui portat libros), uel si in hoc manumittatur, ut procurator sit.*
⁴⁵ (7303) *Spendusae uixit m(enses) V. d(ies) XXVI, Spendo Torquatian(us) et Primigenia filiae dulcissimae fecer(unt). loc(us) dat(us) a dominis et decurionib(us)*; (7297) *d. m. s. Panope ornatrix Torquate Q. Volusi, uixit annis XXII et Phoebe a speculum uixit annis XXXVII, Spendo contubernalibus suis bene merentibus fecit et sibi loc. d. dec. decu.*: apparently, Spendo had two *contubernales* before his union with Primigenia: vd. Chap. 5.
⁴⁶ Saller and Shaw, 1984, 139.

⁴⁷ Cf., Plin., *HN.* 7, 52, §177: *e duobus fratribus equestris ordinis Corfidiis maiori accidisse ut uideretur expirasse, apertoque testamento recitatum heredem minorem funeri institisse.*
⁴⁸ Suet., *Aug.* 34, *leges retractauit et quasdam ex integro sanxit, ut sumptuariam et de adulteriis et de pudicitia, de ambitu, de maritandis ordinibus*; Dio, 54, 16; Tac. *Ann.* 3, 25; Brunt, 1971, 136-140.
⁴⁹ Freedmen were in principle ordered to leave at least half of their property to patrons by testament, and if a freedman was of Latin status, all his property went to his patron. But having children helped them to escape from this obligation. If a freedman had one son or daughter, a patron could claim half of the property, if he had two, a third; only if he had three children was a patron finally excluded from the inheritance. In the case of freedwomen, the patron became the guardian of his freedwoman, and could claim all her property, since she could not make a will without the patron's approval. Under the *lex Papia Poppaea*, a freedwoman was released from a patron's control only if she gave birth to 'four' children; Gai. *Inst.* 3, 41-44; Gardner, 1993, 21; Watson, 1987, 35-39; on the procedure of *iteratio* of Junian Latins, Gaius, *Inst.* 1, 29; vd. Chapter 4, n. 9.
⁵⁰ vd. Chapter 5, n. 3.

the general reluctance towards marriage among the contemporary upper class). The *columbarium* as the communal burial facility and the *collegium domesticum* as the unity of servile dependants were to enable those who did not have families to rely on for commemorations and give them a sense of community. The prospect that they would be buried in a place where they were perpetually surrounded by fellow members of their household would have been at least comforting to them.

Conclusion: the union of slaves and freedmen, and the possible threat it presented

Having thus looked at the evidence of the *collegia domestica*, one may wonder about its possible implications in terms of social and 'home' security. Aristocratic masters in the early Empire still had fresh memories of the political disturbances during the late republic centred on the *collegia*,[51] and were obsessed with the widespread notion of 'slaves as enemies'. Attempts were repeatedly made during the Principate to dissolve all of the previously notorious guilds, except those of long-standing and of strictly legitimate purpose, and ban any new formations.[52] In such a social atmosphere, the idea of the *collegium* being organised by their own slaves and freedmen might perhaps have left the large-scale slave owners with a certain degree of uneasiness. The execution of 400 slaves of the murdered senator Pedanius Secundus during the reign of Nero reflects the fears of masters who could not penetrate the community of slaves.[53] At another point, it was proposed in the senate to distinguish slaves from the free by forcing slaves to wear identical dress, but the senators eventually rejected it because they thought this might give them visible unity.[54] Masters were well aware that the *familia* represented a potentially tight community.

The *collegia* thus organised and run by slaves and freedmen were primarily for funeral matters, and the extent of their activities would have been largely limited to that area. Nonetheless, as the *collegia* in general also functioned to bring people together, the *collegia domestica* symbolise the association and enjoyment of a limited degree of solidarity and autonomy of slaves and freedmen, away from the aristocratic master/patron. Certainly, a 'common identity' or 'class consciousness' in a Marxist sense never developed among Roman slaves; at a general level, slaves' social positions and wealth were so diverse that they failed to recognise their common legal status. Moreover, Roman slaves enjoyed a significantly high possibility of manumission and integration into society compared to other slave-owning societies, and this allowed their status in slavery to be transient. Roman literature, for example Plautus, seems to illustrate discord between slaves, rather than their unity. Slaves or freedmen thus did not form a 'class', but I think that they still formed their own 'communities'. At the level of everyday life, they must have experienced aspects of association, of a shared life between themselves, which did not involve aristocratic masters.[55] Such was probably the background in which their *collegia domestica* operated.

Even though they might be left with a certain nervousness towards the *collegium* by their *familia*, the elite masters put a priority on ensuring adequate burial for their numerous servants. The purpose of the *collegia domestica* was also to avoid reliance on external undertakers and so to ensure the ideal of household self-sufficiency. Whilst the creation of *collegia* in general was difficult in the early Empire, the *collegium domesticum* was in a sense a good alternative since it remained within the domain of private individuals and household. For this practical reason, it was probably less threatening than it sounds that slaves and freedmen in the *collegia domestica* used the titles of formal public organisations with officials equivalent to those of the *collegia* in the city or in other Roman municipalities, which were ultimately those of the Roman government. Like the *collegia* organised by the imperial or public slaves and freedmen, the often informal but virtual unions of the slaves and freedmen of elite households reflected the privilege and trust that accompanied the membership of the notable elite *domus*.

---

[51] Lintott, 1968, 77-79; Vanderbroeck, 1987, 59-61, 67-76; Brunt, 1974, 74-102; Treggiari, 1969, 168-177.
[52] Suet., *Caes.* 42, 3, *cuncta collegia praeter antiquitus constituta distraxit*; id., *Aug.* 32, 1, *et plurimae factiones titulo collegi noui ad nullius non facinoris societatem coibant... ergastula recognouit, collegia praeter antiqua et legitima dissoluit*; Dio, 54, 2, 3; Suet., *Tib.* 8; Tac., *Ann.* 14, 17, Nero dissolved the *collegia* illegally organised in Pompeii; Plin., *Ep.* 10, 33-34, cautiouisly suggested the benefit of organising a *collegium* of firefighters, no more than 150 men, but Trajan declined his suggestion, for fear of turning it into a dangerous political organisation; cf. De Ligt, 2001, 345-358, which argued that, the government's policy in banning all sorts of *collegia* was in fact far more relaxed.
[53] Tac., *Ann.* 14, 44.
[54] Sen. *de clementia*, 1. 24. 1.

[55] In the everyday life of a slave, the sleeping quarters allocated to groups of slaves or to slave familial units would have encouraged an intimacy between slaves, and a certain degree of privacy from the master; Pliny's household had a bedroom (*paedagogium*) shared by several slave boys: Plin., *Ep.* 7, 27, *puer in paedagogio mixtus pluribus dormiebat*; cf., Sen., *Vit. Beat.* 17, 2; Pliny's villa in Laurentum had a living space for his slaves and freedmen: Plin., *Ep.* 2, 17: *reliqua pars lateris huius seruorum libertorumque usibus detinetur plerisque tam mundis, ut accipere hospites possint*; Bradley, 1994, 72-73; cf. Fitzgerald, 2000, 82-3.

Conclusion

The *familia urbana* as envisaged from our examination of the *columbaria* inscriptions may differ from 'slavery' as we understand it in the usual meaning of the word: branded fugitives or chained gangs of agricultural slaves, a sadistic master and a mass of uprooted, helpless slaves, the masters' absolute power and the slaves' subjection, or moralising anecdotes concerning masters' affection towards slaves and slaves' loyalty. The *columbaria* inscriptions do not indicate any of these images, or rather, counter them. What we can infer from the *columbaria* and epitaphs is neither cruel treatment (they were equipped with welfare of burials) nor humane relationship (burials are necessities, and aristocratic masters did not commemorate nor were commemorated by their servile dependants). While uprooted and alienated, family life and friendship were not impossible in slavery.

In the former period, great slave wars ingrained in the Roman public psyche a shock horror realisation of what they were potentially capable of. Slaves or masters with first-hand memory of the united cause or the terror at the outcome of Spartacus' revolt (73BC), let alone the great Sicilian slave wars (135-132, 104-100BC), were no longer alive. Fewer and fewer slaves now, perhaps, were those who experienced brutal enslavement by war. Certainly, at the same time, the threat of slaves as potential enemies was not altogether a thing of the past. Though the memory of rebellious slaves in Sicily or at Capua had faded in the distance, eye-witnesses of the recent calamities of civil war had not forgotten the slave gangs that the late-republican leaders used for their own political purposes. In fact, a slave uprising, instigated by an ex-praetorian guard, was reported in Brundisium during the reign of Tiberius, precisely the period when many of the *columbaria* were established; it was fortunate luck on the part of Rome that the conspiracy was checked at the outset. Then there continued to be desperate slave gladiators always visible in the arena.[1]

However, as the political system shifts to the Principate, the Augustan *pax Romana*, the sort of slaves and freedmen was gradually emerging, from whom everyone had much to fear. They were a handful of slaves and freedmen in the imperial household who had the practical potential to wield enormous power and cause greater damage than a mere slave revolt. Those buried in the *columbaria* are one privileged group of slaves, but the gulf between imperial (Livia's) and new Augustan aristocratic households (the Statilii, Volusii, and others) widens in the course of the first century AD, as the standing of the latter becomes terribly precarious before imperial power and is eventually replaced with new ones in one way or another. This shifting social and political landscape represents a blurring in the concept of slavery – the situation of the state and Roman aristocracy headed, under notorious emperors after Augustus, towards exactly what Cicero and republicans had feared as 'slavery' to a tyranny, though they could no longer cry out for freedom and fight for it with as much confidence as a century before. 'Slaveries' permeated to more than one dimension of society, freedom and slavery no longer so clear-cut in the consciousness of the Romans in this period.

In the background of the *columbaria*, there was a greater transformation of the city, with a number of public buildings constructed or repaired on the initiative of Augustus. He also encouraged his family members and trusted generals to contribute; T. Statilius Taurus' amphitheatre was one of these great public constructions by triumphant generals. The family's ownership of the *horti* on the Esquiline might also be seen in that context, i.e., as part of the project of remodelling the city, as leading to the improved sanitation and landscape of the region, like the adjacent *horti* of Maecenas. It was on the periphery of these building activities during this period that the *columbaria* were established one after another. The Statilian *columbarium* in particular was located in close proximity to the family's *horti*, which may suggest that the whole region was the family's territory or at least their selection of the places for the *columbarium* and *horti* was well co-ordinated. Another contributing factor

---

[1] In Brundisium: Tac. *Ann.* 4, 27; an attempted revolt by gladiators at Praeneste in AD 64: Tac. *Ann.* 15, 46.

to the popular construction of the *columbaria* might have been the ongoing project of repairing the old highways, sponsored by Augustus himself alongside other triumphant generals, as they were usually located along the major roads.[2]

As for the underlying motives in establishing the *columbaria* on the part of the aristocratic masters, it would be relevant to turn to Augustus' social policy of encouraging stable family life and having children.[3] In this context, the welfare to provide funerals and enable servile dependants to leave memorials with adequate funeral facilities may be considered as the aristocratic masters' (or Livia's etc.) gesture of regard for family. Undertaking commemorative rituals for family members and frequenting the *columbaria* for such purposes would naturally strengthen the sense of *pietas* in slaves and freedmen, who were supposed to be 'kin-less' on another ideology. We saw a varying proportion of individuals mention their familial ties (Table 5.2), and commemoration of the deceased was most frequently made by spouses (*coniunx* or *contubernalis*) and secondly by parents or by children (Table 5.1).

But it remains unclear whether the individuals in the *columbaria* as a whole represent exemplary family-oriented associations or a reflection of the mood of celibacy in society. There were indeed many who did not mention any ties of family, and the communal burial facilities of the *columbaria* and the unity of servile dependants as *collegia domestica* were also meant to make things easier for those who did not have enough savings (*peculia*) or family to rely on for commemoration. Even though indications of the operation of the *collegia* are actually very few, such co-operative bodies seem to have been ubiquitous, whatever the degree of formality involved (Table 7.1). The extent of their activities might have been greatly limited, in accordance with the negative connotation that the *collegia* and slaves might invoke as potential enemies. The priority, however, centred on ensuring the adequate burial of their numerous servants, and corporate organisation was necessary to carry them out smoothly. By extension of this practical necessity, servile dependants associated with the elite households were entrusted to carry out the business concerning their burials and the very act of leaving their epitaphs. At the same time, the operations of the *collegia domestica*, namely undertaking the burials of the domestics by themselves, represent the way the large *domus* liked to proceed in dealing with every necessity of life. Self-sufficiency and autonomy was the traditional ideal and aspiration of the large *domus*. In this sense, the range of occupations found in the epitaphs of a *columbarium* might be an indicator of the strength of the household: by possession of skilled slaves and freedmen, the household strived to avoid relying on external contractors or *mercenarii*.

In such a large, though not necessarily systematically centralised, living unit of *domus*, with household staff increased more than ever, the hierarchy and ownership that held them together were essentially complex. We saw the levels of ownership structure and hierarchy among servile dependants. About 30% of all the Statilian servants recorded their masters or patrons, and more than half of them belonged not to the aristocratic masters but to 'intermediate owners', namely slaves or freedmen of the Statilii (Chap. 4). A disseminated ownership structure of this kind sustained the workforce for the *domus* and mobilised them in a more flexible manner.

There was a certain degree of mixture of 'native' born and foreign born in the *domus*, though actual evidence of '*vernae*' (home-born) and 'foreigners' in the *columbaria* is very small (Chap. 5 and 6). The wars against barbarians were now significantly reduced, which might have resulted in a shift in the sources of slaves, from foreign captives of war to home-born. Rather than reducing the arrival of foreigners, the peace ultimately encouraged Rome to be a cosmopolitan city, where people from various regions (many as slaves) could be seen without being a potential threat. According to the accounts of literary authors and also a bulk of inscriptions left by freedmen, the free population of Rome appears to have been racially mixed to a large extent by the time of the Principate.

Augustus' legislation on the manumission of slaves was allegedly (according to Suetonius) intended to prevent the Roman citizen body being contaminated by former slaves, many of whom were of non-Italian origin.[4] The *lex Fufia Caninia* of 2 BC and the *lex Aelia Sentia* in AD 4 regulated the number of slaves that a master could manumit by will and the methods of formal manumission and age of the candidates. These laws might have created greater obstacles to a slave on the route to citizenship, and many freedmen supposedly became not freed Roman citizens but intermediate Junian Latins, the status formally created by either Augustus or Tiberius. If this legislation contributed to relativising and loosening status distinctions and created a farrago of free, servile, and semi-servile status, that situation might be echoed in the *columbaria*, where individuals show little concern about specifying their legal status.

The Principate emasculated the aristocratic families, and the senate no longer possessed the political powers of old. We do not find any *nomenclator* in the epitaphs of the *columbaria* that might have been used for

---

[2] Suet. *Aug.* 29 and 30; Eck, 1984, 140; Purcell, 1985.

[3] Suet. *Aug.* 34, *leges retractavit et quasdam ex integro sanxit, ut sumptuariam et de adulteriis et de pudicitia, de ambitu, de maritandis ordinibus*; Dio, 54, 16; Tac. *Ann.* 3, 25; Brunt, 1971, 136-140; Augustus' policy was that freedwomen who bore four children (for free-born women three children) were exempted from the guardianship; moreover, women over twenty and men over twenty-five were punished if unmarried. Although these regulations were not applied to slaves, they become liable as soon as they were manumitted.

[4] Suet. *Aug.* 40, 3-4, *magni praeterea existimans sincerum atque ab omni colluvione peregrini ac servilis sanguinis incorruptum servare populum, et civitates Romanas parcissime dedit et manumittendi modum terminavi*; cf. Dio, 55, 13.

election campaigns in the former period. The bodyguards (*Germani*) and litter-carriers (*lecticarii*) of the Statilii were a rare heritage from the new man Taurus, perhaps already felt awkward in the generations of his descendants in the post-Augustan period.

A process of transition in onomastic practice is also witnessed in the *columbaria* epitaphs. The Statilii were one of those families with new styles of nomenclature (discarding traditional *praenomen* and adopting *cognomen* of maternal *gens*), while the Volusii continued to follow the conventional mode (differentiating the *praenomina* as personal names). Their freedmen in adopting the aristocratic masters' nomenclature duly receive the *praenomina* – even the little-used 'Titus' of the Statilii –, though without much use: instead, the *cognomen*, that had been their personal name in slavery, functioned as the individual signifier.

The early Empire, when the servile dependants of some prominent aristocratic families ran the *columbaria* on the outskirts of Rome, was a period of transition in many ways. Familiar and unchanging, however, as represented in the inscriptions of the *columbaria*, is perhaps the status of women and children. Women, especially as children, in the *columbaria*, seem to have been accorded lesser value: we found almost universally in the *columbaria* the female population to be a half of the male population (Table 5.3), and fewer girls than boys under the age of fourteen are known among those with a record of age of death (Fig. 5.1.1-3). Such an apparent imbalance of males and females might indicate that female children were unwanted and likely to be sold or sent away. It is rare to find more than one daughter (unlike sons) from the same parents in the *columbaria* epitaphs (Table 5.4). More women received commemoration as wife or mother than men as husband or fathers (Table 5.5), and 90 % of all job-title holders were men (Table 3.1), which indicates that women were mainly appreciated for their role as spouse and mother. The *familia urbana* was centred on males, and women and children were essentially to fall subordinate to men in that structure. The servile familial units that bound men, women, and children, often embraced the aspect of ownership, and also conversely, those bound in ownership might accompany ties of family.

The servile dependants of a large household present a paradox for modern scholars as well as for Roman aristocratic masters. They might be insignificant as individuals and readily replaceable, but they constituted an essential human resource for the autonomous system of a large living unit. They were domestics and freedmen with shared nomen, but they were also considered permanent outsiders and some were in fact of foreign birth. They might be mere instruments and property, but they were human souls and formed a community, comprising women, children, and also the old. Even though they lived in the shadow of the powerful Romans, the inscriptions of the *columbaria* as a whole present powerful testimonies of their presence, and furthermore testimonies of private aspects of their aristocratic masters' lives.

Appendix
Inscriptions relating to the *familia* of the Statilii

I reproduce below the inscriptions relating to the *familia* of the Statilii from the recent edition by Caldelli and Ricci, 1999, 83-134. For each inscription the first number is an adapted form of the numeration of Caldelli and Ricci and the second is their number in *CIL* VI.

A. Inscriptions from the *columbarium* of the Statilii

A1. Structure (N)

Podium plaque

(A001) (6275)
Hic est ille situs / qui qualis amicus / amico quaque fide / fuerit, mors fuit indicio. / f(unus) f(ecit) / Faustus Erotis / dispensatoris vicarius.

(A002) (6349)
Daphne, sarcinatri(x).

(A003) (6362)
Ossa / Italiae textric(is).

(A004) (6494)
Opacus Aulici f(ilius), / annorum sex.

(A005) (6507)
Preima Afra.

(A006) (6395)
Hilara Hermiae / vicaria, an(norum) XIIII.

(A007) (6459)
Grata Iucundi l(iberta).

(A008) (6528)
T. Statilius Tauri l(ibertus) Dapnis.

(A009) (6226)
Charito, custos de amphiteat(ro).

(A010) (6444)
Faustus Bassiani.

(A011) (6530)
T. Statilius Diogenes.

(A012) (6577)
Statilia Sappho, Alypus f(ecit?), / 'Erotis f(ilius?)'.

(A013) (6594)
[---pat]rono benemere/nti.

(A014) (6379)
Cladus Elate f(ilius) / vixit ann(is) V, d(iebus) XIIX.

Wall plaque

(A015) (6213)
Familia T. Statili Tauri / patris, ex d(ecreto) d(ecurionum), / Antoniae M. l. Chryse, in / bonore (!) Statili Storacis, / ollam dederunt.

(A016) (6251)
Ossa sita / Licini / coloratoris.

(A017) (6256)
Apthonus, cub(icularius) / Tauri pat(ris).

(A018) (6256)
Clarus, cubicular(ius) / Tauri adulescentis.

(A019) (6263)
Menophilus, / cubic(ularius) vix(it) an(nis) XXX. / Phil[---], unct(or) / fi[lio fec(it)?].

(A020) (6276)
Suavis Erotis dispensatoris vern(a), / annor(um) XII, quoius ossa hic / sunt sita.

(A021) (6278)
Philemo Posidippi / dispensator, vixit an(nis) XX.

(A022) (6302)
Aba, lectic(arius).

(A023) (6306)
[As]tragalo, lectik(ario), / Afriano; / de suo f(ecerunt). // [The?]ophilus, [Dio?]genes, // Musaeus, / Agatho.

(A024) (6314)
Nothi, librari a manu. / Non optata tibi coniunx monimenta locavit / ultima, in aeternis sedibus ut maneant / spe frustra gavisa Nothi quem prima ferentem / aetatis Pluton invidus eripuit. / Hunc etiam flevit quae qualis turba et honorem / supremum digne funeris inposuit.

(A025) (6315)
Philargyrus, / librarius, / Catullianus.

(A026) (6316)
Zena Sutorianus / mag(ister), quaest(or), / ad locationes.

(A027) (6321)
Laches, / mensor, / uixsit (!) an(n)o(s) XVII.

(A028) (6338)
Prima Sura / Alexandri l(iberti) pist(oris) (scil. serva?).

(A029) (6346)
Urbana veteran(a), / quasillaria; / heic ossa sita sunt.

(A030) (6377)
Hilara Iasonis vicaria. / Clemens, unctor, fecit.

(A031) (6387)
[---]+ticus Dicaeo, / [vi]cario suo.

(A032) (6423)
Ossa sita sunt Clement(is) / Hilarionis fili nato(!) / Athenaine. Vixit annos / III, menses VII. Quei / spiritum exsolvit / hora qua natus est.

(A033) (6424)
Clite Corneliae l(iberta).

(A034) (6429)
Cratiste / T. Statilio / Eroni, patrono.

(A035) (6431)
Dapnis Sura, / vixit ann(is) XXVII.

(A036) (6436)
Have! / Erotis Boeotiani / ossa hic sunt sita. / Secunda coniugi suo fecit.

(A037) (6437)
Esychus Tauri ser(us).

(A038) (6440)
Euticus Aprodisiae / coniugi suae.

(A039) (6446)
Fausto Storaci(s) / l(iberto), vixit ann(is) XIIII.

(A040) (6490)
Nemesis / Nicenis Tauri l(ibertae) / ancilla.

(A041) (6515)
Salviae l(ibertae) / ossa hic sita sunt. / [---] feci(t).

(A042) (6548 & 6609)
Quoat vixit, vixit suaviter. / T. Statilius Tauri / lib(ertus) Eros Parra, vixit probe, / pudenter, amicus amico, placuit / suis; have et tu, vale et tu. Fecit / Hetereia P. l. Chreste viro suo.

(A043) (6582)
Terpusa Longini (scil. serva?).

(A044) (6592)
Si qua manent obitis V+[---] / praemia sub terris [---] / iudicat id coniunx, erepta qua sibi maerens / devovet invisi noxsia (!) regna dei.

(A045) (6293)
Protogenes, horrearius, / Hipparchi vicarius.

(A046) (6392)
Felicla Hipparci / vicaria.

(A047) (6214)
T. Statilius Tauri l(ibertus) / Diodotus / magister, q(uaestor) in familia, / vivos sibi et Augeni / coniugi suae fecit. // Vedusia Tauri / sororis l(iberta) / Auge vixit annos L. / Bonitatem suam / et fidem bonam secum apstulit. // Have et tu memineris.

(A048) (6285)
Zabda / faber.

(A049) (6243)
Neo / T. Statili / Tauri ser(vus), / balneator.

(A050) (6339)
Acte, / quasil(laria).

(A051) (6587)
Ossa / Tychenis.

(A052) (6261)
Hilarionis, / Posidippi, cub(icularii), / ossa hic sita sunt; / vixit ann(is) XX.

(A053) (6277)
Gratus, / Posidippi, disp(ensator).

(A054) (6386)
[..]mmunis / [Epa]phrae hic vicari / [o]ssa sita.

(A055) (6409)
Apate.

(A056) (6584)
Teucher / Hilarianus / h(ic) s(itus) est.

(A057) (6246)
Eros, cocus, / Posidippi ser(vus), / hic situs est.

(A058) (6274)
Eros, T. Statili / Posidippi ser(vus), / disp(ensator).

(A059) (6578)
Statilia / Sura.

(A060) (6329)
Philocalus, / paedagogus.

(A061) (6310)
Medus, / lecticarius.

(A062) (6509)
Primi ossa / hic sita sunt.

(A063) (6234)
Pothus, / Germanus, / hic situs est.

(A064) (6236)
Suebus, / Germanus, / hic situs est.

(A065) (6232)
Clemens, / Germanus, / hic situs est.

(A066) (6215)
Statilia Ammia hic / sepulta est, quoius sepult(urae) / curam egerunt conleg(ium) / commorient(ium): Cerdo, ins(ularius), / vir eius, Bathyllus, atriens(is), / Musaeus, ost(iarius), Eros, ins(ularius), Philocal[us], / unctor.

(A067) (6216)
Philologus, / cellarius, / ex conlegio / commorientes (!).

(A068) (6227)
Menander l(ibertus) / ostiarius/ ab amphiteatr(o).

(A069) (6230)
Ossa / Casti, Germ(ani).

(A070) (6235)
Strenuus, / Germanus, / v(ixit) a(nnis) XXX.

(A071) (6238)
Pamphilus, / asturconarius.

(A072) (6239)
Antigonus, / atriensis, / Candianu(s).

(A073) (6240)
Felici, atriesi (!), / Hilarus / mag(istro) suo.

(A074) (6249)
Zena, / cocus.

(A075) (6250)
Statiliae T. l. Hilarae / Amarantus, colorat(or), / Philologus, atriesis (!) coniugi posuer(unt). / Bene adquiescas Hilara; si quid sapiunt Inferi, / tu nostri memento. Nos numquam obliviscemur tui.

(A076) (6252)
Hic situs est / Milanio, comoedus. / Calliste fecit.

(A077) (6253)
Τύραννος κωμωδὸς / ἔζησεν ἔτη IH. / Τῆς (!) εἶσεν (!) φιλίς / χρυσέρως καὶ παιδὸς Ἀρέτης (!) τήνδ' ἐπὶ τῷ μνή/μης (!) εἴνεκ' ἔθηκε Πᾶρον.

(A078) (6254)
Alter, cubicul(arius), / dulcissimus, / v(ixit) a(nnis) XIIX. Ossa hic sita sunt. Aster, mag(ister) // 'v(isit)'.

(A079) (6255)
Alter, cubicul(arius), / v(ixit) a(nnis) XVIII. / Aster, mag(ister).

(A080) (6258)
Eutychus, / cubicularius, / Aphrodisio fratri / suo, 'velario', fecit.

(A081) (6260)
Glyconis, cubiclari (!), / hic ossa sita sunt. / Donata fecit.

(A082) (6280)
Felix ex / Albano / Diogaes f(ilius).

(A083) (6283)
Bassus, fab(er).

(A084) (6284)
Gratus, fa[ber]; / h(ic) o(ssa) [s(ita) s(unt)].

(A085) (6287)
Donatus, / fullo, / Tironianus.

(A086) (6289)
Hilari, / fullonis, oss(a) / sita sunt.

(A087) (6295)
Metrogenes, / horrearius.

(A088) (6296)
Demostenes, / insularius.

(A089) (6298)
Felicis, insul(arii), / ossa sita sun[t].

(A090) (6299)
Eros, insularius (!) / ex horteis Pompeia[nis].

(A091) (6303)
Agathoni, lecticar(io) / Tauri, fecerunt / Caliste, vicaria, et / Philologus et Felix

(A092) (6304)
Alcimus, / lecticarius, / [vix(it) a]n(nis) XXXX.

(A093) (6308)
[I]ucundus Tauri [l(ibertus)], / [l]ecticarius. Quandi/us vixit vir fuit et se et / alios vindicavi (!). Quan/dius vixit honeste vixit. / Callista et Philologus dant.

(A094) (6309)
Laetus, / lecticarius.

(A095) (6311)
Phileros Paplago (!), lecticarius.

(A096) (6313)
Iucundae, / lecticari(ae), / ossa.
---cf. CIL VI (*Trucundae lecticari*)

(A097) (6318)
Nicepor, / marmorarius.

(A098) (6333)
Felix, pediseq(uus), / Gabinianus.

(A099) (6340)
Auge, Sura, / quasillaria.

(A100) (6342)
Italia, quasillaria, / visit ann(is) XX; / Scaeva, tabellarius Tauri, / coniugi suae fecit.

(A101) (6343)
Messia Dardana, / quasillaria; / fecit Iacinthus, / unctor, Dardanus.

(A102) (6345)
Sige, quasillar(ia); / Faustus legit / ossa.

(A103) (6347)
Tyranni salar(ii?) / ossa hic sita sunt. / Clymene uxor / titl(um) (!) fec(it).

(A104) (6348)
Attalus, / sarcinator.

(A105) (6352)
Barnaeus, / Sisennae / strator, Patern(ianus).

(A106) (6353)
Alexander, / structor.

(A107) (6355)
Diomedes, / sutor.

(A108) (6356)
Scirtus, / symphoniacus, / Cornelianus.

(A109) (6360)
Secundus, / tetor (!), Ta<u>rianu(s), / Terti frater, / hic {T} situs.

(A110) (6361)
[..]lvionis, / text(oris), ossa / hic sita sunt.

(A111) (6363)
Acasti, fabri / tignuari.

(A112) (6364)
Anteros, / faber tig(nuarius).

(A113) (6367)
Primus, / tonsor.

(A114) (6371)
Euticus Corneliae / veteranus. Fecerunt / fratres et Zena, velarius.

(A115) (6320)
Secunda / Thyrso, medico, / merenti.

(A116) (6380)
Philadelphus, / unctor, / v(ixit) ann(is) XX, o(ssa) h(ic) s(ita) s(unt).

(A117) (6382)
Postestatis Salvianae. / Posuit Rufio, unctor / Tauri f(ilii).

(A118) (6384)
Amarantus, / Pasicratis / vicarius.

(A119) (6388)
Heramo, / Peloris / veicarius.

(A120) (6389)
Iucundus, / vicarius, / vixit ann(is) XIIX.

(A121) (6391)
Zethus, Amaranthi / vicarius. Ossa hic sita.

(A122) (6393)
Helena, / Pansae vicaria.

(A123) (6398)
Optata, Chresti / Auct(iani) vicar(ia), / vixit annos III. / Mater dedit.

(A124) (6399)
Rufa, / Menandri / Saeni (scil. servi) vicaria, / an(ni) I.

(A125) (6400)
[S]ecunda, Scurrae vi[c(aria)], / hic sita est. / Viixit (!) an(nis) XVII[II].

(A126) (6401)
Tertia, vicar(ia) / Clonni.

(A127) (6403)
Ampelium, / hic sita est.

(A128) (6405)
Anthrax / Sosian(us), hic.

(A129) (6407)
Antigonaes l(ibertae) / ossa hic sita sunt.

(A130) (6411)
Aucta Varillae (scil. serva?).

(A131) (6412)
Auctae ossa heic sita sunt.

(A132) (6414)
Aufidia / Prima.

(A133) (6415)
Beata, Posidip(pi) (scil. serva).

(A134) (6416)
Berullus.

(A135) (6420)
Cedrus, / vixit an(nis) XIX.

(A136) (6421)
Chryseros / Dorcadis libert(us) / hic insitus est / annorum VIIII.

(A137) (6426)
Condicio, Posidippi / liberti (scil. servus), / vixit annos V.

(A138) (6430)
Crhesimus (!) / Teucrhianus (!) / hic est.

(A139) (6432)
Dionysius.

(A140) (6435)
Eros Attico suo; / [d]ominus calamitosus fecit. / Quantum fuit carus / [d]eclaravit supremus dies. / Ossa hic sita sunt. [E]ros Philerotianus At<t>ico fecit.

(A141) (6441)
D(is) M(anibus) / Fatalis. / Faustus pater / et Euochia ma/ter filio piissimo / fecerunt.

(A142) (6443)
Faustilli, Daphninis (scil. servi), hic / ossua sita sunt. Annorum / natus fuit VII, fecit / illi suos (!) tata p(ius?)

(A143) (6445)
Faustus, fili[us].

(A144) (6447)
Fausta, / d(ecurio).

(A145) (6448)
Ossa / Faustaes heic / sita sunt.

(A146) (6451)
Felicula, / Dionysiae (scil. serva?).

(A147) (6452)
Felix, Daphi (scil. servus), / annorum XX, / heic situs est. Calliste / mater fecit.

(A148) (6453)
Felix / Lepontia.

(A149) (6454)
Felix, / Statiliae f(iliae) (scil. servus).

(A150) (6455)
[C?]asti, L. Foli Philippi ser(vus), ollas duas.

(A151) (6456)
Ossa Gatis / hic sita sunt.

(A152) (6457)
Gemella, salve. / Salvete mei parentes / et tu salve quisquis es.

(A153) (6458)
Graphis Varillae

(A154) (6461)
Hannibalis ossa hic.

(A155) (6462)
Helena.

(A156) (6463)
Helena, / v(ixit) a(nnis) XVII.

(A157) (6464)
Helena, / Philotaes (scil. serva?).

(A158) (6467)
Heracla Catulli / Tauri l(iberti) servos. / Quod quisque vestrum mortuo optarit / mihi, id illi di faciant semper vivo et mortuo.

(A159) (6468)
Hermeros / Niceroti / fratri, v(ixit) a(nnis) XXV.

(A160) (6470)
Heureticus, / vixit a(nnis) VIII.

(A161) (6471)
Hilarae / Lepontiae / hic ossa.

(A162) (6473)
Hymen, Corvini (scil. servus), / v(ixit) a(nnis) XX.

(A163) (6476)
Iazemus, / Posidippi / lib(erti) (scil. servus).

APPENDIX: INSCRIPTIONS RELATING TO THE *FAMILIA* OF THE STATILII

(A164) (6482)
Diis Manibus. C. Iunius Eug[enes ---]/ Iuniae Statutae, l(ibertae) suae bene m[erenti et ---] / Iucundo et Plotiae Amoenae o[---] / sub fastigio sibi et suiis (!) [---].

(A165) (6483)
Laudica, / Cilicissa.

(A166) (6484)
[---]artae / [ossa] sita sunt.
cf. Solin, 1996, 603, [M]artae

(A167) (6485)
[-M]emmi[---] / Memmia[---] / et[---].

(A168) (6488)
Moschin[is] / ossa hic /sita sunt.

(A169) (6489)
Musa l(iberta).

(A170) (6491)
Nessalis / ossa hic / sita sunt.

(A171) (6492)
Ossa / Nicenis hic sita sunt. / Superi viv<i>te valete, / Inferi havete, recipite Nicenem.

(A172) (6496)
Pascusa, ann(orum) VII, / heic sita est.

(A173) (6497)
Pastoris ossa sita sunt hic.

(A174) (6500)
Phileroti / Blanda / posuit.

(A175) (6501)
Phyllis / heic sita est.

(A176) (6505)
Pontia / Nardis.

(A177) (6506)
Pothus, / d(ecurio).

(A178) (6514)
Rufionis Siculi / ossa / heic sunt sita.

(A179) (6518)
Ossa hic / Secundae.

(A180) (6524)
T. Statilius / Anuptes / Artemae l(ibertae).

(A181) (6526)
T. Statiliu[s] / Carus.

(A182) (6527)
T. Statilius / Celadus.

(A183) (6535)
T. Statilius / Posidippi l(ibertus) Eros.

(A184) (6536)
T. Statilius / T. l. Faustus.

(A185) (6544)
T. Statilio Hermeroti / fratri suo, / Eutychis soror dat.

(A186) (6545)
Diis Manibus. / T. Statilio Ianuario / Statilia Lale / liberto suo bene / merenti, vixit ann(is) XX.

(A187) (6549)
[T. St]atilius Dasi l(ibertus) / [P]hiletus, vixit / ann(is) XXV.

(A188) (6550)
T. Statilius Tauri / l(ibertus) Princeps Minor, / hic humatus est.

(A189) (6551)
T. Statilius / Romanus.

(A190) (6552)
T. Statilius / Salvius.

(A191) (6554)
T. Statili / Zabinae / ossa hic sita sunt.

(A192) (6555)
Statilia T. f. / `Agaphima´.

(A193) (6559)
Statilia Corvi[ni l(iberta)] / Damis, / vixsit (!) annu(m) [I], / menses IIII, dies [---].

(A194) (6560)
------ / [---] ++ [---] / [S]tatilia T. [l.] / [E]rotis con[iux].

(A195) (6563)
Statilia Fausta / Clari l(iberta).

(A196) (6564)
Statilia Pagani / l(iberta) Fausta / et Tarentinus / Catlus.

(A197) (6573)
Statiliaes Philemaes, / Malchionis l(ibertae), / ossua hic sita sunt, bonaes / feminaes, have vale.

(A198) (6575)
Iunoni / Statiliae Polynoes.

(A199) (6581)
Stephanus / l(ibertus).

(A200) (6585)
Therpsicor, / Nice, / lite h(ic) s(itae) e(st) (!).

(A201) (6590)
Urbana, Posid(ippi) (scil. serva), / vixit annos / XXVII.

(A202) (6222)
M. Iunius Veiento, / ex d(ecreto) d(ecurionum); v(ixit) a(nnis) XIII, / infelix parentibus.

(A203) (6224)
Erotis, actari, hic ossa / sita sunt. / Urbana, Sosicratis vicar(ia), / posuit titulum.

(A204) (6225)
Eros libertus ad aedificia. Γαίος Οὐεδούσιος παιδά με πενταετῆ ὀλίγη ἐκρύψατο κροσσός καλλίστου ταχέως ἀντιάσαντ᾽ Ἀΐδεω. Οὔνομα δὴ δίζησαι ἐνὶ πρωτοίσι μέμης (!). [Ia]m spes es externis semper committimus oris.

(A205) (6233)
Nothi (!), / Germanu[s].

(A206) (6319)
Hic sunt ossa / sita Spudenis / Lysae medici filiae. // Immatura sinu, tellus, levis accipe Grati / ossa et legitimo more sepulta fove. / Quattuor huic cursus Phoebeos fata negarun(t), / ereptum sibi quem luget uterque parens. / Quid prodest vixisse in amabilitate facetum / cunctaque blanditiis emeruisse suis? / Num potuit dilectus ob haec perducere lucem / longius? Heu Ditis foeda rapina feri.

(A207) (6378)
Epaphrae, Tauri unctori, facit mulier / infelix amori suo dulcissimo filio / et amico continenter. Clades, Elates / filius, vixit annos V, dies XVIII.

(A208) (6273)
T. Statilius / T. l. / Optatus, / a manu, / v(ixit) a(nnis) XXVI. // ʽIucun<d>us, / disp(ensator) / Corviniʼ.

(A209) (6291)
T. Statilius / Iucund"[u]"s, ad / hereditates.

(A210) (6301)
T. Statilius Tauri l(ibertus) / Spinther, supra lec(ticarios), / T. Statilius Crescens f(ilius).

(A211) (6327)
Gemellus, Messallinae / Tauri f(iliae) paedagogus.

(A212) (6330)
T. Statilius / Zabda, /paedag(ogus) Statiliae.

(A213) (6354)
T. Statilius Nicepor, / faber struct(or) parietar(ius).

(A214) (6373)
T. Statilius / T. l. Hilarus / Cor(vini?), vest(iarius).

(A215) (6376)
Antiocho / magistro, / unctores.

(A216) (6402)
Alcestes / Chresti Tauri (scil. servi vicarius) / v(ixit) a(nnis) IIII.

(A217) (6413)
M. Aufidius Felix, / ʽv(ixit)ʼ Pantuleia Arbuscula.

(A218) (6427)
Constans Statili / Bassi (scil. servus), vix(it) ann(is) IIII.

(A218) (6472)
Himerus / Milonis f(ilius), / vixit annos / sex. // {Felicu} / Statilia Felicula / Milonis l(iberta).

(A220) (6495)
D(is) M(anibus). G. Pantuleius / Sotericus f(ecit) filio suo / pientissimo Victorino, / q(ui) vixit annis II, d(iebus) q(---).

(A221) (6512)
Rosa fecit / Zenae et Antiocho.

(A222) (6521)
[T. Sta]tilius / [---] + A / ------?

(A223) (6531)
T. Statilius / Diogenes / Sossianus.

(A224) (6532)
[T. S]tatilius Suavis / lib(ertus) Entellus / [qui?] vix(it) ann(is) XII.

(A225) (6537)
T. Statilius / [------] / [------?] // Feliculae / [------] / [-----?].

(A226) (6538)
T. Statilius / T.l. «[Felix]».

(A227) (6542)
T. Statilius Tyli l(iberti) f(ilius) / Saturninus, vix(it) a(nnis) V, / d(iebus) IIC.

(A228) (6546)
T. Statilius / Lucrio.

(A229) (6565)
Statil(ia) Fortunata / Heraclaes uxor, / vix(it) an(nis) XXIIII.

(A230) (6576)
Statilia Capsulae / l(iberta) Prepusa. // Statilia / Capsulae / et ((duorum mulierum)) l(iberta) Sabina, / vix(it) a(nnis) XIIII.

(A231) (6583)
D(is) M(anibus). / Tettiae Teleteni / coniugi beneme/[renti, qu]ae vixit / [ann(is) ---] / ---

(A232) (6307)
Bithus, / Tauri lect(icarius), / v(ixit) a(nnis) XL.

(A233) (6350)
Musa, / sarcinatrix, / hic sita est.

(A234) (6480)
Iucunda / Hilari (scil. serva).

(A235) (6504)
Polus, / vix(it) ann(is) VII.

(A236) (6394)
Hellas, Epinici / vicaria.

(A237) (6588)
Dis Man(ibus) / Vitalis, vix(it) / an(nis) XII, dieb(us) / LII. C. Cor/nelius Syn/neros (!) fecit / vernae suae / et sibi po<s>ter/isque suis.

(A238) (6460)
Gymnasionis, / Statili Chaereae (scil. servi). / Posit (!) T. Statilius / Hilarus.

(A239) (6422)
D(is) M(anibus). / Claudiae / Caenidi. / T. Statilius / Pharnaces / coniugi / b(ene) m(erenti) p(osuit).

(A240) (6474)
Ia / Aucti l(iberta), / v(ixit) a(nnis) XXX.

(A241) (6305)
Ascla, lecticar(ius), / vixit ann(is) XXXX.

(A242) (6328)
Ossa. / Iasullus Philerotis lib(ertus), / Sisennae paedagogus.

(A243) (6486)
Modestus. / Eunus funus fec[it].

(A244) (6517)
D(is) M(anibus) Secundi, v(ixit) a(nnis) XII, m(ensibus) III, d(iebus) X. Ti. Claudius Apollonius et Ti. Claud[ius] [...].

(A245) (6417)
Bithynicus / Corvini (scil. servus), / Egnatia posit (!).

(A246) (6331)
[St]atilia T. l. Tyranis / paedagoga / Statiliaes.

(A247) (6487)
Modesto / L. Norbani Quadrati l(iberto), / vix(it) a(nnis) XXX. / Amerimnus Norbani (scil. servus) / amico suo carissimo.

(A248) (6539)
T. Statilius / Felix, / vixit annis XXV. / Statilia Nice / filio suo carissimo / bene merenti fecit.

(A249) (6541)
T. Statilius / Gamillus, / vix(it) an(no) I, m(ensibus) IIX.

(A250) (6556)
Statilia / Ariadne / T. Statili / Attis l(iberta)

(A251) (6568)
Statilia / Quadrati libert(i) l(iberta) / Ichmas, v(ixit) a(nnis) XL.

(A252) (6570)
[Stat]ilia Sisennae [---] / [---]yris l. Lesbi[ae] / [---] + V+ [---] / ------.

(A253) (6390)
Modestus, / Chresti Tauri / (scil. servi) vicarius.

(A254) (6410)
Appollonius (!) / [Po]sidippi / ser(vus).

(A255) (6217)
Chius l(ibertus), Sisennae / silentiarius / ex conlegio hic situs est. / Curatores / Musaeus, ostiar(ius), dec(urio), / Amaranthus, colorat(or), l(ibertus), / Eros, insular(ius), dec(urio), / de suo dant.

(A256) (6269)
T. Statilius T. l. / Men«[a]», Aucti frater / dispens(ator), an(nis) XIIX.

(A257) (6288)
Ossa / Fausti, fullonis, / hic sita sunt. / Galyme«[d]»es Tauri l(ibertus) / fecit «[c]»ognato suo.

(A258) (6220)
Antiochi l(iberti) hic ossa sita / sunt. Amici contulerunt / curatoribus Pansa l(iberto), / Cisso l(iberto), Heracleone l(iberto), / Theophilo, Mithridate, / Salvio, Nicarcho, Agathone, / Philotimo, Musaeo. / Consumptum est in funere et in ossibus e[t i]n novendi{n}(alibus) / MCCCCLXXXX.

(A259) (6247)
Hilaro, / coco, / Barbiano.

(A260) (6547)
T. Statili / Mamae.

(A261) (6557)
Statilia / Athenais, / mater Campani.

(A262) (6241)
Lentiscus, ex horteis / atriensis.

(A263) (6282)
Hectoris, ex ortis (!), / ossa hic sunt.

(A264) (6286)
Ophilio, / fartor.

(A265) (6259)
Felicis, / cubiculari, / ossa h(ic) s(ita) s(unt).

(A266) (6397)
Faustio, vern(a) / Deucalionis, / vixit an(nis) V. Ossa tibi / bene quiescant et matri.

(A267) (6262)
Iucundus, / Posidippi ser(vus), / cubucularius (!), / verna, annor(um) XXI.

(A268) (6279)
Stablio, / Posidipi l(ibertus), / disp(ensator).

(A269) (6396)
Irene, vicar(ia) / Deucalionis. / Faustio filius posuit.

(A270) (6479)
Isidorus, / Posidipp(i) / lib(ertus).

(A271) (6525)
T. Statilius / Posidippi l(ibertus) / Apella.

(A272) (6406)
Anthus / T. Statili Chresti (scil. servus), / vix(it) ann(is) XV.

(A273) (6466)
Helpis T. / Statili l(iberta).

(A274) (6244)
T. Statilius Corvini / lib(ertus) Epaphra, / calator XVvir(orum).

(A275) (6279)
Stati[lia] / Faust[a], / Aucti d[isp(ensatoris) (scil. uxor?)].

(A276) (6370)
Sasa, ex / hortis / topiariu[s].

(A277) (6475)
Ianuari/`us´ Posidippi l(ibertus), / v(ixit) a(nnis) IXV (!).

(A278) (6266)
T. Statili [---], / Aucti d[isp(ensatoris) ---].

(A279) (6271)
Cebes, / dispe(nsator), vix(it) an(nis) XXXV.

(A280) (6281)
Eros Teuc(rianus), ex / hortis / Scatonianis.

(A281) (6337)
Adratus, / pistor.

(A282) (6359)
T. Statilius / Pothus, / tabular(ius). // T. Statilius / Ephebus, / vix(it) ann(nis) XXI.

(A283) (6369)
Felix, / topiarius.

(A284) (6374)
T. Statilius / Malchio, / ad vestem. // T. Stati[lius] / Melic«[rh]»[us] / [[[------]]].

(A285) (6478)
Irena, / Apolloni f(ilia).

(A286) (6272)
Falernus, / dis(ensator) / Statiliae.

(A287) (6334)
Iphic[---], / pedi[sequ-].

(A288) (6341)
Hedone, / quasillaria, / vix(it) ann(is) XXX.

(A289) (6365)
Flaccus, faber / tignuarius, / Cornelianus.

(A290) (6366)
Cadmi, tonsoris; / mater fecit filio suo et Poplari.

(A291) (6368)
[E]rotis, tostricis, / hic ossa sita sunt.

(A292) (6465)
Helpis, / Bassi an[c(illa)].

(A293) (6540)
T. Statilius / Felix, / Statilia Prima, [T. St]atilius T. f. Felix.

(A294) (6312)
Potamo, / Sisennae / lect(icarius).

(A295) (6231)
Cirratus, / Germanus, / hic situs est.

(A296) (6335)
Logas, / Messallin(ae) / pedis(equa), v(ixit) a(nnis) XVI, / Aprodisia (!) mater / fecit.

(A297) (6404)
Anteros / Milensiae / suae.

(A298) (6425)
Comes, / Alexandri / liberti ser(vus).

(A299) (6586)
Tima / Bassi (scil. serva?).

(A300) (6229)
Felix, German(us), / armiger Tauri f(ilii) / hic situs est.

(A301) (6510)
Prima Erotis (scil. serva?), / Cappadoca.

(A302) (6513)
Rosae / libertae.

(A303) (6534)
T. Statilius / T. l. Eros, / hic situs est.

(A304) (6569)
Statilia / Agathlonis l(iberta) / Iucunda.

(A305) (6218)
Antiochus, / lecticarius / de conlegio.

(A306) (6219)
T. Statilius / Anoptes, pistor de conleg(io).

(A307) (6439)
Eupemus / Bassi ser(vus), / vix(it) an(nis) II, men(sibus) V.

(A308) (6265)
Teres, / cubicul(arius).

(A309) (6300)
Felix, / Messalinae / lanipend(us?)

(A310) (6498)
Peregrinus / Posidippi ser(vus), / vix(it) ann(is) XX.

(A311) (6572)
Statilia / Martha / Alexandri l(iberta).

(A312) (6519)
Secunda, / Thraecida (!)

(A313) (6228)
Euenus, Chresti / Auctiani vicar(ius), / de amphiteatro (!), / v(ixit) a(nnis) XXV.

(A314) (6325)
Secunda, / opstetrix / Statiliae Maioris.

(A315) (6508)
Primigenius / Tiphi l(ibertus).

(A316) (6428)
L. Cornelius / L. l. Alexsander.

(A317) (6449)
Felicio, / vix(it) a(nnis) X.

(A318) (6332)
Eutrophus, / ped(isequus).

(A319) (6292)
Felix, horrearius, / Hipparchi vicarius.

(A320) (6385)
Apollinaris / Chresti Auctiani / vicarius, v(ixit) a(nnis) XXV.

(A321) (6434)
Egloge / Narcissi anc(illa).

(A322) (6450)
Felicla / Alexandri l(iberti) / ancilla.

(A323) (6469)
Hermion[e] / C. Minuci Galli (scil. serva), / Philadelpho, / avonculo suo, ob / pietatem erga in se (!).

(A324) (6533)
T. Statilius / Eros, / vix(it) an(nis) LX.

(A325) (6529)
T. Statilius Dasius, / vix(it) ann(is) XXX, / Cale coniunx fec(it).

(A326) (6553)
T. Statilius / Timaeus.

(A327) (6372)
T. Statilius / Dasius Tauri l(ibertus), / ad vestem avi.

(A328) (6268)
T. Statilius Epicrates, / Aucti disp(ensatoris) frater.

(A329) (6543)
T. Statilius / Heracleo, / [S]isennae l(ibertus).

(A330) (6358)
Sophro, Sisennae / Statili ser(vus), tabul(arius); / Psyche soror et / Optata coniunx fecer(unt).

(A331) (6523)
T. Statilius Thespi l(ibertus) / Alexis.

(A332) (6520)
Sestiliae Aptae, / vix(it) a(nnis) XL, / Ti. Iulius Aug. l. / Philantropus / coniugi carissimae.

(A333) (6579)
Statilia / Quadrati / liberti l(iberta) / Venusta, vix(it) an(nis) XVII.

(A334) (6237)
Urbani, Germani, / ossa hic sita sunt.

(A335) (6267)
Aphia, mater / Aucti l(iberti), / dispensatoris.

(A336) (6477)
Iovincae, / Theophili / et Cissi (scil. servae).

(A337) (6351)
Phyllis, Statiliae / sarcinatr(ix), / Sophro coniugi suae / merenti.

(A338) (6433)
Egloge / Hilari. (scil. serva?).

(A339) (6481)
Iucunda, / l(iberta).

(A340) (6336)
Posis, / Statiliaes / pedisequa.

(A341) (6242)
Primus, / atriesis (!).

(A342) (6326)
Optata, Pasaes / ostiaria. Fecerunt / amici.

(A343) (6383)
Ismyrne, / veterana.

(A344) (6264)
[T.] Statilius Phileros, / Corneliaes / cubicularius.

(A345) (6324)
Atticus f(ilius) / Stactes nutricis, / Sisennae f(ilii) conlacteus, / `v(ixit) ann(is) IV´.

(A346) (6375)
Statilia / Rufilla / T. Statilii / Heraclae, viat(oris), uxor.

(A347) (6571)
Statilia Lychoris / hic sita est; / T. Statiliu(s) Carus, / v(ixit) a(nnis) VIIII / cum mama sua.

(A348) (6566)
Diis Manibus / Statiliae Hilarae, / Attice posuit / matri suae bene merenti.

(A349) (6294)
Menander, / horrearius.

(A350) (6567)
Statilia / Hilara, Cissi (scil. uxor), / v(ixit) a(nnis) XXXX.

(A351) (6562)
Statilia / Helladis l(iberta) / Eucumene.

(A352) (6297)
Diogenes, / insularius.

(A353) (6322)
Boethus, / Corneliaes (scil. servus), / a monumento.

(A354) (6408)
Antiochus hic / situs est, vixit / annos XXXV.

(A355) (6493)
Onesimus, / Posidippi / T. Statili ser(vus), / vixit an(nis) VII.

(A356) (6223)
[---]o Primo et Cn. Fulv[io---] / [---im]agines posuit et coler[e---].

(A357) (6317)
Anthus Zenae / Sutoriani (scil. servus?).

(A358) (6344)
Plecte, / quasilaria (!).

(A359) (6357)
Diomedi, tabell(ario), / contubernales / dant.

(A360) (6365a=9415)
T. Statili / Tauri l(iberti) / Antiochi, / fab(er) tig(nari). // Statiliae / T. l. Muntanae.

(A361) (6419)
L. Calpurn(ius) / Abascantus / L. Calpurnio Nedym(o) / patrono benemerenti / fecit.

(A362) (6502)
Desinite aequales Plocami lugere sepulti / fata frequentatis funeris exsequiis! / In requiem excessi. Quod quaeritis, id repetitum / apstulit iniustus creditor ante diem. / Compositos tantum cineres humus integat, oro, / inque vicem pietas vestra parentis eat.

(A363) (6511)
Psycarionis hic / ossua (!) sita sunt.

(A364) (6516)
D(is) M(anibus). / Salutari vernae suo / carissimo, vix(it) a(nnis) II, m(ensibus) VI, / d(iebus) XXV. fecer(unt) / C. Caecilius Atimetus et Manlia / Terpne sibi suis posterisq(ue) eorum.

(A365) (6561)
Statilia Erotis, / T. Statili Chresti / Barbiani liberta.

(A366) (6580)
Stat[ilia---], / vix(it) [ann(is)---].

(A367) (6589)
Dis Manib(us), / Vitelia (!) / Nereis fecit / ------.

(A368) (6593)
Viva viro placui prima et carissum(a) coniunx / quoius in ore animam frigida deposui. / Ille mihi lachrimans morientia lumin(a) pressit. / Post obitum satis hac femina laude nitet.

(A369) (6574)
Statilia / Posidippi / l(iberta) Phoebe, v(ixit) a(nnis) XII.

Urns

(A370) (6323)
Echonis, Statiliae / Minoris fili / nutr<i>x.

(A371) (6381)
Plebeia Statilia, / Philerotis liberti, / unctoris, et Artagenis / filia, vixit annos / duos et menses sex.

(A372) (6522)
[T.? Stati]lius Tau[ri l. ---] / [Sta]tiliae [---] / ------.

(A373) (6591)
Zmyrna Post/tumiana (!)

Others

(A374) (6245)
Epaphra, / puer / capsa(rius).

Materials unidentifiable or unavailable

(A375) (6248)
Nireus, / [Ph]ilerotis l(iberti), coci, ser(vus), / vix(it) ann(is) V.

(A376) (6290)
Posporus, fullo.

(A377) (6418)
Bonaes.

(A378) (6438)
Eupemus.

(A379) (6499)
Phileros.

(A380) (6503)
Polonus, / vix(it) ann(is) VII.

(A381) (6558)
Statilia / Tauri l. / Bassa, / Zmaragdi (scil. uxor), // T. Statilius / Thallus. / v(ixit) a(nnis) XXIV.

∞ ∞ ∞ ∞ ∞

A2. Structure (O)

Wall plaques

(A382) (6599)
[---Cor]neliai (scil. liberta?), / [vix(it) a]nn(is) XX.

(A383) (6595)
Epapho, / Corvini a manu, / ann(orum) XXXV. / Diodorus, conser(vus), / cubicularius, / fecit.

(A384) (6600)
D(is) [M(anibus)]. / Cornelia[e---] / Eutych[---] / coniu[gi---] / ------.

(A385) (6607)
Sext[ia---] / [-----] / T. Sexti[---] / coniu[gi---] / -----

(A386) (6608)
D(is) [M(anibus)] / Sosii Elp[---] / et Tych+ [---] / Elpidi [---] / et si[bi et ---].

(A387) (6611)
C. Valerius / C. f. / Cosanus.

(A388) (6614)
Dis / Manibus / [------].

(A389) (6615)
[Sosi?]strati, / [cu]bicl(ari) (!) / [ossa] hic / [sita sunt].

(A390) (6606)
Hic si[tus ets] / Nomas, [q(ui) v(ixit) ann(is)] / XX[---], Sex. Vib[---] / mer[enti ---].

(A391) (6610)
T. Statilius Karus, / annorum novem / ++[---]++[---]/------.

(A392) (6598)
Ti. Claudi / Bathylli.

(A393) (6597)
P. Baebius / Onesimus / sibi et suis.

(A394) (6596)
Dis manibus. / Sperato, tabulario, / Messallinae Neronis (scil. uxoris) / servo, vixit annis XXX, / Statilia Felicula coniunx / bene merenti fecit.

(A395) (6613)
Urbanus.

(A396) (6602)
Fortunatae / Fructus fecit.

(A397) (6604)
Invento, / Tauri Statili servo, / Prima conservo suo / merenti fecit, v(ixit) a(nnis) XXXV.

(A398) (6616)
------ / [---con]iugi / [---quoc]um vixit / [---] XXIIX.

(A399) (6601)
------? / [---]s Dio/[---D]icaeo-sy/[ne---] bene / [meren]ti / [------].

(A400) (6612)
Valeria Prima sibi et / C. Valerio C. f. Cosano patrono et / P. Camelio Salvillo viro carissim(o) et / Primigeniae delicio suo et / libertis libertabus posterisq(ue) eorum.

Stone slabs

(A401) (6603)
Herma(s), / T. Statili Tauri (scil. servus), / vixit annis / XVIII. / Ossa.

(A402) (6605) Iuliae Tyche. / Rhesus filius / matri fecit.

(A403) (6617)
Q. Fictorius / Onesimus / T. Statilio / Cesto / posuit.

(A404) (6618)
T. Statilius / Trophimus / Chrotidi / contubernali / bene merenti / fecit.

Altars

(A405) (6619)
Diis / Manibus / Primi, / Messallinae / Neronis (scil. uxoris) ser(vi) vern(ae), / opsonat(oris) / vix(it) ann(is) XXI. / Statilius Hesychus, / patruus, p(osuit) d(e) s(uo).

(A406) (6620)
Dis manibus / Statiliae / Messallinae l(ibertae) / Primillae. / Haec vixit ann(is) X, / m(ensibus) VII, d(iebus) XVIIII. / Hesychus pater fecit.

(A407) (6621)
Diis Manibus / Iuliae Mansuetae / et Graecini filii; / Martialis Abascanti / C. Nymphidi Sabini / praef(ecti) p(raetorio) / ser(vus) vicarius, / coniugi et filio.

∞ ∞ ∞ ∞ ∞

A3. Structure (P)

Wall plaques

(A408) (6625)
Dis Manibus. / Comico Onesimi / Messallinae Nero/nis (scil. uxoris) lib(erti) ser(vo). Fecit / Pantagathus / conservo b(ene) m(erenti).

(A409) (6627)
Helenus / Cornelianus, / vixit ann(is) XXXI.

(A410) (6628)
Dis Man(ibus). / Hermes et / Statilia Donata / T. Statilio Dionico / parenti et contuber(nali) / et Dicaeosyone (!) servae / benemerentibus.

(A411) (6629)
Olia Gemella, vixit annos / XVI, Olia P. l. Paralia, mater; / sibi et filiae fecit.

(A412) (6630)
Pedan[i---] / Prim[---].

(A413) (6631)
RECTO: Quintia A. l. / Sperata.
VERSO: Vix(it) ann(is) XXV, / Quintia / Sperata / A. Quinti / Pamphili l(iberta).

(A414) (6635)
Threptus Statiliae / Rhodes alumnus, / vixit an(nos) X et mens(es) duo.

(A415) (6636)
------ / [b(ene)] m(erenti) f(ecit) / Verecundus, / q(ui) v(ixit) a(nnis) XVII, m(ensibus) V, / d(iebus) XXIX.

(A416) (6622)
D(is) M(anibus). / L. Abuccius / Alexander / fecit / Clodiae Agathe / coniugi b(ene)m(eren)t(i).

(A417) (6623)
C. Galerius + [---] / Artemisia [---], / vixit an[n(is)] XLII, / perit sub sabuc(a) (!).

(A418) (6633)
Diis M[ani]bus / T. Statili [---]geni / ++[---]a coniugi suo / [---] fecit, / [---]XXXVII, d(iebus) IX.

(A419) (6632)
T. Statilius Tauri l(ibertus) Mystes / filis suis piissimiis: / T. Statilio Mysti, / vixit annis XXXV; // T. Statilio Thallo, / vixit annis XXXVI.

(A420) (6624)
Coeliae Catulli l(ibertae) / Agathemeridis.

(A421) (6637)
D(is) M(anibus) s(acrum). / A. Vibio Capitoni, / vix(it) ann(is) IIII, m(ensibus) V, d(iebus) XI. / A. Vibius Capito, pater, fecit / et sibi posterisque suis.

Stone slabs

(A422) (6626)
Diis / Manib[us] / Galeriae / Hygiae.

(A423) (6634)
D(is) M(anibus). / Statilia Pia / Statiliae Topy/rae (!) matri be/ne merenti fe/cit. Vixit annis / XXXIIII, mens(ibus) VIII.

(A424) (6640)
D(is) M(anibus). F(ecit?) / Statilia Hegema / T. Statilio / Felici c(ari)s(simo); / v(ixit) a(nnis) XXXXV, / s(ibi) p(osterisque) s(uis).

Urns

(A425) (6638)
Corinthias / Statili Faustionis / et Statiliae Hedones / delicium, vixit / ann(is) VIIII.

(A426) (6639)
D(is) M(anibus). Iuliae Eleutheridi / dominae, Menophilus / Aug(usti) n(ostri) despensator (!) / Ciliciae.

Others

(A427)
Antistia / ((mulieris)) l(iberta) / Lais.

∞ ∞ ∞ ∞ ∞

A4. Inscriptions from the *columbarium* but omitted in the editions of Caldelli and Ricci, but included in *CIL* VI.

(A428) (6221)
Donatus Tauri German. / hic situs est sodales ei funus / fecerunt hom. CXXX ✕ CCXXV / curatoribus Maximo Helicone Dapno.

(A429) (6442)
D. M. Faustini Faustus pater et Euuochia mater filio pissimo fecer.

B. Inscriptions relating to slaves and freedmen of the Statilii discovered elsewhere

(B001) (6208)
Cellia Aetheatice / T. Statili Chresti / coniux fida viro.

(B002) (9775)
Doris, Statiliae Mino[ris] / pediseq(ua); / Erotis, ad inpediment[a], / vixit an(nis) XXIIII.

(B003) (17401)
Eutychae Statiliae (scil. servae) / Nardinus / delicio, / vixit an(nis) / III, m(ensibus) IIII.

(B004) (22272=2344)
Masae Tauri l. ossa heic sita sunt.

(B005) (33185)
Mylo Tauri ser(vus). // T. Statilius Hyacinthus.

(B006) (8952)
Amoenus, Messallinae / Ti. Claudi Caesaris (scil. uxoris) / ab ornamentis

(B007) (9191)
T. Statili / Cirrati / l(iberti) Germ(ani), armig(eri) / Tauri (scil. filii); // Donat[l], / dispen[s(atoris)] / Messalin[ae] / Tauri (scil. filiae).

(B008) (9287)
T. Statilius / Tauri l. Synistor, / supra cubicl(arios) (!).

(B009) (9842)
Agrimatio, / Statiliaes / Tauri f. Messalinae / pumilio.

(B010) (9922)
Alexander, / Tauri tabul(arius), / vixit ann(is) XXV, / Prisca contub(ernalis) d(e) s(uo) fecit.

(B011) (10386)
Statilia (!) Storge / contubernali / Statili Mystis, / decur(ionis).

(B012) (19363)
Herma Statiliae / sibi et suae / conservae Palladioni I (!).

(B013) (19754)
Iucunda / Messallinae.

(B014) (26758)
T. Statilius Tauri l. / Cnidus, / Statilia T. l. / Philematium.

(B015) (26760)
T. Statilio Tauri l. / Eleuthero, / Statilia Storge coliberto suo.

(B016) (26771)
T. Statilio / Corvini l. / Nereo. // (vacat)

(B017) (26784)
Statilia Tauri l. / Albana, pia in suos hic requiscit v(ixit) a(nnis) III.

(B018) (26787)
Statiliae T. Hilari l. / Iucundae, / fe[m]inae fidisimae, vixit cara suis ann(is) / XXVIIII.

(B019) (26915)
Diis manibus / Successae / Messalinae Neronis (scil. uxoris) lib(ertae). / Epaphroditus, / Prisca, Onesime, / matri piissimae fecerunt.

(B020) (28661a)
[- Vettius] M. Tucci l. Prim[---] / [sibi] et [---] M. l. Logo, / [---] Tauri l. Chio, / et Vettiae Urbanae f. / <<[Antesti Abascanti (scil. uxori)]>> / [libert]abusque postereis[que] / et C. Antesti Repe[ntini].

(B021) (38303)
D(is) [M(anibus)]. / Ela[ino] / Messall[inae] / Neronis (scil.uxoris) ser(vo).

(B022a) (9412)
T. Statili(us) Tauri / l. Antiochi, fabri / tib(nuarii). In fr(onte) p(edes) XII, in ag(ro) p(edes) XI[I].

(B022b) (9413)
T. Statili / Tauri l. / Antiochi, fab(ri) / tig(nuarii). / In f(ronte) p(edes) XII, in ag(ro) p(edes) XII.

(B022c) (9414)
T. Statili(us) / Tauri l. / Antiochi, / fab(ri) tig(nuarii). In fr(onte) p(edes) XII, in agr(o) p(edes) XII.

(B022d) (9415=6365a)
T. Statili / Tauri l. / Antiochi, / fab(ri) /tig(nuarii). // Statiliae / T.l. / Muntanae.

(B023) (9808)
T. Statilius / Eros, pistor, / Caninianus. // Statilia / Zotiche.

(B024) (9883)
Statilia / Calliste, / sarcinatr(ix).

(B025) (9913)
T. Statilius / Tyrannus, sumpt(uarius). // Statilia / T. l. Prisca, / Severi (scil. uxor), / Severae T.f. / mater.

(B026) (26764)
T. Statili / Eudaemonis.

(B027) (26765)
T. Statilius / Faustus.

(B028) (26767)
T. Statilius / Hialissus.

(B029) (26770)
T. Statilius Metra; / v(ivit) Statilia Chreste; / v(ivit) Statilia Vitalis.

(B030) (26777)
T. Statilius / Sanius (!).

(B031-B032) – fragmental inscriptions, to be disregarded here

(B033)
D(is) M(anibus) / Statiliae / Leae, / C. Statilius Anthi/mas benemerenti / fecit.

(B034)
Dis Manibus / Erasti C. Statili / Messalini ser(vi); / Artia, mater, filio / piissimo fecet (!); / vix(it) / annis XVI, dies / XIIV.

(B035) (26790)
Statiliae / Methe, v(ixit) a(nnis) XX, / Primigenius / Agrippinae (scil. servus) / coniugi fec(it).

(B036) (4654)
D(is) M(anibus). Fortuna/ta, mater, f(ecit) / T. Statilio Prisco / filio.

(B037) (16091)
Diis Manibus. // Cordia Peregrina / T. Statilio Latino, / coniugi karissi/mo, vix(it) an(nis) XXXV. / Cordia Peregrina / sibi et suis poste/risque eorum. // Teredia Sosime / fecit filio suo et / M. Teredio Rodoni, / patrono benemere(nti), / sibi et posterisque suis. // Petronia / Epinoe / v(ixit) a(nnis) XXII.

(B038) (20149)
D(is) M(anibus). / Ti. Iulius Nepos se vibus conparav/it sibi et suis libert(is) liberta(bus) posterisq(ue) / eorum itemque Statiliis liberti(s) / libertabus coiugis suae quond/am et C. Iulio Hilaro amico dulcissi/mo et liber(tis) liberta(bus) eius in portion/e locorum duorum et iudeici (!) sicu(t) / donationi (!) ei factae continetur.

(B039) (26772)
D(is) M(anibus). / T. Statilio Pietati, / v(ixit) a(nnis) X, d(iebus) XXVII, h(oris) III. / T. Statilius Blastus / filio / pientissimo / fecit.

(B040) – fragmental inscription, to be disregarded here

Unpublished inscriptions

(B041)
Statilia / Secunda / Statilio / Decembro / f(ilio) suo fecit; / vix(it) ann(is) IX, / mens(ibus) VI.

(B042)
Dis / Manibus. / T. Statilio / Eutycho. / Fecit Stati/lia Prisca / patrono [...].

APPENDIX: INSCRIPTIONS RELATING TO THE *FAMILIA* OF THE STATILII

(B043)
D(is) M(anibus) / Statilio Martino con/[i]ugi benemerenti. Fe(cit) / [Sta]tilia Grat(a), cum [qua] vixit a[nnis...?] [...].

(B044-47) – fragmental inscriptions, to be disregarded here

(B048)
Statilia M.l. / Nice ollam sibi emit. // St[atilia ...?] / [...].

Concordance of the Statilian inscriptions

1. The *columbarium* of the Statilii (from structure O, N, P)

CIL VI / in this book		
6213 / A015	6260 / A081	6308 / A093
6214 / A047	6261 / A052	6309 / A094
6215 / A066	6262 / A267	6310 / A061
6216 / A067	6263 / A019	6311 / A095
6217 / A255	6264 / A344	6312 / A294
6218 / A305	6265 / A308	6313 / A096
6219 / A306	6266 / A278	6314 / A024
6220 / A258	6267 / A335	6315 / A025
6221 / A428*	6268 / A328	6316 / A026
6222 / A202	6269 / A256	6317 / A357
6223 / A356	6271 / A279	6318 / A097
6224 / A203	6272 / A286	6319 / A206
6225 / A204	6273 / A208	6320 / A115
6226 / A009	6274 / A058	6321 / A027
6227 / A068	6275 / A001	6322 / A353
6228 / A313	6276 / A020	6323 / A370
6229 / A300	6277 / A053	6324 / A345
6230 / A069	6278 / A021	6325 / A314
6231 / A295	6279 / A268	6326 / A342
6232 / A065	6279 / A275	6327 / A211
6233 / A205	6280 / A082	6328 / A242
6234 / A063	6281 / A280	6329 / A060
6235 / A070	6282 / A263	6330 / A212
6236 / A064	6283 / A083	6331 / A246
6237 / A334	6284 / A084	6332 / A318
6238 / A071	6285 / A048	6333 / A098
6239 / A072	6286 / A264	6334 / A287
6240 / A073	6287 / A085	6335 / A296
6241 / A262	6288 / A257	6336 / A340
6242 / A341	6289 / A086	6337 / A281
6243 / A049	6290 / A376	6338 / A028
6244 / A274	6291 / A209	6339 / A050
6245 / A374	6292 / A319	6340 / A099
6246 / A057	6293 / A045	6341 / A288
6247 / A259	6294 / A349	6342 / A100
6248 / A375	6295 / A087	6343 / A101
6249 / A074	6296 / A088	6344 / A358
6250 / A075	6297 / A352	6345 / A102
6251 / A016	6298 / A089	6346 / A029
6252 / A076	6299 / A090	6347 / A103
6253 / A077	6300 / A309	6348 / A104
6254 / A078	6301 / A210	6349 / A002
6255 / A079	6302 / A022	6350 / A233
6256 / A017	6303 / A091	6351 / A337
6256 / A018	6304 / A092	6352 / A105
6258 / A080	6305 / A241	6353 / A106
6259 / A265	6306 / A023	6354 / A213
	6307 / A232	6355 / A107

6356 / A108	6411 / A130	6467 / A158
6357 / A359	6412 / A131	6468 / A159
6358 / A330	6413 / A217	6469 / A323
6359 / A282	6414 / A132	6470 / A160
6360 / A109	6415 / A133	6471 / A161
6361 / A110	6416 / A134	6472 / A219
6362 / A003	6417 / A245	6473 / A162
6363 / A111	6418 / A377	6474 / A240
6364 / A112	6419 / A361	6475 / A277
6365 / A289	6420 / A135	6476 / A163
6365a=9415 / A360	6421 / A136	6477 / A336
6366 / A290	6422 / A239	6478 / A285
6367 / A113	6423 / A032	6479 / A270
6368 / A291	6424 / A033	6480 / A234
6369 / A283	6425 / A298	6481 / A339
6370 / A276	6426 / A137	6482 / A164
6371 / A114	6427 / A218	6483 / A165
6372 / A327	6428 / A316	6484 / A166
6373 / A214	6429 / A034	6485 / A167
6374 / A284	6430 / A138	6486 / A243
6375 / A346	6431 / A035	6487 / A247
6376 / A215	6432 / A139	6488 / A168
6377 / A030	6433 / A338	6489 / A169
6378 / A207	6434 / A321	6490 / A040
6379 / A014	6435 / A140	6491 / A170
6380 / A116	6436 / A036	6492 / A171
6381 / A371	6437 / A037	6493 / A355
6382 / A117	6438 / A378	6494 / A004
6383 / A343	6439 / A307	6495 / A220
6384 / A118	6440 / A038	6496 / A172
6385 / A320	6441 / A141	6497 / A173
6386 / A054	6442 / A429*	6498 / A310
6387 / A031	6443 / A142	6499 / A379
6388 / A119	6444 / A010	6500 / A174
6389 / A120	6445 / A143	6501 / A175
6390 / A253	6446 / A039	6502 / A362
6391 / A121	6447 / A144	6503 / A380
6392 / A046	6448 / A145	6504 / A235
6393 / A122	6449 / A317	6505 / A176
6394 / A236	6450 / A322	6506 / A177
6395 / A006	6451 / A146	6507 / A005
6396 / A269	6452 / A147	6508 / A315
6397 / A266	6453 / A148	6509 / A062
6398 / A123	6454 / A149	6510 / A301
6399 / A124	6455 / A150	6511 / A363
6400 / A125	6456 / A151	6512 / A221
6401 / A126	6457 / A152	6513 / A302
6402 / A216	6458 / A153	6514 / A178
6403 / A127	6459 / A007	6515 / A041
6404 / A297	6460 / A238	6516 / A364
6405 / A128	6461 / A154	6517 / A244
6406 / A272	6462 / A155	6518 / A179
6407 / A129	6463 / A156	6519 / A312
6408 / A354	6464 / A157	6520 / A332
6409 / A055	6465 / A292	6521 / A222
6410 / A254	6466 / A273	6522 / A372

6523 / A331	6563 / A195	6603 / A401
6524 / A180	6564 / A196	6604 / A397
6525 / A271	6565 / A229	6605 / A402
6526 / A181	6566 / A348	6606 / A390
6527 / A182	6567 / A350	6607 / A385
6528 / A008	6568 / A251	6608 / A386
6529 / A325	6569 / A304	6609=6548 / A042
6530 / A011	6570 / A252	6610 / A391
6531 / A223	6571 / A347	6611 / A387
6532 / A224	6572 / A311	6612 / A400
6533 / A324	6573 / A197	6613 / A395
6534 / A303	6574 / A369	6614 / A388
6535 / A183	6575 / A198	6615 / A389
6536 / A184	6576 / A230	6616 / A398
6537 / A225	6577 / A012	6617 / A403
6538 / A226	6578 / A059	6618 / A404
6539 / A248	6579 / A333	6619 / A405
6540 / A293	6580 / A366	6620 / A406
6541 / A249	6581 / A199	6621 / A407
6542 / A227	6582 / A043	6622 / A416
6543 / A329	6583 / A231	6623 / A417
6544 / A185	6584 / A056	6624 / A420
6545 / A186	6585 / A200	6625 / A408
6546 / A228	6586 / A299	6626 / A422
6547 / A260	6587 / A051	6627 / A409
6548 =6609 / A042	6588 / A237	6628 / A410
6549 / A187	6589 / A367	6629 / A411
6550 / A188	6590 / A201	6630 / A412
6551 / A189	6591 / A373	6631 / A413
6552 / A190	6592 / A044	6632 / A419
6553 / A326	6593 / A368	6633 / A418
6554 / A191	6594 / A013	6634 / A423
6555 / A192	6595 / A383	6635 / A414
6556 / A250	6596 / A394	6636 / A415
6557 / A261	6597 / A393	6637 / A421
6558 / A381	6598 / A392	6638 / A425
6559 / A193	6599 / A382	6639 / A426
6560 / A194	6600 / A384	6640 / A424
6561 / A365	6601 / A399	- / A427
6562 / A351	6602 / A396	

2. Inscriptions relating to the Statilii (from outside the *columbarium* or unknown place)

CIL number / in this book		
4654 / B036	9913 / B025	26765 / B027
6208 / B001	9922 / B010	26767 / B028
8952 / B006	9415=6365a / B022d	26770 / B029
9191 / B007	10386 / B011	26771 / B016
9287 / B008	16091 / B037	26772 / B039
9412 / B022a	17401 / B003	26777 / B030
9413 / B022b	19363 / B012	26784 / B017
9414 / B022c	19754 / B013	26787 / B018
9775 / B002	20149 / B038	26790 / B035
9808 / B023	22272=2344 / B004	26915 / B019
9842 / B009	26758 / B014	28661a / B020
9883 / B024	26760 / B015	33185 / B005
	26764 / B026	38303 / B021

Bibliography

Astin, A. E. (1978), *Cato the Censor*. Oxford.

Aubert, J. (1994), *Business Managers in Ancient Rome; A Social and Economic Study of Institores, 200 B.C. – A.D. 250*. Leiden.

Baldwin, B. (1978), 'Trimalchio's domestic staff', *Acta Classica* 21: 87-97.

Barrett, A. A. (2002), *Livia, First Lady of Imperial Rome*. London.

Barrow, R. H. (1928), *Slavery in the Roman Empire*. London.

Bassett, S. (ed.) (1992), *Death in Towns – Urban Responses to the Dying and the Dead, 100-1600*. London.

Bauman, R. A. (1992), *Women and Politics in Ancient Rome*. London.

Bellen, H. (1981), *Die germanische Leibwache der römischen Kaiser des julisch-claudishen Hauses*. Mainz.

Benario, H. W. (1970), 'The family of Statilius Taurus', *Classical World* 64: 73-76.

Bianchini, F. (1991), *Camera ed inscrizioni sepulcrali de' liberti, servi, ed ufficiali della casa di Augusto scoperte nella via Appia*. Naples. Reprint of original 1727 edition, with introduction by J. Kolendo.

Boatwright, M. T. (1982), 'The Lucii Volusii Saturnini and Tacitus', in *I Volusii Saturnini: Una famiglia romana della prima età imperiale*, Bari, pp.7-16.

Bodel, J. (1994), *Graveyards and Groves, a Study of the Lex Lucerina* (*American Journal of Ancient History* 11), Cambridge.

———. (2001), *Epigraphic Evidence. Ancient History from Inscriptions*. London.

———. (2003), Review of H. Solin, *Die Stadtrömischen Sklavennamen*, *Bryn Mawr Classical Review* (http://ccat.sas.upenn.edu/bmcr/2003/2003-01-03.html)

Bosworth, A. B. (2002), 'Vespasian and the slave trade', *CQ* 52: 350-357.

Bradley, K. (1986), 'Wet-nursing at Rome: a study in social relations', in Rawson, 1986a, 201-229.

———. (1987a), *Slaves and Masters in the Roman Empire*. Oxford.

———. (1987b), 'On the Roman slave supply and slavebreeding', *Slavery and Abolition* 8: 42-64.

———. (1991), 'Remarriage and the structure of the upper-class Roman family', in Rawson, 1991, 79-98.

———. (1994), *Slavery and Society at Rome*. Cambridge.

———. (2000), 'Animalising the slave: the truth of fiction', *JRS* 90: 110-125.

Bradley, M. (2002), 'It all comes out in the wash; looking harder at the Roman *fullonica*', *Journal of Roman Archaeology* 15: 21-44.

Brunt, P. A. (1961), 'Charges of provincial maladministration under the early Principate', *Historia* 10: 189-223.

———. (1966), 'The Roman mob', in Finley, 1974, 74-102.

———. (1971), *Italian Manpower, 225BC – AD14*. Oxford.

———. (1980), 'Free labour and public works', *JRS* 70: 83-100.

Buckland, W. W. (1908), *The Roman Law of Slavery*. Cambridge.

Buonocore, M. (1984), *Schiavi e liberti dei Volusi Saturnini – le iscrizioni del colombario sulla via Appia antica*. Rome.

Bush, M. L. (ed.) (1996), *Serfdom and Slavery*. London.

Caldelii, M. L. and Ricci, C. (1999), *Monumentum familiae Statiliorum*. Rome.

Carter, J. M. (1982), *Suetonius: Divus Augustus*. Bristol.

Chilton, C. W. (1955), 'The Roman law of treason under the early Principate', *JRS* 45: 73-81.

Cooley, A. (2000), *The Epigraphic Landscape of Roman Italy*. London.

Corbier, M. (2001), 'Child exposure and abandonment', in Dixon (ed.), 2001, 52-73.

Cotter, W. (1996), 'The *collegia* and Roman law', in Kloppenborg and Wilson, 1996, 74-89.

Crook, J. (1955), *Consilium Principis*. Cambridge.

———. (1967), *Law and Life of Rome*. Ithaca.

Croom, A. T. (2000), *Roman Clothing and Fashion*. Charleston.

D'Arms, J. H. (1981), *Commerce and Social Standing in Ancient Rome*. London.

Dixon, S. (1988), *The Roman Mother*. London.

———. (1992), *The Roman Family*. London.

———. (2001a), *Reading Roman Women. Sources, Genres and Real Life*. London.

———. (ed.) (2001b), *Childhood, Class and Kin in the Roman World*. London.

———. (2001c), 'The 'other' Romans and their family values', in Dixon (ed.), 2001b, 1-17.

Duff, A. M. (1928), *Freedmen in the Roman Empire*. Oxford.

Duncan-Jones, R. (1982), *The Economy of the Roman Empire*. Cambridge. 2nd edn.

Eck, W. (1972), 'Die Familie der Volusii Saturnini in neuen Inschriften aus Lucus Feroniae', *Hermes* 100: 461-484.

———. (1981), 'Miscellanea Prosopographica', *ZPE* 42: 227-256.

———. (1984), 'Senatorial self-representation: developments in the Augustan period', in Millar and Segal, 1984, 129-167.

———. (1997a), 'Rome and the outside world: senatorial families and the world they lived in', in Rawson and Weaver, 1997, 73-100.

———. (1997b), '*Cum dignitate otium*: senatorial *domus* in imperial Rome,' *Scripta Classica Israelica* 16: 162-190.

Evans, J. K. (1991), *War, Women and Children in Ancient Rome*. London.

Farrar, L. (1998), *Ancient Roman Gardens*. Stroud.

Finley, M. (ed.) (1960), *Slavery in Classical Antiquity*. Cambridge.

———. (1973), *The Ancient Economy*. London.

———. (ed.) (1974), *Studies in Ancient Society*. London.

———. (ed.) (1976), *Studies in Roman Property*. Cambridge.

———. (1998), *Ancient Slavery and Modern Ideology*. Princeton.

Fitzgerald, W. (2000), *Slavery and the Roman Literary Imagination*. Cambridge.

Flory, M. B. (1978), 'Family in *familia*: kinship and community in slavery', *AJAH* 3: 78-95.

———. (1988), 'The meaning of Augusta in the Julio-Claudian period', *AJAH* 13: 113-138.

Frank, T. (1916), 'Race mixture in the Roman Empire', *American Historical Review* 21: 689-708.

———. (1936), *An Economic Survey of Ancient Rome*. vol. ii. Baltimore.

Fraschetti, A. (ed.) (1994), *Roman Women*. London.

———. (1994), 'Livia the politician', in Fraschetti (ed.), 1994, 100-117.

Frier, B. (1982), 'Roman life expectancy: Ulpian's evidence'. *Harvard Studies in Classical Philology* 86: 213-251.

Gardner, J. (1993), *Being a Roman Citizen*. London.

Gardner, J. and Wiedemann, T. (1991), *The Roman Household: a Sourcebook*. London.

Garland, A. (1992), 'Cicero's *familia urbana*', *G&R*, 39-2: 163-172.

Garnsey, P. (1976), 'Urban property investment', in Finley, 1976: 123-136.

———. (ed.) (1980a), *Non-Slave Labour in the Greco-Roman World*. Cambridge.

———. (1980b), 'Non-slave labour in the Roman world', in Garnsey, 1980, 34-47.

———. (1981), 'Independent freedmen and the economy of Roman Italy under the Principate', *Klio* 63: 359-371.

George, M. (1997), '*Servus* and *domus*: the slave in the Roman house', in Laurence and Wallace-Hadrill, 1997, 15-24.

Gordon, M. (1924), 'The nationality of slaves under the early Roman Empire', in Finley, 1960, 93-111.

Grimal, P. P. (1969), *Les jardins romains*. Paris.

Gummerus, H. (1920), 'Die Bauspekulation des Crassus', *Klio* 16: 190-192.

Harris, W. V. (1980), 'Towards a study of the Roman slave trade', *Memoirs of the American Academy* 36: 117-140.

———. (1994), 'Child-exposure in the Roman Empire', *JRS* 84: 1-22.

———. (1999), 'Demography, geography and the sources of Roman slaves', *JRS* 89: 62-75.

Herrmann-Otto, E. (1997), *Ex Ancilla Natus*. Stuttgart.

von Hesberg, H., and Zanker, P. (1985), *Römische Gräberstrassen*. München.

Hope, V. (2000), 'Fighting for identity: the funerary commemoration of Italian gladiators' in Cooley (ed.), 2000, 93-113.

———. (2001), *Constructing Identity: The Roman Funerary Monuments of Aquileia, Mainz, and Nimes*. Oxford.

Hopkins, K. (1978), *Conquerors and Slaves*. Cambridge.

———. (1983), *Death and Renewal*. Cambridge.

———. (1993), 'Novel evidence for Roman slavery', *Past and Present* 138: 3-27.

Huttunen, P. (1974), *The Social Strata in the Imperial City of Rome*. Oulu.

Jones, A. H. M., ed. by P. A. Brunt (1973), *The Roman Economy: Studies in Ancient Economic and Administrative History*. Oxford.

Joshel, S. R. (1992), *Work, Identity, and Legal status at Rome*. London.

Joshel, S. R. and Murnaghan, S. (eds.) (1998), *Women and Slaves in Greco-Roman Culture*. London.

Kajanto, I. (1965), *The Latin Cognomina*. Helsinki.

Kajava, M. (1989), 'Cornelia and Taurus at Thespiae', *ZPE* 79: 139-149.

Kampen, N. (1981), *Image and Status: Roman Working Women in Ostia*. Berlin.

Kaster, R. A. (1995), *C. Suetonius Tranquillus, De Grammaticus et Rhetoribus*. Oxford.

Kepartová, J. (1986), 'Ein Beitrag zu den Forschungen über die *familia Volusiorum Saturninorum*', *Klio* 68: 281-283.

Keppie, L. (1991), *Understanding Roman Inscriptions*. London.

Kertzer, D. I. and Saller, R. P. (eds.) (1991), *The Family in Italy, from Antiquity to the Present*. London.

Kienast, D. (1982), *Augustus, Prinzeps und Monarch*. Darmstadt.

———. (1990), *Römische Kaisertabelle*. Darmstadt.

Kloppenborg, J. S. and Wilson, S. G. (eds.) (1996), *Voluntary Associations in the Graeco-Roman World*. London.

Lanciani, R. (1889), *Ancient Rome in the light of recent discoveries*. London.

Laurence, R. and Wallace-Hadrill, A. (eds.) (1997), *Domestic Space in the Roman World: Pompeii and Beyond*. Portsmouth.

Levick, B. (1976), *Tiberius the Politician*. London.

De Ligt, L. (2001), 'D. 47, 22, 1, pr.-1 and the formation of semi-public *collegia*', *Latomus* 60: 345-358.

Lintott, A. (1968), *Violence in Republican Rome*. Oxford.

Loane, H. J. (1938), *Industry and Commerce of the City of Rome (50BC-200AD)*. Baltimore.

Laurence, R. (1994), *Roman Pompeii, Space and Society*. London.

Martin, D. B. (1996), 'The construction of the ancient family: methodological considerations', *JRS* 86: 40-60.

Maxey, M. (1938), *Occupations of the Lower Classes in Roman Society*. Chicago.

McWilliam, J. (2001), 'Children among the dead: the influence of urban life on the commemoration of children on tombstone inscriptions', in Dixon (ed.), 2001, 74-75.

Merola, F. R. (1990), *Servo parere*. Camerino.

Miller, F. (1981), 'The world of the Golden Ass', *JRS* 71: 63-75.

Millar, F. and Segal, E. (eds.) (1984), *Caesar Augustus, Seven Aspects*. Oxford.

Morris, I. (1992), *Death-Ritual and Social Structure in Classical Antiquity*. Cambridge.

Mottershead, J. (1986), *Suetonius, Claudius*. Bristol.

Murison, C. (1992), *Suetonius, Galba; Otho; Vitellius*. Bristol.

Nash, E. (1968), *Pictorial Dictionary of Ancient Rome*, vol. I, II. London.

Nielsen, H. S. (1995), 'The physical context of Roman epitaphs and the structure of 'the Roman family'', in *Analecta Romana Instituti Danici* 23: 35-60.

———. (1997), 'Interpreting Epithets in Roman Epitaphs', in Rawson and Weaver, 1997, 169-204.

Nippel, W. (1995), *Public Order in Ancient Rome*. Cambridge.

Noy, D. (2000), *Foreigners at Rome*. London.

Parker, H. (1998), 'Loyal slaves and loyal wives: the crisis of the outsider-within and Roman *exemplum* literature', in Joshel and Murnaghan, 1998, 152-173.

Parri, L. (1998), 'Iscrizioni funerarie, colombari e liberti il terzo ipogeo di Vigna Codini ed alcuni dei suoi epitaffi', *Atene e Roma* 43: 51-60.

Patterson, J. R. (1992), 'Patronage, *collegia* and burial in Imperial Rome', in Bassett, 1992, 5-27.

Patterson, O. (1982), *Slavery and Social Death*. Cambridge.

Platner, S. B. (revised by T. Ashby) (1929), *A Topographical Dictionary of Ancient Rome*. London.

Pomeroy, S. (1975), *Goddesses, Whores, Wives, and Slaves*. London.

Purcell, N. (1985), 'Tomb and suburb', in von Hesberg and Zanker, 1985, 25-41.

———. (1986), 'Livia and the womanhood of Rome,' *Proceedings of the Cambridge Philological Society* 212: 78-105.

Rawson, B. (1966), 'Family life among the lower classes at Rome in the first two centuries of the Empire', *CP* 61: 71-83.

———. (1974), 'Roman concubinage and other *de facto* marriages', *TAPA* 104: 279-305.

———. (ed.) (1986a), *The Family in Ancient Rome*. London.

———. (1986b), 'Children in the Roman *familia*', in Rawson, 1986a, 170-200.

———. (ed.) (1991), *Marriage, Divorce, and Children in Ancient Rome*. Oxford.

Rawson, B. and Weaver, P. R. C. (eds.) (1997), *The Roman Family in Italy*. Oxford.

Rawson, E. (1979), 'L. Cornelius Sisenna and the early first century BC', *CQ* 29: 327-46, reprinted in E. Rawson, 1991, 363-388.

———. (1991), *Roman Culture and Society*. Oxford.

Reynolds, P. K. (1926), *The Vigiles of Imperial Rome*. London.

Rich, J. W. (1990), *Cassius Dio, The Augustan Settlement*. Warminster.

Richardson, L. jr. (1992), *A New Topographical Dictionary of Ancient Rome*. London.

Rickman, G. (1971), *Roman Granaries and Store Buildings*. Cambridge.

———. (1980), *The Corn Supply of Ancient Rome*. Oxford.

Royden, H. L. (1988), *The Magistrates of the Roman Professional Collegia in Italy from the First to the Third Century AD*. Pisa.

Rutledge, S. H. (2001), *Imperial Inquisitions*. London.

Saller, R. P. and Shaw, B. D. (1984), 'Tombstones and Roman family relations in the Principate: civilians, soldiers, and slaves', *JRS* 74: 124-156.

Saller, R. P. (1987a), 'Slavery and the Roman family', *Slavery and Abolition* 8: 65-87.

———. (1987b), 'Men's age at marriage and its consequences in the Roman family', *CP* 82: 21-34.

———. (1991), 'Corporal punishment, authority, and obedience in the Roman household', in Rawson, 1991, 144-165.

———. (1994), *Patriarchy, property and death in the Roman family*. Cambridge.

———. (1996), 'The hierarchical household in Roman society: a study of domestic slavery', in Bush, 1996, 112-129.

———. (1998), 'Symbols of gender and status hierarchies in the Roman household', in Joshel and Murnaghan, 1998, 85-91.

Salomies, O. (2001), 'Names and identities: Onomastics and prosopography', in Bodel, 2001, 73-94.

Sandys, J. E. (1969), *Latin Epigraphy. An Introduction to the Study of Latin Inscriptions*. London. 2nd. edn. Revised by S. G. Campbell.

Salway, B. (1994), 'What's in a name? A survey of Roman onomastic practice from c. 700 B.C. to A.D. 700', *JRS* 84: 124-145.

Scheidel, W. (1995-1996), 'The most silent women of Greece and Rome: rural labour and women's life in the ancient world (I), (II)', *G&R* 42, 202-217; 43, 1-10.

———. (1997), 'Quantifying the sources of slaves in the early Roman Empire', *JRS* 87: 156-169.

Schiess, T. (1888), *Die römischen Collegia Funeraticia nach den Inschriften*. Münich.

Schumacher, L. (1982), *Servus Index*. Wiesbaden.

Shatzman, I. (1972), 'The Roman general's authority over booty', *Historia* 21: 177-205.

———. (1975), *Senatorial Wealth and Roman Politics*. Brussels.

Shaw, B. D. (1987), 'The age of Roman girls at marriage: some reconsiderations,' *JRS* 77: 30-46.

———. (1991), 'The cultural meaning of death', in Kertzer and Saller, 1991, 66-90.

Shelton, J.-A. (1998), *As the Roman Did: A Sourcebook in Roman Social History*. Oxford. 2nd edn.

Sherwin-White, A. N. (1967), *Racial Prejudice in Imperial Rome*. Cambridge.

Solin, H. (1982), *Die griechischen Personennamen in Rom. Ein Namenbuch*. vol. I-III. Berlin.

———. (1989), 'Namenwechsel und besondere Vornamen römischer Senatoren', *Philologus* 133: 252-259.

———. (1996), *Die stadtrömischen Sklavennamen*. vol. I-III. Stuttgart.

Speidel, M. P., (1984), '*Germani corporis custodes*', *Germania* 62: 31-45.

———. (1989), 'The soldiers' servants', *Ancient Society* 20: 239-247.

Strong, D. E. (1968), 'The administration of public building in Rome during late Republic and early Empire', *BICS* 15: 97-109.

Sutherland, C. H. V. (1984), *The Roman Imperial Coinage*. London. 2nd edn.

Syme, R. (1939), *The Roman Revolution*. Oxford.

———. (1958), *Tacitus*. Oxford.

———. (1986), *The Augustan Aristocracy*. Oxford.

Talbert, R. J. A. (1984), *The Senate of Imperial Rome*. Princeton.

Taylor, L. R. (1961), 'Freedmen and freeborn in the epitaphs of imperial Rome,' *American Journal of Philology* 82: 113-32.

Thompson, F. H. (2003), *The Archaeology of Greek and Roman Slavery*. London.

Toynbee, J. M. C. (1971), *Death and Burial in the Roman World*. London.

Treggiari, S. (1969), *Roman Freedmen during the Late Republic*. Oxford.

———. (1973), 'Domestic staff at Rome in the Julio-Claudian period, 27 B.C. to A.D. 68', *Social History* 6: 241-255.

———. (1975a), 'Jobs in the household of Livia', *Papers of the British School at Rome* 43: 48-77.

———. (1975b), 'Family life among the staff of the Volusii', *TAPA* 105: 393-401.

———. (1976), 'Jobs for women', *AJAH* 1: 76-104.

———. (1979a), 'Lower class women in the Roman economy', *Florilegium* 1: 65-86.

———. (1979b), 'Questions on women domestics in the Roman West', in *Schiavitù, manomissione e classi dipendenti nel mondo antico*, Rome, pp.185-201.

———. (1980), 'Urban labour in Rome: *Mercennarii* and *Tabernarii*', in Garnsey, 1980, 48-64.

———. (1991), *Roman Marriage*. Oxford.

Vanderbroeck, P. J. J. (1987), *Popular Leadership and Collective Behavior in the Late Roman Republic (ca. 80-50BC)*. Amsterdam.

Veyne, P. (1961), 'Vie de Trimalchion', *Annales* 16: 213-247.

———. (1979), 'Mythe et réalité de l'autarcie a Rome'. *Revue des Etudes Anciennes* 81: 261-280.

Vogel-Weidemann, U. (1982), *Die Statthalter von Africa und Asia in den Jahren 14-68 n.Chr.* Bonn.

Vogt, J. (1974), tr. by Wiedemann, T., *Ancient Slavery and the Ideal of Man*. Oxford.

Vout, C. (1996), 'The myth of the toga: understanding the history of Roman dress', *G&R* 43: 204-220.

Wallon, H. (1988), *Histoire de l'esclavage dans l'antiquité*. Paris.

Waltzing, J. P. (1895-1900), *Etude historique sur les corporations professionnelles chez les Romains depuis les origines jusqu'à la chute de l'Empire d'Occident*. 4 vols. Louvain.

Watson, A. (1987), *Roman Slave Law*. London.

Weaver, P. R. C. (1972), *Familia Caesaris*. Cambridge.

———. (1990), 'Where have all the Junian Latins gone? Nomenclature and Status in the Early Empire', *Chiron* 20: 275-305.

———. (1997), 'Children of Junian Latins', in Rawson and Weaver, 1997, 55-72.

Westermann, W. L. (1955), *The Slave Systems of Greek and Roman Antiquity*. Philadelphia.

Wiedemann, T. E. J. (1985), 'The regularity of manumission at Rome', *CQ* 35: 162-175.

———. (1989), *Adults and Children in the Roman Empire*. London.

Wiseman, T. P. (1971), *New Men in the Roman Senate, 139BC – AD14*. Oxford.

———. (ed.) (1985a), *Roman Political Life, 90 BC-AD 69*. Exeter.

———. (1985b), 'Competition and Co-operation', in Wiseman (ed.), 1985a, 3-19.

———. (1985c), 'Who was Crassicius Pansa?', *TAPA* 115: 187-196.

www.ingramcontent.com/pod-product-compliance
Lightning Source LLC
Chambersburg PA
CBHW041706290426
44108CB00027B/2873